THE WAR FOR SOUTH VIET NAM

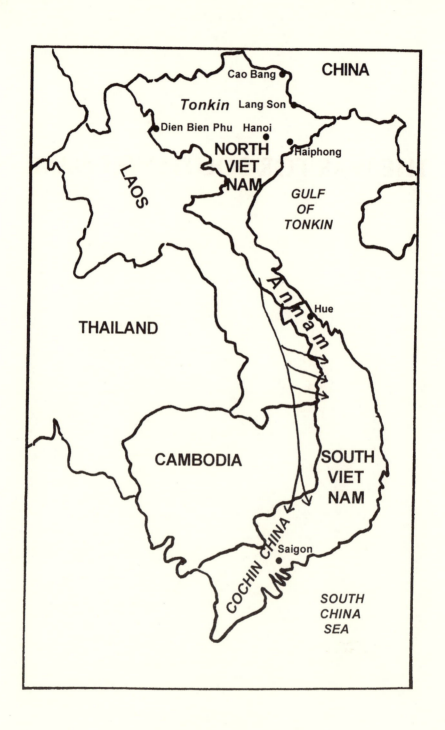

THE WAR FOR SOUTH VIET NAM
1954–1975

Revised Edition

Anthony James Joes

PRAEGER

Westport, Connecticut
London

Library of Congress Cataloging-in-Publication Data

Joes, Anthony James.
  The war for South Viet Nam, 1954–1975 / Anthony James Joes.—Rev. ed.
    p.   cm.
  Includes bibliographical references and index.
  ISBN 0–275–96806–5 (alk. paper)—ISBN 0–275–96807–3 (pbk. : alk. paper)
    1. Vietnamese Conflict, 1961–1975.   2. Vietnam—History—1945–1975.   I. Title.
DS557.7.J63   2001
959.704'3—dc21   00–058006

British Library Cataloguing in Publication Data is available.

Library of Congress Catalog Card Number: 00–058006
ISBN: 0–275–96806–5
      0–275–96807–3 (pbk.)

First published in 2001

Praeger Publishers, 88 Post Road West, Westport, CT 06881
An imprint of Greenwood Publishing Group, Inc.
www.praeger.com

Printed in the United States of America

The paper used in this book complies with the
Permanent Paper Standard issued by the National
Information Standards Organization (Z39.48–1984).

10 9 8 7 6 5 4 3 2 1

To the Vietnamese people,
who have paid so much

Contents

Preface to the Second Edition

Saigon fell to the North Vietnamese Army in April 1975. A decade and a half later, the Cold War ended, and the Soviet Union itself disappeared. Ten years after that, the United States entered upon a new century, a new millennium. Nevertheless, the Americans have not come to closure on their Southeast Asian experience. Viet Nam destroyed two presidencies, each of which had attained power by electoral landslides. It broke apart the old New Deal coalition. It accounts for the U.S. Army's reluctance today to deploy to places like Bosnia and Kosovo. It still deeply affects the educational system, the media, and the general orientation toward governmental authority. Years ago a distinguished student of these affairs declared, "We must disenthrall ourselves from Viet Nam."[1] But the spectre of Viet Nam still haunts America.

Much excellent work has come forth on this subject since the first edition of this book appeared in 1989. Nevertheless, the quality of discussion and debate about Viet Nam in American society at large has not improved very much. That is a situation so fraught with peril that any effort, however inadequate, to challenge some of the clichés and stereotypes that befog the Vietnamese struggles may be worthwhile. Hence the new edition of this book.

The text and notes of this edition contain new material, and many of the most useful recent works appear in the bibliography. Nevertheless, in order to keep the book concise and accessible, the focus remains on those aspects of the subject that continue to appear to me, as a political scientist, most salient and instructive: the nature of Vietnamese Communism, the defeat of the French, the assassination of Diem, the Tet Offensive, the Ho Chi Minh Trail, the South Vietnamese army. The fundamental approach of the book remains unchanged: although the Americanization of the war was unnecessary, the U.S. general

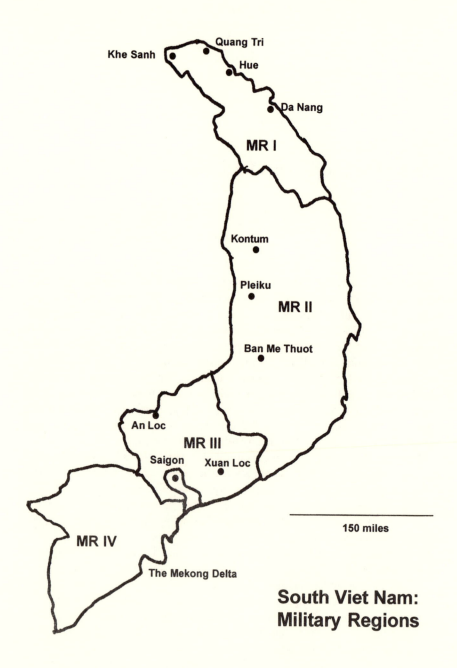

South Viet Nam:
Military Regions

strategy inappropriate, and the South Vietnamese allies deficient, the American abandonment of those allies to their fate was dishonorable.

I wish especially to thank the many generous reviewers of the first edition, Heather Ruland Staines of Praeger Publishers for supporting the idea of a second one, and Mrs. Anne Szewczyk of Saint Joseph's University for invaluable assistance with the maps.

Preface to the First Edition:
The Challenge of Viet Nam

"Few internal conflicts in modern times have received as much publicity and have been as little understood as the fighting in Viet Nam."[1] Penned more than 20 years ago by a keen observer of Vietnamese affairs, these words are still true today.

South Viet Nam was a state to whose defense five presidents of the United States made public commitment, and to which four sent U.S. military forces. South Viet Nam fought for its independence for over 20 years against great odds, and then suffered defeat and conquest. Even (or especially) for those who proclaim this defeat to have been inevitable—whatever that term is intended to mean—the question still remains: why did the South fall in 1975, and not 1965, or 1985?

It is the principal thesis of this book that the conquest of South Viet Nam was not "inevitable." On the contrary, given the kind of assistance the United States has extended to Korea or Israel over the past decades, South Viet Nam was, at the very least after 1968, a viable enterprise. Paradoxically, and unfortunately, as its power to resist conquest by Hanoi was increasing, support for South Viet Nam inside the United States was decreasing. The United States spent scores of billions of dollars on the defense of South Viet Nam; it suffered the loss of over 50,000 of its troops. In proportion to population, South Viet Nam lost 40 times as many soldiers as the Americans. Yet in 1975 the United States, after causing so much blood and treasure to be expended and after allowing so many South Vietnamese to expose themselves as opponents of a Communist takeover, abandoned the South to conquest by the North Vietnamese army.

No matter how they evaluate the wisdom of the initial U.S. involvement in

Viet Nam, many Americans today continue to be deeply troubled by that act of abandonment.

A related thesis of the book is that pressure to abandon the South Vietnamese derived in large part from a faulty presentation of the war to the American public, including a false image of the armed forces of South Viet Nam. In large part, this flawed perception derived from the U.S. strategy for fighting guerrillas and regular Communist military units. Therefore a great deal of attention is devoted to the military aspects of the conflict, especially to the much-neglected South Vietnamese army and militia.

This book does not try to be a history of the successive wars in Viet Nam. It does not raise, let alone answer, every question concerning those conflicts. My principal conscious purpose has been to challenge some current myths about the struggle for South Viet Nam, myths that threaten to become engraved, mainly through repetition, on the American mind.

We are still too close to those days and those events to see all things clearly. Nevertheless, over the past 15 years much passion has dissipated and much evidence has come to light, so that perhaps we can more calmly entertain ideas that but a few years ago would have been considered much too controversial.

It is therefore to reflection, not to recrimination, that I invite the reader.

Acknowledgments

In trying to come to grips with Viet Nam I have benefited greatly from conversations and debates with many persons, some of whom might prefer not to be publicly associated with this book. But I must give special thanks to the research staff of St. Joseph's University Library for their efficiency and patience, as well as to Professor Peter Woolley of Fairleigh Dickinson University, and my long-suffering spouse, Chris, for uncovering many lapses and errors in various drafts of the manuscript.

For all its remaining inadequacies, I alone am responsible.

THE WAR FOR SOUTH VIET NAM

1

Viet Nam before 1945

The political function of Communism is not to overthrow authority but
to fill the vacuum of authority.

—Samuel P. Huntington
Political Order in Changing Societies

THE TWO RICE BASKETS

Viet Nam has a territory of 127,000 square miles, with former North Viet Nam
roughly equal in size to the state of Georgia, and South Viet Nam to the state
of Washington. With its northernmost point on the same latitude as Miami and
the southernmost point on the latitude of the Panama Canal, Viet Nam is more
than 1,000 miles in length, roughly the distance from Rome to Copenhagen, or
Boston to Jacksonville. But the country is very narrow for its length, tapering
from 300 miles wide at the broadest to less than 50 miles at the narrowest point.
In essence, Viet Nam is two deltas, those of the Red River and the Mekong,
joined by a narrow, mountain-bound coastal strip. The country is even narrower
than these figures indicate, or than a map shows: 80 percent of the population
lives on only 20 percent of the land area, mostly clustered in the great deltas
and within a few miles of the sea. Hardly any Vietnamese live in the mountains,
owing partly to the presence of malaria-bearing mosquitoes; the sparse mountain
population is composed almost entirely of ethnic minorities.

Topographically, therefore, Viet Nam resembles a barbell. The Vietnamese
use another simile, more revealing of the basis of life in the country: for them,
Viet Nam is a carrying pole with a basket of rice at both ends. Burma, Thailand,
and Viet Nam collectively have long been a rice bowl of Asia. Even so, they
could have produced a lot more; only about half the land area is cleared for

cultivation, and agricultural methods are ancient. That is why the Japanese produce five tons of rice per hectare, while the Vietnamese produce only two.

The great outside world knew or cared little about Viet Nam before World War II, and most Americans discovered it no earlier than 1954, or even years after. Nevertheless, Viet Nam, along with the rest of Southeast Asia, lies at the crossroads of communications between the Pacific Basin and the Indian Subcontinent.

In an area only half the size of Brazil, the nations of Southeast Asia contain close to 400 million people, more than the combined population of the former Soviet Union and all its European satellites. Yet relative to the rest of the continent, Southeast Asia is underpopulated; almost all of Laos, for instance, and much of Viet Nam is covered by virgin rainforest. Although most of its people are poor, the region itself is rich, with the rubber of Malaya, the petroleum of Indonesia, the rice of Burma and Viet Nam, and much else besides. It was the desire of the Japanese to possess this strategically located and resource-rich area that produced Pearl Harbor and the Pacific War.

On the eve of World War II, in all of Southeast Asia, only Thailand was an independent state. The British ruled over Malaya, Singapore, and Burma; the Dutch held sprawling Indonesia; the Americans were in the Philippines; while the French had established themselves in Laos, Cambodia, and the Vietnamese regions of Tonkin, Annam, and Cochinchina. Within a few years of the end of the war, the Americans had granted independence to the Philippines and the British were emancipating their empire; largely for this reason, postwar Communist insurgencies in Malaya, Burma, and the Philippines were unsuccessful. The Dutch decided to resist the drive for Indonesian independence, but the task soon proved beyond their capacity. Of the prewar colonial powers, only the French made the commitment to retain their Southeast Asian holdings and sustained that commitment by force of arms.

BEFORE THE EUROPEANS

Until the arrival of the French, Viet Nam was ruled by a mandarin class, not hereditary but open to any who could pass a qualifying examination (in Chinese). The mandarinate maintained order and dispensed an approximation of justice; there were no cruel punishments, no great extremes of wealth and poverty, and ownership of land was widespread. Nevertheless, the literary education and antique values of the mandarins froze Viet Nam in the past.

The central monarchical government exercised power for the most part only in religious and military affairs.[1] But it was far from easy for even this limited government to hold the country together, because "the Vietnamese are as conscious of region as the Indian is of caste."[2] Centuries before the Geneva partition, "the political, psychological, moral and economic differences between the North and the South" constituted a "profound reality."[3]

Northern Vietnamese see themselves as dynamic and southerners as rather lazy and slow-witted. Southerners view northerners as aggressive, money-hungry, harder-working, and more enduring. They perceive themselves as more pacific than the militant inhabitants of the Red River Delta, possessing in their enjoyment of the bounties and beauties of nature the secret of true happiness.[4] The roots of these widely held perceptions lie in both the geography and the history of the country: the centers of population of Viet Nam are almost a thousand miles apart, and the southernmost provinces of the country were acquired by the Vietnamese relatively recently.

MARCH TO THE SOUTH

Sun Yat-sen, founder of the Chinese Republic, once remarked that "the Vietnamese are slaves by nature."[5] Their history of warfare with their more powerful Chinese neighbors seems to belie this characterization; so does the great March to the South, "Nam Tien," the 500-year period (A.D. 1400–1900) during which the Vietnamese pushed their way by conquest from Tonkin all the way down eventually to the Ca Mau Peninsula. The Vietnamese completed the conquest of the southern part of their present territory (Cochinchina) relatively recently, only about a century before the arrival of the French. This late arrival of the Vietnamese into the area accounts in part for deeply felt regional diversity; so does the fact that as the French strengthened their presence in Viet Nam, they pursued different policies in the different regions of the country.

The long push south by the Vietnamese into Cochinchina involved the conquest or displacement of its Khmer (Cambodian) inhabitants. The Vietnamese conquered Saigon from the Khmers in 1698: in the 1970s, as many as a half-million ethnic Khmers still remained within southern Vietnamese territory. Their presence, along with that of many Chinese and the hill tribes, adds ethnic diversity to regional peculiarity. Viet Nam might eventually have conquered all of Cambodia; the French offered protection against Vietnamese imperialism to Cambodia as well as to Laos, which largely explains how the French were able to occupy those states with relatively little native opposition.[6]

TWO VIET NAMS

Vietnamese regionalism, rooted in geography and ethnicity, found itself reinforced by centuries of political division and warfare. During the sixteenth century, two rival Vietnamese states, one northern and one southern, contended for dominance. These states united toward the end of the century, but in 1620 Viet Nam split apart once more, roughly along the 18th parallel. For the following 50 years the northern state, with its capital at Hanoi, fruitlessly attempted to conquer the south. The north had the support of the Dutch, while the southern kingdom received aid from the Portuguese. In the 1780s, the conquest of Hanoi by the south reunited the Vietnamese into a single state.[7]

Gen. Nguyen Anh founded the last Vietnamese imperial dynasty. Ascending the throne in the first decade of the nineteenth century, with the help of French military advisers, he assumed the title of Emperor Gia Long and conferred on Viet Nam its present name.

In the 500 years before the statesmen of Geneva partitioned Viet Nam along the 17th parallel, there had been only about three decades during which a single government controlled the whole of present-day Vietnamese territory, and only 100 years of unity out of the past 4,000.[8] The Communists in Hanoi succeeded in convincing many Westerners that an independent state in southern Viet Nam was some sort of temporary and intolerable aberration, but that was quite incorrect; centuries of partition between the 16th and 18th parallels meant that "the present division [1954–75], by historical criteria, is normal, not exceptional."[9] The Vietnamese Communists recognized the geographical and historical diversity within Viet Nam when, founding their party in 1930, they organized separate branches in Tonkin, Annam, and Cochinchina.

THE COMING OF THE FRENCH

In the sixteenth century, Japan was the center of Catholic missionary activities in Asia. In the early 1600s, however, the rulers of Japan decided to close their country off from the outside world and employed the most vigorous methods to dissuade missionaries from trying to enter. Thus, by what was in effect an accident, the attention of the Catholic world, especially as embodied in well-organized French missionary efforts, turned to Viet Nam. It proved relatively easy to convert Vietnamese Buddhists, including monks, to Christianity; by 1660 there were 400,000 Catholics in Tonkin alone,[10] and French Jesuit missionaries invented the present written Vietnamese language. By the eve of the Second World War, Catholics constituted a tenth of the entire Vietnamese population, and fully 50 percent in some provinces.[11]

Beginning in the 1830s, the predictable nativist reaction was in full swing: thousands of Vietnamese converts and scores of French priests were murdered. The protection of endangered French citizens provided the justification for Napoleon III to occupy parts of the country; by 1859, French troops had established themselves in Saigon, only a small town then but with an excellent harbor, and in much of the surrounding territory.[12] Less than a decade later the French had taken control of all the provinces of Cochinchina, and within a few years Tonkin and Annam were tightly within the French orbit as well. At the end of the century, Annam was an indirect protectorate under its emperor, Tonkin was a direct protectorate with a French governor ruling in place of the emperor, and Cochinchina was a French colony, ruled straight from Paris.

The record of an imperial power in one of its colonies never looks the same to the colonizers and the colonized. Any effort to assess objectively such a record immediately embroils one in bitter controversy, and nowhere is this truer than in regard to the French presence in Viet Nam. (As one might expect, some of the most trenchant critics of French rule in Indochina have been Frenchmen.)

On the one hand, apologists for French rule in Indochina are not without ammunition in their battle. Critics of French imperialism in Southeast Asia (and elsewhere) like to contrast the idyllic pre-colonial and pre-capitalist village society with the disruptions wrought by contact with the Europeans and their economic rapacity.[13] But in fact, pre-colonial life was not so very nice for most peasants, nor was capitalism (that is, the introduction of the national market) always harmful.[14] The French brought peace and order, the indispensable prerequisites of justice and prosperity. French scientists did much good work fighting tropical diseases. The colonial government introduced modern methods of sanitation and hygiene, and built hospitals and dispensaries; health services under the French in fact were free and unsurpassed in quality anywhere in Southeast Asia. The French extended the dike system, built canals, drained large districts and irrigated others, thus converting a great deal of wasteland into food-producing areas, especially in Cochinchina.[15] A noted Indian historian of European imperialism has written that in the first three decades of the twentieth century, the French administration of Indochina was as good as in any colonial area in the world.[16]

On the other hand, French imperial policy envisioned Indochina as a source of raw materials and a market for the goods of French industry; the imperial tariff system caused Indochinese to pay more for imported goods. French policies eventually produced a semi-industrialized north, where native workers had to sign three-year contracts by which they could be sent far from home and family, under strict discipline, in poor conditions, and for low wages. In the south, the development of large estates created both the curse of absentee landlordism and a new class of sharecroppers.

Under this system, the standard of living of the peasants—90 percent of the population—was quite low. By the time French rule came to an end, less than a quarter of the Vietnamese population was literate. At least one distinguished historian maintains that the Vietnamese were actually worse off at the end of the colonial regime than at the beginning. A most telling indictment of French rule is their government opium monopoly, which encouraged the Vietnamese to buy and use the drug while opium smoking was illegal in France itself. (In partial mitigation of this disgraceful practice, it might be noted that other European governments in Southeast Asia did the same thing, and opium smoking was legal in independent Siam.)[17]

In any case, whatever else the French were doing in Indochina, and especially Viet Nam, they were not making money out of the enterprise. For the French economy as a whole, Indochina was a drain, not a source, of wealth.[18] In 1913, France's trade with all her colonies was 11 percent of its total external trade, and total external trade amounted to but 3 percent of French GNP.[19] With the shadow of German hegemony growing ever darker across the continent of Europe, the driving force behind French imperialism in Southeast Asia and elsewhere was not the quest for wealth but the search for prestige.[20]

As the spectre of a second world war began to dominate the horizon, the

French had clearly failed to achieve their own professed aims in Southeast Asia: the modernization of the economy and the unity of Indochina under the rule of law.[21] Not only were the French aliens in Viet Nam, as the Americans were in the Philippines and the British in India; they had done very little indeed to prepare the Vietnamese or the other Indochinese peoples for independence, or even for home rule. Following the worst of all courses, they had trained a new Vietnamese elite in French values and by French methods, then frustrated the aspirations of this new class by reserving all the important positions in Viet Nam, and many of the unimportant ones, for Frenchmen. Thus they had blocked the aspirations of Vietnamese, from Ho Chi Minh to Ngo Dinh Diem, to exercise power over their own people. The French themselves therefore provided some of the essentials required by Vilfredo Pareto in his theory of revolution (the accumulation of frustrated elements in the population), while the impending invasion by the Japanese would supply the rest (the progressive debility of the forces of order).[22] And by making the expression of political discontents illegal, the French played directly into the hands of the Communists, well trained in the arts of clandestine organization. Thus, in any final evaluation of colonial rule in Viet Nam, the contribution the French themselves made to the rise of a Communist-dominated revolutionary movement must hold a primary place.

2

The Viet Minh

Men do not become tyrants in order that they may not have to suffer
from the cold.

—Aristotle

Today the War; tomorrow the Revolution.

—Mussolini

THE ORIGINS OF THE VIETNAMESE REVOLUTION

To make a successful revolution requires at least three conditions. First, there
must be a *revolutionary situation*: this often results from a perceived intolerable
gap between what large numbers of persons want from their government, and
what they receive. Second, there must be a leadership group, a *revolutionary
elite*, which, from whatever motives, effectively expresses, focuses, and orga-
nizes dissatisfaction by means of a revolutionary ideology. Third, there must be
a *crisis*: some calamity or series of events that for a time visibly weakens the
government's ability to exercise control in the old way, opening the path for an
armed challenge by the revolutionary elite. Without all three of these conditions,
a revolutionary outbreak may well occur, but it will almost certainly not be
successful.[1] In nineteenth-century Viet Nam, armed resistance to the empire-
building French occurred under the leadership of the indigenous aristocratic
mandarin class. This feudal and parochial group was disdainful and perhaps
afraid of the peasant masses, and hence could not produce an effective revolutionary ideology. A major revolutionary movement was thus not possible until
the appearance of a Vietnamese elite that was nationally oriented in vision and
frustrated enough to articulate a program that could appeal to the mass of the

population, the peasantry, upon whose traditional village life the French colonial economic system of plantation and factory was encroaching. Ironically enough, it was the French themselves who produced the native elite that would fashion such an ideology, find peasant support, and eventually drive them out of Viet Nam.

The French, through state schools and religious academies, had by the end of the First World War created a sizeable stratum of European-educated Vietnamese. And during that conflict, many Vietnamese had served with the armies of France in Europe, learned much about the great outside world, and returned home to find conditions in their country very disillusioning. The new Vietnamese elite found itself denied the positions and power to which it felt entitled by its French education and French military service. Comparative figures on the European presence in Asia are revealing. In 1925, the British were governing 325 million Indians with a force of 5,000 European civil servants; the French employed the same number to govern only 30 million Vietnamese.[2] A decade later, three times as many Frenchmen held government posts in Viet Nam as Englishmen in India.[3] There were even French traffic policemen in Hanoi as late as the 1950s.[4] Many positions in the civil service or in private enterprise, and all of the top ones, were closed to Vietnamese. Where they did get jobs in these organizations, they usually found themselves subordinate to Frenchmen with less education than themselves, and they received one-half to one-fifth the salary paid to Frenchmen in similar positions.[5] The French talked a good deal, and taught their Vietnamese pupils, about liberty, equality, and fraternity, but the educated Vietnamese was at best a second-class citizen in his own country. And if he wished he could contemplate the situation in the Philippines, an American possession where almost all the government services—police, health, education, and so on—were staffed and run by Filipinos.[6] The future leaders of revolution in Viet Nam were, like those who made the Nazi and Bolshevik revolutions, frustrated in their desires for upward mobility. "For most of those who became revolutionaries, it was clear that their own opportunities for advancement were inseparably bound up with eliminating French rule in Vietnam."[7] The modern obsession with economics and fixation on the class struggle have caused many to miss the extent to which the political conflicts of this century have been fueled by the desire of intellectuals to get into power; nevertheless, the underemployment and lack of status of educated Vietnamese, and roadblocks to positions of authority for them, are at the root of the Vietnamese revolution.[8]

Twentieth-century nationalism in Viet Nam had always been strongly influenced by outside forces: from France, from the Soviet Union, and especially from China, both Nationalist and Maoist. For instance, many of the leaders of the new Communist party that Ho Chi Minh sent into Viet Nam were graduates of Chiang Kai-shek's military academy at Whampoa; these included Pham Van Dong, born in 1906 into an aristocratic mandarin family yet destined to hold major offices in Communist North Viet Nam. Another example of foreign influence on Vietnamese nationalism is the VNQDD, the Nationalist Party of Viet Nam, founded in Hanoi in 1927 under the direct inspiration of Chiang's Kuomintang party.

Early nationalist movements in Viet Nam were urban and elitist, with little idea of the necessity or the means to appeal to the peasantry. The VNQDD's peasant program, for example, seems to have consisted mainly of extorting money from the well-to-do and then lending it to peasants, in order to obligate them to the party.[9] The inability to come up with a long-range and realistic revolutionary strategy resulted in adventuristic and premature uprisings: in 1930, one such poorly coordinated effort by VNQDD ended with a crushing defeat at the hands of the French. The revolt's leaders—those who escaped—fled to China, where they remained until the middle of World War II.

Besides their almost exclusively urban composition and lack of good revolutionary theory, several other factors prevented the emergence of non-communist nationalists, such as the VNQDD, as a powerful force, and therefore opened the way for the capture of the growing nationalist sentiment by Ho and the Communists. First, French rule in Viet Nam permitted no channel whereby Vietnamese could work and organize peacefully to express the desire for political change and opposition to perpetual French domination. Unlike the situation in India or the Philippines, public advocacy of independence for Viet Nam was treated as treason.[10] This French policy therefore gave a tremendous advantage to those with the will and ability to engage in illegal, clandestine organization. VNQDD leadership, with little organizational experience (and weakened, like the rest of the non-communist nationalist movement, by internal factionalism) could not flourish in the face of efficient French repression. The non-communist nationalists were periodically decimated by the French police; the Vietnamese Communists, in contrast, with a party based on tight discipline and a leadership trained abroad in the tactics of Leninist subversion, were able to hang on and even expand. Additionally, Vietnamese Communists had ideological allies and defenders in the French parliament, while the non-communist nationalists did not. This international Communist linkage would become of major importance when the Communist-backed Popular Front cabinets held power in France in the late 1930s. Finally, when exiled VNQDD leaders returned to their native country in the van of Chinese Nationalist occupation forces in 1945, they soon found themselves thoroughly discredited among their own people by the arrogance of those troops, and their looting. The eventual withdrawal of the Chinese from northern Viet Nam left the VNQDD exposed to attack by the French police and by the Vietnamese Communists as well. By the summer of 1946 they were almost completely destroyed. It is another one of the rich ironies of the whole Vietnamese revolution that the French would search desperately in the 1950s for an effective nationalist alternative to the Communists, an alternative that, by their persecution from the 1920s to the 1940s, they had all but eliminated.

HO CHI MINH

The man who above all others would benefit from the failure of non-communist nationalism in Viet Nam was Ho Chi Minh. He was born in 1890, in Nghe An province, an old-time hotbed of revolution on the central coast; his real name was Nguyen That Thanh. As a revolutionary he would take many aliases until finally settling on Ho Chi Minh, meaning "he who shines." Ho was a descendant of scholars and government bureaucrats; his father, an ardent nationalist, sent Ho to the best high school in Viet Nam, at Hue.[11] Rejected as a young man for a position with the French administration, Ho embarked upon a strange odyssey that was to take him all around the world and eventually to total power in Hanoi.

In 1911, Ho took a job on a French steamship. He was not to return to his country for 30 years. During his steamer voyage to Europe, Ho associated with seamen from Brittany and Cornwall; finding them as illiterate and superstitious as any Vietnamese peasant, Ho lost his awe of white men. In London, he worked as a pastry cook for the great Escoffier, and he may have spent some time in Harlem, in New York City. He helped found the French Communist Party at Tours. He went to Moscow and took courses in the certainties of Marxism and the techniques of Leninism at the University of the Toilers of the East. Becoming active in the Comintern, he anticipated Mao by many years in proclaiming that the Asian revolution would have to be based on the peasantry, not on Marx's urban proletariat.[12] He visited Vietnamese settlements in Thailand disguised as a Buddhist monk, and he fled from Chiang's China to Stalin's Soviet Union by crossing the forbidding Gobi Desert. Arrested in Hong Kong in 1932 and held for extradition to French Viet Nam, he was defended all the way to the Privy Council in London by none other than Sir Stafford Cripps. Cripps got Ho off the hook by presenting him as a political refugee and thus not subject to extradition. This was indeed very fortunate for Ho, because the French had him under sentence of death. Back in Moscow once again, he attended the famous Lenin School. Re-entering China, he served for a time with Mao's Eighth Route Army. During all these adventures, he learned to speak passable Russian, English, and Mandarin Chinese, in addition to his own Vietnamese tongue and French, which he had learned as a boy. Ho's experience of the outside world was far greater than that of any other Vietnamese leader; indeed, it was much broader than that of any of the world-class Communist leaders, including Stalin and Mao.

Ho first entered upon the world political stage at the Versailles peace conference after the First World War, when he was still a young man. He had journeyed to Paris to petition President Wilson on the subject of Vietnamese independence. Brushed aside by the statesmen of the victorious Allied Powers, he nevertheless won for himself much notoriety and prestige among the sizeable group of Vietnamese resident in France. And here, perhaps for the first time, Ho was attracted to Communism, because that ideology—and its Soviet proponents come recently to power—seemed to provide the only international support for Vietnamese national aspirations.[13] Lenin was indeed interested in independence for the Asians, but for rather complicated reasons. Like all Marxists born in the nineteenth century, Lenin was totally Eurocentric. When he, like Marx, used phrases like "the history of all peoples," he meant "the history of the Europeans." Lenin and other Marxists had long been puzzled by the continuing failure of the European proletariat, even after the Russians had given them the example in 1917, to rise up and carry out the revolution, the inevitability of which had been so powerfully explained by Marx himself. Lenin's explanation for this proletarian failure was that the ruling capitalists of Europe had bribed the upper strata of their respective proletariats with some of the loot stolen from the subject peoples of their colonial empires. Clearly, then, reasoned Lenin, if the overseas empires could be broken up, the European proletariat would be deprived of its imperialist bribes and sink back into "immiseration." Then the long-desired revolution would arrive. That is what Lenin meant when he said, "The road to Paris lies through Peking" (and if he didn't actually say it, he should have). In the summer of 1920 Ho read Lenin's "Theses on the National and Colonial Question," and this probably more than anything else first turned him to Communism.[14] Of course, Lenin never applied his ideas about the liberation of oppressed nationalities to the oppressed nationalities of Russia; by definition, oppression was another capitalist monopoly. Nevertheless, Communism "seemed to offer racial equality to subject peoples," and that was its fundamental appeal in Viet Nam not only after the First World War but after the second.[15] Elected as a delegate to the Eighteenth Congress of the French Socialist Party at Tours in December 1920, Ho joined the walkout that resulted in the foundation of the French Communist Party and thus became "the first Vietnamese Communist."

All his life Ho remained unmarried and ascetic; his one personal weakness seemed to be the chainsmoking of American cigarettes. His image as one who sacrificed all personal comforts and private desires in an unquenchable patriotic fire, willing to struggle for his principles at no matter what cost in the blood of his countrymen, would paradoxically endear him in the 1960s to a generation of American and European students whose lifestyles were anything but ascetic, who viewed the patriotism of their own countrymen as a contemptible anachronism, and who otherwise found the shedding of blood for any political cause obscene. The image of Ho as a self-sacrificing ascetic, however, is not accepted in its entirety by all commentators. One American scholar has recorded his opinion that "mendacity was a cornerstone of Ho's career."[16] He had had in his wanderings several incredibly narrow escapes from Western prisons, stimulating accusations that from time to time he had purchased his freedom by acting as a police informer. More specifically, some maintain that Ho betrayed noncommunist Vietnamese revolutionaries, including Trotskyites, to the French authorities, for money.[17] One of those believed to have been thus betrayed was the nationalist hero Phan Boi Chau, called by Bernard Fall "Viet Nam's Sun Yat-sen." Fall also questioned the truth of Ho's saintly self-denial: the Hanoi regime told the world that Ho lived and slept in a small peasant hut right beside the former French governor's palace, but Fall said that in July 1962 he walked all around the grounds of that building but failed to find that little hut.[18]

THE COMMUNIST PARTY OF VIET NAM

Ho Chi Minh would float to power on a tidal wave of nationalist sentiment, but the craft that would carry him was the Communist Party of Viet Nam. This craft did not look at all seaworthy as the decade of the 1920s came to an end; in fact, it was broken into three parts, each claiming to represent authentic Marxism-Leninism. On orders from Moscow, the three squabbling factions came together in January 1930 to form the "Indochinese Communist Party," with a membership of 211.[19] Then the tiny, newly united party was nearly wiped out by its involvement with the ill-prepared nationalist uprisings of 1930. French police repression, vigorous and effective, was aided to a considerable extent by betrayal within the party: "Virtually the entire Party Central Committee had been sold out by fellow Communists."[20]

Vietnamese Communism was different from other anti-French organizations in the country: "It was a subversive movement launched from outside Viet Nam by the Soviet Government as an instrument for embarrassing France."[21] In the 1930s and after, the close association of the Vietnamese Communists with foreign Communist states would be of enormous, even decisive, advantage to it. But subservience to Moscow was not without its costs. The strategy of Vietnamese Communism was made in Moscow, and Moscow refused to allow East Asian realities to interfere with its total absorption with the European scene.[22] In terms of promoting world revolution, Moscow's leadership, institutionalized in the Communist International, or "Comintern," was a total failure, especially in Western and Central Europe. In those areas, Moscow's policy of attacking the Socialists both weakened the working class and isolated the local Communists. European Communism was weaker in 1939, after 20 years of Comintern leadership, than it had been in 1919. Moscow expected Asian Communist parties as a matter of course to jump and dance to every change in its international line, regardless of what disasters that line might provoke in their respective countries.

Ho Chi Minh, outside Viet Nam during the 1930s, was spared the humiliation and political damage that would have resulted from having had to explain and enforce the everchanging Moscow directives. Reflecting deeply on the trauma of the 1930–31 uprising and its suppression, he derived two fundamental lessons from that experience. First, no force generated inside Viet Nam alone could defeat the French; some international upheaval would be necessary, such as the First World War, which had made possible the Bolshevik seizure of power in Russia. Second, the party must be ready for such an eventuality by perfecting a tightly disciplined, tested organization of revolutionaries.

In 1936, the party received unexpected and spectacular assistance with its preparations: the Communist-backed Popular Front government came to power in France and soon proclaimed a general amnesty for political prisoners in Viet Nam. All the subversives so painstakingly rounded up after 1930 were now released, permitted to organize openly and insert themselves into the mainstream of Vietnamese politics—all this with the blessings of the rhetoricians in the Paris Assembly.

Even while deriving valuable lessons from the past, even while receiving valuable favors from friends in France, the Vietnamese Communists, like the nationalists, remained a very small operation indeed. Pre–World War II nationalism in Viet Nam was very much an urban affair, which is to say that it affected hardly at all the great majority of the population. The power of Marxism-Leninism in colonial and underdeveloped areas, in the 1930s as in the 1980s, lay not in popularity among the peasantry, nor even among the proletariat (which of course was very small), but rather in its attraction for the urban intellectuals. Many of these intellectuals found themselves excluded from participation in the capitalist economy, where important positions were reserved for Europeans. As capitalism in Viet Nam wore an alien face, so Marxist condemnation of capitalism and consignment of it to oblivion struck a responsive cord.[23] Excluded from full participation in the world of the French, Viet Nam's intellectuals were at the same time cut off by their education, aspirations, and style of living from the traditional Vietnamese past. Marxism provided a psychological as well as political haven for many such persons: "To be a Marxist represented a grand gesture of contempt for the corrupt past as well as the humiliating present."[24] Most of all, Marxism-Leninism represented for Vietnamese intellectuals a vision—indeed, a promise—of power, the power from which they were excluded. In those days as in these, Communist revolutionary theory, even in peasant societies such as Viet Nam, insists on "the leadership role of the proletariat," which means in fact the leadership role of the party—that is, of the intellectuals who were and remain its core and soul.

In the circumstances prevailing in the Viet Nam of the late 1930s, Communism derived little benefit from its attraction for the small urban educated class. The party remained hardly more than a sect centered in Hanoi and a few other cities. Then, in August 1939, the world was stupefied by the Hitler-Stalin pact. Dutiful Communists in France and in Viet Nam supported Moscow's alliance with the former hated enemy and hence became openly the enemies of the French state. French authorities in Hanoi reacted with predictable speed and severity, casting leaders and members alike of the party into prison. Those who escaped had to leave the comfort of their cafés and teahouses to shelter in the despised and unfamiliar countryside, an exodus that would in the not distant future produce the most momentous consequences.[25]

THE JAPANESE AND THE REVOLUTION

In June 1940, France fell before the onslaught of Hitler's juggernaut. The following August, the Japanese government demanded that French authorities in Hanoi grant Japanese troops the right to occupy Viet Nam's major cities and strategic points. Cut off from any hope of outside assistance, the French had no choice but to accede to Japanese desires. These and subsequent events are absolutely crucial to understanding how a Vietnamese revolution became possible, and why it took the form and course that it did. Without the sweeping aside of French power in 1940, without the public humiliation of the once-invincible French authorities, without this stripping of the French of their Mandate of Heaven—and all this at the hands of an Asian people—it is very difficult to imagine how a Vietnamese national revolution would have succeeded, especially one under the leadership of the Communist Party. But the Japanese entrance into the world war, and into Viet Nam, gave the small but well-disciplined Vietnamese Communist Party its chance: The Japanese produced the crisis of the regime.

The response of the Communists to this sudden-but-long-prepared-for opportunity was the Eighth Plenum, which took place at Pac Bo in May 1941. At this crucial assembly, the leaders of Vietnamese Communism made two major decisions, from which all else would follow. First, the struggle between classes must be subordinated to the struggle for national independence. Second, all anti-Japanese groups and individuals, Communist and non-Communist alike, must unite in a total crusade against the national enemy. As the vehicle for this unity, the Communists established a new front organization called the League for the Independence of Viet Nam, or Viet Minh for short.

To exchange their Communist clothes for the robes of nationalism was perhaps the most important decision Ho and his followers ever made, because "in terms of revolutionary strategy, Communism has succeeded only when it has been able to co-opt a national liberation struggle, and has failed whenever it was opposed to or isolated from a national liberation struggle such as those in Israel, Algeria, Indonesia, and Burma."[26] In the short run, the substitution of national independence for class war at the heart of the Communist message brought the party many advantages. The appeal to nationalism—opposition to the predatory Japanese occupation and to the French, whose weakness, whose very presence in Viet Nam made the Japanese occupation possible—helped transcend the many regional, ethnic, and class divisions among the Vietnamese, and without transcending these divisions no national revolution could succeed. The cause of national independence was more attractive to young intellectuals than class struggle alone had ever been.[27] And most of all, the promise to get rid of the French and distribute their wealth and property provided an essential tool whereby the intellectuals who led the Communist Party could fashion the all-important alliance with the peasant majority, upon whose shoulders the burden of any realistic revolutionary strategy would have to be placed.[28]

In creating this Viet Minh front organization, Ho and his followers were pursuing "the primary political tactic of communist revolutionaries since the time of Lenin."[29] The purpose of the Viet Minh, like the purpose of any Communist front, was to attract, by means of widely accepted symbols and slogans, non-Communist nationalists and democratic elements into an alliance that they would not normally want to make. Through this alliance, the Communists would be able to gain favorable attention and access to groups formerly indifferent to or suspicious of them, and thus broaden their support, not on the basis of Communist goals but of their temporarily adopted nationalist aims. Once such a front was established, the Communists, by means of their superior discipline, self-consciousness, and cohesion, their clarity of purpose and ruthlessness of means, would first manipulate and eventually dominate it.

The front tactic was thus ideally suited to carrying out Lenin's "Two-Stage Theory" of revolution in colonial areas. Stage One was the "bourgeois" revolution, by which a broad, inter-class coalition (like the Viet Minh) came to power. Stage Two was the "real" revolution, in which "the workers," led by (or sometimes substituted by) "the vanguard of the proletariat"—that is, the intellectuals who made up the leadership of the party—took over.

In accordance with these tactics, the Communists declared that if Viet Nam did not achieve national independence, then no class within it would achieve what it needed or wanted. The salvation of the working class, of the peasantry and of the bourgeoisie all depended on national liberation.[30] Class war must be submerged into a "racial patriotism."[31] Thus the Communists dropped their call for general land seizures in favor of the seizure of French-owned lands only and mere reduced rents for the rest.

The Japanese army was in control of the cities, and therefore any revolutionary action would have to take the form of guerrilla warfare in the rural areas—hence the Viet Minh promise to distribute foreign-owned lands to the peasants. Thus Ho turned away from the Bolshevik, or Petrograd, Model of revolution—the seizure of power in the capital city by a well-trained force of workers led by intellectuals. In its place Ho adopted what would some day be known the world over as the Maoist model of revolution.[32] All the elements of that model that would become so well known were taking form: a united national liberation front, guerrilla warfare, the beginnings of a party army, and a secure base area. This decision by Ho to turn away from a metropolitan strategy based on the workers toward a rural strategy based on the peasantry made the Vietnamese revolution possible.[33]

Theory—correct revolutionary theory—is the most important thing in the world to Marxist revolutionaries. Lenin said, "No revolutionary theory, no revolution." He meant it, and his followers have believed it, with good reason. Thus all these tremendous changes in the strategy and tactics of the Vietnamese revolution had to be fitted in—somehow—with correct Marxist theory as interpreted by Lenin and understood by the directors of the Comintern. Ho Chi Minh was no theorist; responsibilities for theoretical orthodoxy fell principally to his collaborator, Truong Chinh. But no matter how winding the roads over which he led his followers, Ho never lost control. His dominance was based on his vast experience of the world, his good contacts in Moscow, and his international reputation as a revolutionary leader. But above all, his contribution to Vietnamese Communism lay in his genius as an organizational tactician. When it came to building fronts, cementing alliances, attaching non-Communist organizations to his own party, or simply swallowing up rival groups whole, Ho had no equals, certainly not in Viet Nam.

By the end of 1941, with Viet Nam fairly tightly in the grip of the Japanese, most nationalist leaders who were not associated with the Viet Minh had fled to China, entered into collaboration with the French, or retired from political life. But persisting in its revolutionary strategy, the Viet Minh grew. Soon it had a monopoly of all serious anti-Japanese armed resistance, and it would reap rich political rewards for this record. General Giap, the schoolteacher-turned-military commander of Viet Minh forces, had several hundred men in his National Salvation Army by the end of 1943,[34] and exercised close to undisputed control over the three remote border provinces of Cao Bang, Lang Son, and Bac Kan. As the war entered its final phase, the Americans began parachuting arms to this little Viet Minh army.

For most of their occupation, the Japanese had been content to use the French as their instruments. In March 1945, however, they disarmed and locked up all the French forces in the country they could lay hands on. Since the Japanese did not have anything like enough troops to control both the cities and the countryside, Giap's forces were now free to grow at a rapid rate. By the middle of 1945, he commanded 5,000 trained men and exercised political control over perhaps one million peasants in the border areas. The fact that the Viet Minh actually exercised control over Vietnamese territory, no matter how small a portion, helped to legitimize it in the popular eye as a true alternative government, an enormous advantage for the Viet Minh over the other nationalist groups.[35]

The Japanese occupation produced yet another tremendous, and predictable, windfall for the Viet Minh: famine. The Japanese had been taking rice out of Viet Nam for their farflung wartime purposes and had forced many peasants to produce not rice but jute for Japanese industrial needs. In the winter of 1944–45 a serious famine broke out in the northern provinces. Estimates of those who died reach two million, out of Tonkin's population of perhaps nine million. The relationship between hunger and the outbreak of revolution in France and Russia is well known, and the Viet Minh would have benefited from this terrible situation even if it had sat still and done nothing. But in many places the Viet Minh led demonstrations in front of government granaries, sometimes seizing the grain and distributing it to the multitudes, in this way winning attention and gratitude. Viet Minh agitation during the famine was a "key to the development of the movement in rural areas throughout the north,"[36] and it provided, along with the front's campaign for national independence, the basis for what popular support it enjoyed in 1945. Still, by August of that year, the Viet Minh remained a small operation.

Meanwhile, having cast aside the last vestiges of French rule, the Japanese approached former Annamese emperor Bao Dai and offered him independence under Japanese protection. On March 11, 1945, Bao Dai proclaimed the independence of the empire of Annam and Tonkin, while Cochinchina remained under Japanese control. French power had disappeared, and defeat was impending for the Japanese; thus a political vacuum was being created in Viet Nam, a vacuum into which the Viet Minh, with its small but disciplined and devoted numbers, would soon march.

THE AUGUST REVOLUTION

No Vietnamese revolutionary group, including the Viet Minh and the VNQDD, had a mass following in Viet Nam, or even in Tonkin, in 1945. The decisive events of that fateful time were all very much the work of elite minorities.[37] But this was no obstacle, or even problem, for the Communists. For Marxist-Leninists, a revolutionary situation did not necessarily mean that there was great support for the revolutionaries, only that there was little or no support for the government. It was this absence of support that the Communists sought to manipulate, or create. In such conditions, the role of armed forces, those of the government and those of the revolution, became crucial.[38]

The circumstances for a Communist seizure of power in Hanoi in August 1945 were extremely propitious. After years of nationalist agitation, the humiliation of the French in 1940, the hardships of the Japanese occupation, and especially the terrible famine, a revolutionary situation was clearly at hand. The revolutionary elite was present in the form of the small but determined forces of the Viet Minh. Now, with the imprisonment of the French in March 1945 and the unexpected surrender of the Japanese Empire on August 15, the revolutionary crisis had appeared. On the night of August 18, Viet Minh troops moved into Hanoi and the next day proclaimed their control over the city. The police and militia of the Bao Dai government wavered in the face of the Communists' speed and discipline. Most importantly of all, the 30,000 Japanese troops in the city stood indifferently aside as the Viet Minh took over control of government buildings and strategic points around the city. On August 28, Ho Chi Minh announced the Provisional Government of the Democratic Republic of Viet Nam. Some Communists had wanted to imitate the Lenin of 1917 and set up an exclusively Communist cabinet; but Ho insisted that some non-Communist members be included, while keeping all key offices safely in the hands of the party. Ho also demanded that Emperor Bao Dai abdicate, and that gentleman complied with his demand. But then, acting on the principle that the front through which the Communists were working must be as broad as possible, Ho immediately appointed Bao Dai "Supreme Political Adviser" to the new regime. Finally, on September 2, 1945, in a moving ceremony before a vast Hanoi crowd, Ho proclaimed the independence of Viet Nam under the leadership of the Viet Minh.

Two outstanding circumstances permitted the August Revolution and shaped its course. First, the daring takeover of Hanoi resembled a coup much more than the great revolutions in history. It was an elitist movement, with a small number of well-drilled activists grasping the symbols of power amidst the confusion of their enemies. Notably absent, in Hanoi and especially in Saigon, in the events of August was the participation of middle-class elements.

Second, the August Revolution took place thanks to the temporary weakness, or absence, of those who could have opposed it. It was the imprisonment of the French and the neutrality of the Japanese, not the strength of the Viet Minh, that ensured the success of the August takeover.[39] Just as the First World War had made possible the October Revolution in Petrograd, so the Second World War made possible the August Revolution in Hanoi.

The seizure of Hanoi represented a sudden, if brief, switch back from a rural strategy to the old Bolshevik model of revolution. But unlike the revolutionaries in Petrograd in October 1917, the Viet Minh could not hold onto the capital. It would eventually be forced back into the jungles and mountains of northern Viet Nam, not to re-enter Hanoi again until the final capitulation of the French after many years and many, many deaths. Nevertheless, the August Revolution and the possession of government power in Hanoi, however briefly it all lasted, transformed the image of the Viet Minh from a revolutionary sect to a contender for national power and indeed the embodiment of the national cause. For many Vietnamese, including conscious anti-Communists, the choice now seemed to have narrowed down to a stark one: allow the discredited French to return or join (or at least support) the Viet Minh. At the same time, nobody outside of the Viet Minh, and probably only a handful of people inside it, were aware of the extent to which the Viet Minh was under Communist control.[40] Thus, in those heady and emotional days following the proclamation of independence, many Catholics, including some bishops, offered the Ho regime their tentative support.[41]

After the August Revolution, but before the return of the French, the Viet Minh made good use of the Japanese. Many Japanese officers had viewed the Second World War in profoundly racial terms, a colossal struggle between the people of East Asia and those of the North Atlantic. Imperial Japan had failed in its mighty effort to oust the detestable Caucasians from their Asian colonies, but the struggle might be carried on nonetheless through the agency of local nationalist groups like the Viet Minh. Hence all over East Asia in the waning days of the summer of 1945 the Japanese handed over great quantities of arms and ammunition to such organizations. In this manner the Viet Minh obtained, among other things, 31,000 rifles and 18 tanks.[42]

As the turn of the year approached, an increasing number of French forces were arriving in Viet Nam, especially around Saigon. Aware that an open breach with the French would result in the immediate loss of Hanoi (and perhaps much else), Ho decided on compromise. He and French representative Jean Sainteny negotiated the famous agreement of March 6, 1946. By this accord, France recognized the Democratic Republic of Viet Nam, consisting of at least Tonkin and Annam, as a free state—with an army, a parliament, and a treasury of its own. For his part, Ho accepted the stationing of a modest number of French armed forces north of the 16th parallel for five years, the training of the DRVN troops by French officers, and Vietnamese membership in the French Union (a Gallic version of the British Commonwealth). Ho also conceded that a plebiscite should be held in Cochinchina to determine if the people of that area wished to join the DRVN.

The Ho-Sainteny agreement recognized the legitimacy of Ho's government, but it fell short of granting complete independence. There was much opposition to it, even within the Viet Minh. General Giap called the agreement a new Brest-Litovsk, after the disastrous treaty Lenin signed with the German army in 1918. (Aside from purely frontist tactics, Ho had appointed non–Viet Minh members to his new February cabinet precisely because he foresaw the opposition that this "surrender" to the French would generate and didn't want all the blame to fall on the Viet Minh.)[43]

With the signing of the agreement, the triumph of the Communists and their Viet Minh front over the non-Communist nationalists seemed complete. Ho's skilled leadership, the attractiveness of Marxist philosophy to French-educated intellectuals, the temporary submersion of true Communist goals within the vessel of national independence—all had been important factors in this outcome. But so had Communist hostility toward non-Communist nationalists. The Communists had been for years betraying the latter to the French authorities. This policy had been particularly devastating against the VNQDD.[44] But to consolidate its victory and achieve total dominance over the Vietnamese nationalist movement, the Viet Minh increasingly relied on more direct methods. One needs to remember that the Communists had no wish whatsoever to be one component in a Vietnamese national movement and government; they desired an independent Viet Nam *only if it was completely controlled by them*. "Indeed, the fight for independence was for them only a vehicle for the conquest of power."[45] To this end, they carried out a deliberate campaign to destroy the noncommunist nationalists, murdering rivals or potential rivals by the score. "The elimination of their opponents was one of the most common means the Communists used to establish Viet Minh control over the entire nationalist movement."[46]

This dominance-through-murder policy was quite successful. "The Stalinists [Viet Minh] saw to it that those whose brilliance might have dimmed their own luster were buried in good time."[47] Not only was the Viet Minh able to establish control of the anti-French movement, but it also severely weakened the future state of South Viet Nam. This "Communist policy of killing all true nationalist opponents of the Viet Minh" deprived that state of the services of many who might have given it vigor and safety.[48] The Viet Minh also sought through assassination to decapitate the indigenous religious sects; it executed the leader of the powerful Hoa Hao, and corpses of sect members could be viewed floating down the Mekong River tied together in bundles, like logs.[49] And for good measure the Communists killed every Trotskyite they could locate.

The Communist destruction of the leadership of independent groups was very effective in the short run; in the elections of 1946, for example, Ho allegedly received 169,000 votes in Hanoi, whose total population was supposed to be 119,000.[50] But such tactics sowed bitter seeds of uncompromising hostility to the Viet Minh among large sections of the Vietnamese population, especially in the south.

The First Indochina War: 1946–1954

We may say that only with guns can the whole world be transformed.
—Mao Zedong

THE OUTBREAK OF FIGHTING

The Ho-Sainteny agreement seemed to promise a peaceful, if not amicable, short-term settlement to the explosive postwar situation in Viet Nam. Yet even while Ho Chi Minh was in Paris negotiating the final details of the agreement, French authorities on the scene were attempting to set up Cochinchina as an independent state, separate from the rest of Viet Nam and under French protection. The man behind this provocative move was Adm. Thierry d'Argenlieu, "the most brilliant mind of the twelfth century," whose appointment as French High Commissioner of Indochina has been called "France's major postwar blunder in Southeast Asia."[1] A hastily gathered assembly proclaimed the autonomous republic of Cochinchina on June 1, 1946. No Viet Minh government, not even Ho's, could long survive if it recognized such a state of affairs as permanent.

On the other side, the French had little enough reason to have confidence in the Viet Minh. In December 1944 Giap's forces had attacked two remote French outposts.[2] In August of the following year, after the signing of the Ho-Sainteny agreement, Viet Minh forces at Bac Ninh destroyed a French convoy on an authorized mission. Then, on November 9, the DRVN proclaimed a constitution without any mention at all of membership in the French Union. There could be no doubt that a real confrontation was coming, especially since the Viet Minh now had around 50,000 men under arms (including several thousand Japanese deserters who assisted General Giap with training and arms production).[3] The most dramatic incident took place at Haiphong in November. In retaliation for several murderous attacks on French soldiers in Hanoi, the French cruiser *Suffren* opened fire on the port of Haiphong. Over 6,000 Vietnamese, mostly civilians, lost their lives through this barbarous act; nobody knows how many were wounded. After the Haiphong incident, there could be no more pretense of French paternalism; it was now to be a naked struggle for power.[4] But however dramatic and regrettable, the shelling of Haiphong has not gone down in the records as the beginning of the war. That event is fixed as December 19, 1946, when Viet Minh troops tried to overwhelm Hanoi, with many grisly assaults on French civilians and concerted attacks on French garrisons all over Indochina.[5] The Socialist prime minister of France, Leon Blum, proclaimed a firm policy of military containment of the rebellion. Now the war was really on.

The seizure of Hanoi in August 1945 was the Leninist phase of the Viet Minh revolution. The retreat into the countryside, where French control had always been weak, was the beginning of the Maoist phase of the revolution. There would be attempts, such as in 1968 and 1972, to return to the Leninist mode and provoke the uprising of the vanguard of the oppressed masses in the great cities. But such uprisings somehow repeatedly failed to occur. In the countryside, the Viet Minh forces quickly and easily adopted the time-tested guerrilla tactics of Mao: speed of movement, surprise, never attacking without overwhelming numbers, always planning any military operation with its political effects uppermost in mind. It was a war of attrition against the French authorities, aiming at gaining control over a greater and greater proportion of the civilian population through persuasion or fear. In addition to their guerrilla units, the Viet Minh were building small conventional forces. These troops generally employed tactics very similar to those of the guerrillas (never fight except when the numbers are with you; slip away from superior forces), the principal difference being that guerrilla units attacked to inflict damage, while conventional forces attacked to annihilate.[6]

THE REVOLUTION DEVELOPS

In the early years of the war, the Viet Minh leadership, faithful to sound frontist tactics, emphasized nationalism and social improvement; it never denied, but never emphasized, the ultimate program of Communization. The Viet Minh seized the lands not of the well-to-do but only of the French and of Vietnamese collaborators, a policy that had its political costs. Many poorer peasants saw little reason to take risks for the Viet Minh if they were not to be given the land they wanted right away, and this despite the wooing of such persons by the Viet Minh with rent reductions and timely assistance to many during the wartime famine.

Faced with this political dilemma, the Viet Minh concentrated on the skillful indoctrination of those peasants who did join up. In the first years, desertions seem to have been few and morale high.[7] The progression of a recruit through the Viet Minh forces usually consisted of service first in a village unit, then in a provincial unit, with the best going ultimately into the conventional army and also perhaps into Communist party membership.

The most serious weakness of the Viet Minh forces after 1946 was the shortage of modern weapons; they simply could not begin to match the French forces in firepower, and under these circumstances they would never be able to defeat them decisively. All this changed when the Chinese Communist armies reached the border of Viet Nam in 1949. For the Viet Minh, Mao's victory across the border in China meant the availability of a sanctuary, improved training, and most of all, military supplies. Ho and the Viet Minh chose this time to proclaim their open and total adhesion to the Communist world under the leadership of Stalin. This act doubtless was encouraged by their Chinese benefactors, and it also won them, for the first time, the open support of the powerful French Communist party (whose chances, however, of coming to power peacefully after 1949 were nil). But on balance this ideological confession was a grave error. In throwing off the mask of the nationalist front and revealing the Stalinist face underneath it, the Communist directors of the Viet Minh paid a tremendous price: they turned the United States decisively and irrevocably against them. Henceforth, for a quarter of a century, the Americans would labor mightily, first by assisting the French, then by helping the southern anti-Communist state, and finally by massive intervention of U.S. forces, to prevent the conquest of all Viet Nam by the avowedly Communist Viet Minh. In bringing all this upon themselves and their country, "the extremists in the Viet Minh movement incurred a grave responsibility to the Vietnamese people."[8]

The principal military leader of the Viet Minh was Vo Nguyen Giap, whose fame from the First Indochina War was to be surpassed only by that of Ho Chi Minh. Giap's career, during which he held high positions both in the Viet Minh armed forces and in the party politburo, illustrates perfectly the Communist insight that military and political considerations are not separate but interpenetrating. Born in 1912, Giap studied at the Lycée National at Hue, the same school attended by Ho and Diem. He then went to the University of Hanoi, where he took a *license en droit* (law degree) in 1937 and considered going on for a doctorate in political economy. But he left the university after marrying the daughter of a professor there and accepted a position as a history teacher at a private school in Hanoi. The war and the Japanese occupation soon swept him up, and he found himself in command of the tiny military forces of the struggling Viet Minh. Whatever his ideological commitment to the revolutionary cause, Giap had profound personal motives for his hostility to the French; they had guillotined his sister-in-law, an anti-French activist, and his wife died in 1943 after a period of French imprisonment.

Giap often boasted that the only military academy he had ever attended was the bush. As one of his biographers points out, the bush is not a bad military school to attend, but it has the serious disadvantage of lacking a library. Hence, while Giap was learning good tactics, he could not broaden his understanding by reading the works of the great strategists. And after the August 1945 seizure of Hanoi, Giap the graduate of the Communist bush liked to appear in public dandily attired in a white duck suit and striped tie.[9]

THE BAO DAI SOLUTION

It was clear enough to the French that if the war came down to the choice of permanent colonialism under France versus independence under the Viet Minh, the French could not hope for a secure victory. They therefore needed a plausible Vietnamese alternative to the Viet Minh, an alternative that would stand for both independence and close cooperation with France, an alternative that could gather together the disparate but cumulatively numerous elements of the Vietnamese population that looked with distaste or horror upon the prospect of a Viet Minh victory. Thus the French abandoned Admiral d'Argenlieu's project for a separate Republic of Cochinchina. (Looking back after all these years, one cannot escape the feeling that, of all the efforts to prevent a totally Communist Viet Nam, this was probably the most likely to have succeeded.) In its place the French offered the so-called Bao Dai solution.

As this book is being written, Bao Dai's image is undoubtedly worse than he deserves. True enough, he became a habitué of nightclubs and less reputable establishments, but that was after he had endured a long series of grave political rebuffs and disappointments. One authoritative student of Viet Nam has called Bao Dai "an underrated man."[10] Having been raised to be emperor, and being very shy, Bao Dai lacked the common touch, especially compared to Ho Chi Minh (although Bao Dai did marry a commoner). However inadequately and unsuccessfully, Bao Dai undoubtedly worked for what he thought was best for his people. It was he, after all, who appointed the intransigent nationalist Ngo Dinh Diem to be his minister of the interior back in the 1930s. And when the Japanese surrendered, Bao Dai sent personal appeals to Charles de Gaulle, President Truman, Chiang Kai-shek, and King George VI, imploring them to recognize the independence of Viet Nam under his leadership. One of the main reasons Bao Dai had abdicated as emperor in the face of Ho Chi Minh's demand was his belief that because the U.S. military mission to Viet Nam spent most of its time at Ho Chi Minh's headquarters in Hanoi, the U.S. government must have been backing Ho.[11] In his abdication message to his people he had written: "We cannot help but have feelings of regret at the thought of the twenty years of our reign, during which we have not been able to render any appreciable service to our country."[12] Yet Ho himself recognized that Bao Dai enjoyed considerable prestige and popular affection; that is why Ho sought to associate him with the new Viet Minh regime by naming him "Supreme Adviser," and they appeared together in public. Bao Dai soon realized he was a figurehead for Communists and fled Viet Nam in March 1946. Now it was the turn of the French to attach him to their cause. Negotiations between the French and the former emperor on the future of Viet Nam caused Ho's government to condemn Bao Dai to death in absentia (December 1947). But in June of the following year, Bao Dai put his signature to a bombshell of a French document that began, "France solemnly recognizes the independence of Viet Nam." The chief of state of this independent Viet Nam was to be Bao Dai himself, who also forced the French to give up the idea that Cochinchina was not a true part of Viet Nam.

Thus "Bao Dai had obtained from the French in two years of negotiating what Ho had not been able to obtain in two years of fighting: the word 'independence.' "[13] Even though the Viet Minh leadership had not yet proclaimed its open adherence to Stalinist Communism, news of Bao Dai's triumph shocked the Viet Minh and caused many of its members to defect.[14]

President Dwight D. Eisenhower once remarked to Secretary of State John Foster Dulles that "the French could win the war in six months if the people were with them."[15] There is a great deal of truth in that observation, but it is not so easy to know who "the people" actually were supporting. In their desperation to find additional manpower, the French had set up a separate Vietnamese army owing political allegiance to Bao Dai and his State of Viet Nam. By 1952 this army consisted of about 80,000 men. Additional scores of thousands of Vietnamese served with the French Union forces. The total number of all Vietnamese in uniform under the command either of the French or of Bao Dai would reach 300,000 by 1954.[16] A Vietnamese military academy was opened in 1949, although few officers came out of it. Vietnamese units in both the French Union and Bao Dai armies were usually infiltrated by Viet Minh agents;[17] also, the French gave their Vietnamese army allies secondhand equipment, further undercutting their morale.[18] Nonetheless, between 1946 and 1950, Vietnamese forces fighting against the Viet Minh incurred about 7,500 casualties a year, a very high rate.[19]

In the south, the French eventually set up a system of warlords, usually local religious sect leaders, to fight the Communists for them; this strategy was not ineffective, but the warlords could flourish only as long as the war went on. Hence they had no real interest in bringing the conflict to a decisive conclusion—an example of the symbiotic relationship between the strength of the Viet Minh and most efforts to destroy them.[20] In Viet Nam as a whole, the Bao Dai– French Union side eventually won the allegiance, or at least the alliance, of the pre-war nationalist parties, the Saigon middle class, the great majority of Catholics, and the powerful southern religious sects. On the other side, General Giap's forces never exceeded 300,000 men, less than 1 percent of the Vietnamese population of those days.[21] It seems that, by 1954, when President Eisenhower made his comment about popular support, the situation in Viet Nam was something like this: a powerful minority favored the Viet Minh; substantial elements opposed the Viet Minh and hence for the time being cooperated with the French; and another group, probably the largest, desired only to be let alone by both sides.

THE FRENCH FORCES

Whatever the constitutional arrangements in Viet Nam, France would of course have to bear the brunt of the war. It would be an understatement to observe that the French conduct of the war was administratively inept. The Ministry of Defense, the Ministry of Overseas France, and other agencies in Paris all exercised shares of control over military affairs.[22] If unity of administration was poor, continuity of command was nonexistent; from 1945 to 1954, French forces in Viet Nam had no less than eight commanders in chief. During that same time, the politicians in Paris, with stunning frivolity, set up and pulled down no less than 16 cabinets.

Beset by overlapping authorities and frequent changes of leadership, the French forces also confronted the classic problem of counter-guerrilla warfare: how to divide one's forces between static defense and mobile operations. Given enough troops under one's command, this problem is not insuperable. But even with the native forces of Bao Dai, the French never had enough troops, because French law forbade the sending of draftees to Indochina.

By 1953, General Giap commanded, as noted, an estimated 300,000 fighters. According to the standard ten-to-one ratio, the French would have needed 3,000,000 troops to achieve victory in Viet Nam, an impossible figure. To reach even an insufficient ratio of three-to-one, they would have needed 900,000. But in fact, French forces consisted of 50,000 French soldiers (out of a population of over 40,000,000), 30,000 colonial troops (mainly Senegalese and North Africans), 20,000 Foreign Legionnaires, and 150,000 Vietnamese, along with 15,000 French naval and air personnel. Even after one adds to these the 150,000 men in Bao Dai's army and another 30,000 in the sect and Catholic militias, the grand total is at most 450,000—precisely half of the totally inadequate three-to-one ratio.

Airpower could have compensated in part for the deficient number of ground troops, but the French had only very limited air capability. As late as 1954, French forces in Viet Nam possessed exactly 10 helicopters. Besides, the Viet Minh usually operated at night, and the French used what airpower they had in direct support of ground troops, to an extent that many French airmen believed was inefficient.[23] (General Chassin, when he was French air commander in Viet Nam, remarked that his air force was going to kill water buffalo because they were the "tractors" of the Viet Minh—a comment that should not be overlooked by those seeking the deeper causes of the French failure in Viet Nam).[24] Nevertheless, in October 1947 French airborne troops descended on Viet Minh headquarters and almost captured both Ho and Giap, one of the great what-ifs in modern history.[25]

The French forces sent to Viet Nam were unprepared for what they encountered. "Our units, organized for warfare in Europe, proved to be ill-suited to . . . a struggle against rebel forces in an Asiatic theatre."[26] The infantry was poorly trained and weighed down by the impedimenta of a Western army.[27] The French Colonial Army had a hallowed tradition of rotating its units among possessions all over the globe. Hence there were very few "area specialists" in its ranks, and this shortage of officers and noncommissioned officers (NCOs) familiar with the realities of Viet Nam made it very difficult to create irregular forces and gather intelligence.[28] The battalions of the Viet Minh fought infrequently, while the French had to be alert and on patrol every night.[29] Time and again, French forces would occupy a village and begin rounding up Viet Minh agents, often with the help of local inhabitants. But then, because of inadequate manpower, they would abandon the place, exposing all the civilians who had helped them to ghastly reprisals. As the conflict dragged on, French infantry units became increasingly dependent on artillery and air support, a sure sign of declining morale.[30] Finally, there appears in the reports of one officer this revealing—and chilling—comment: "Each night the roads were left to the enemy."[31]

FRENCH TACTICS

A favorite French move was to establish outposts far from their base in the Red River Delta (the Hanoi-Haiphong area). Because French airpower was weak, these outposts had to be supplied by convoys. Of course, the Viet Minh responded by ambushing these convoys. Between 1952 and 1954 alone, the French lost 398 armored vehicles.[32] To discourage ambushes, the French begin building strongpoints at places where ambushes had previously occurred. These strongpoints, in turn, needed to be supplied by convoy. Hence, convoys went forth to supply outposts that had been erected to protect the convoys.[33] "The French lived in fear of ambushes to the end of the war."[34]

From time to time the French decided to abandon an outpost, thus creating another great convoy begging to be attacked. These withdrawals produced some of the worst French disasters. At Cao Bang, guarding one of the few passages through the mountainous border with China, the French had a good fort with impressive defenses, natural and manmade. In October 1950, the French high command in Hanoi ordered Cao Bang to be abandoned. Eventually, 1,600 soldiers plus hundreds of civilians left Cao Bang and headed for the city of Lang Son, 85 miles to the south, along a miserable track through the majestic forest. At the same time, 3,500 French Moroccan troops advanced north to meet the party coming from Cao Bang. The two groups linked up, but then the swarming Viet Minh cut them to pieces, "the greatest defeat in the history of French colonial warfare."[35]

The debacle of Cao Bang somehow convinced the French that they should also abandon Lang Son. This city of 100,000 was the main French strongpoint in the entire border region. To avoid alerting the Viet Minh, the French withdrew from the city without first blowing up their munitions. Thus the Viet Minh obtained 10,000 75 mm shells, invaluable gasoline, precious medicines, and much else. It was "France's greatest colonial defeat since Montcalm had died at Quebec."[36] Similar disasters resulted from the abandonment of Hoa Binh in 1952 and Sam Neua in 1953.

The outcome of the border battles gave the Viet Minh unrestricted access to supplies from Communist China. They also suggest that outposts are worse than useless unless they can be safely supplied, and that troops are generally safer inside a strongpoint, fighting off the enemy, than trying to escape that enemy on inadequate roads without air cover.

The French tried to cut the Communists off from the rice and population of the Red River Delta, with a string of fortifications known as the De Lattre Line. This would have been a good idea if the French had possessed sufficient numbers to hold the line tightly, but they did not. Thus the Viet Minh were free to raid the Red River Delta at will and withdraw back to their strongholds. Besides, with the French pursuing their De Lattre Line strategy, the Viet Minh had unimpeded access to its cornucopia at the Chinese border.

Yet all was not going well on the Communist side. General Giap was outstandingly good at logistics, but his limited training in conventional warfare was often a handicap to him when commanding large bodies of troops. Thus in the early 1950s, at the battles of Vinh Yen (a failure that Giap publicly blamed on cowardice on the part of his troops), Mao Khe, and the Day River, the Viet Minh suffered a total of 20,000 casualties. If the French had had the manpower, they could then have launched a possibly decisive counter-offensive against Giap.[37] Instead, the war dragged on, with Giap pursuing more orthodox guerrilla tactics and fighting smaller engagements.

In order to bring the war to a successful conclusion, the French would have had to decide on some combination of the following options: (1) send substantial reinforcements from metropolitan France, (2) create a well-equipped Vietnamese army, (3) close the border with China, through diplomatic or military means, (4) carry out socio-economic reforms to separate the peasantry from the Viet Minh hard core, or (5) retrench into super-enclaves in Cochinchina and the Hanoi-Haiphong Delta area. The French chose none of these paths, attempting instead to fight on in the accustomed way in all areas of Viet Nam.

By the beginning of 1954, after seven years of fighting, the French and their Vietnamese allies clearly could not disperse the Viet Minh, and the Viet Minh could not expel the French. The war had become a stalemate. In these circumstances, the French decided to fight one more outpost battle, at a place called Dien Bien Phu.

DIEN BIEN PHU

The French were getting very tired, and with good reason, of this war that nobody could win. In the French view, their principal problem was that the Communists would rarely engage in regular battles, in which superior French training and firepower would prove decisive (such as in Giap's disaster at Vinh

Yen), but instead engaged mainly in guerrilla fighting, in which the French were at a serious disadvantage. Hence the French high command conceived the idea of building a fortress complex near the Laotian border, in one of the most remote and inaccessible areas of Viet Nam. The fortress would serve two purposes: (1) minimally, it would impede easy passage of Viet Minh troops between Viet Nam and Laos, and (2) much more importantly, the French hoped that General Giap would find this large but isolated outpost an irresistible temptation to a conventional battle. Taking this bait, the Viet Minh would send in its best conventional units, which would of course be totally chewed up by superior French firepower. But the site selected for the fortress at Dien Bien Phu was in a valley; what if the Viet Minh placed heavy artillery on the mountain sides and pounded Dien Bien Phu to pieces at leisure? Impossible: the Viet Minh did not have sufficient artillery or the transport to get it into the jungles on the Laotian border. And even if by some miracle they could bring heavy guns into the area, how could they keep those guns supplied? Besides, let the Communist guns fire once, and French gunners would destroy them quickly and utterly. But what if the siege of Dien Bien Phu should go on and on? Would not its defenders soon run out of ammunition, medicines, everything? No. The French would quickly maul the attackers, but if in fact the battle should become protracted, French airpower would supply the men inside the fortress with their basic needs.

Every single one of these assumptions turned out to be disastrously wrong. One must record, however, that during French preparations of their stronghold at Dien Bien Phu, no foreigners of high rank, including several Americans who visited the place before the battle, ever questioned the basic strategy. The real mistake of the French commander in Viet Nam, General Heuri Navarre, was *"his gross underestimation of the Viet Minh and General Giap."*[38]

But what led General Giap to accept the French challenge and fight a conventional battle around Dien Bien Phu? In the first place, at Dien Bien Phu General Giap would be close to his base, while the French would be far from theirs. The Viet Minh were above all tired of the war and the large casualties it had inflicted upon them. If fighting a major and perhaps decisive battle violated one fundamental Viet Minh principle of warfare, another principle came into play: military action for political impact. The Viet Minh decided to break the stalemate by attacking public opinion in metropolitan France. That is the meaning of the battle of Dien Bien Phu.

In a battle of 56 days, 13,000 Franco-Vietnamese soldiers fought 100,000 Viet Minh troops. The defenders represented perhaps 5 percent of French forces in Indochina, while Giap committed nearly 50 percent of his available combat forces to the siege.[39] The battle began on March 13, 1954—with a Communist artillery bombardment—and the French and Vietnamese defenders knew immediately that they were in deep trouble. The fighting took place according to a predictable scenario: the Communist forces formed a noose around the fortress complex, and one by one they captured its strongpoints until nothing was left to the defenders except an area the size of a football field, and then that too fell. The sufferings of the defenders, French and Vietnamese, especially the

seriously wounded, were profound. Although all the world knew that the outcome of the battle was foregone, throughout the contest hundreds of French and
Vietnamese troops volunteered to be dropped into the doomed fortress. Whatever one may think of the motives of those thousands of Vietnamese who fought
alongside the French against their own countrymen, one cannot deny that many
of them were very brave. An astute observer of this battle has noted that mixed
French-Vietnamese units fought better than purely French or purely Vietnamese
ones, a lesson (one among many) lost on the Americans.[40]

What defeated the defenders of Dien Bien Phu was artillery, a four-to-one
inferiority in artillery to the Communists. The French were utterly astounded at
the ability of the Viet Minh to haul heavy pieces through roadless jungles and
across trackless mountains, and—equally important—to keep these weapons
supplied with shells. The French could not mount a major relief effort on the
ground, since in order to assemble sufficient numbers, they would have had to
strip other and more strategic places. The men inside Dien Bien Phu could have
been saved by massive air attacks on the besiegers, as the marines inside Khe
Sanh would be saved years later. But the most modern French aircraft were too
big and too fast for any airfield in Viet Nam, and the older types were too few.
What French air assistance there was sometimes worked against the defenders.
For instance, on April 15 a French pilot accidentally dropped out of his cockpit
a packet of photographs of the whole battlefield area, including remaining
French positions, photographs that were soon in the hands of General Giap.[41]
Besides, the anti-aircraft fire over Dien Bien Phu was more murderous than that
over Germany during World War II.[42] Many of the Viet Minh anti-aircraft units
had Chinese advisers.[43] One chronicler of the battle says that the Viet Minh
paid for all this effort through the export of opium, which grows abundantly
over the whole area.[44] At last, on May 7, 1954, the remaining defenders gave
up.

Only a very small proportion of French forces in Indochina had been engaged
at Dien Bien Phu. Nevertheless the French, who had watched, fascinated, as the
drama reached its inevitable end, were deeply shaken; as Giap had calculated,
the heart went out of French support for a continuation of the conflict.

In his book *No More Viet Nams*, Richard Nixon states that the United States'
first critical mistake in Viet Nam was not intervening with sea and air power to
save Dien Bien Phu.[45] The United States had been giving substantial financial
support to the French war effort in Viet Nam for years and had fought a significant war of its own against two Communist regimes in Korea. The French
cabinet had requested American air strikes to save Dien Bien Phu. Why, then,
did the Eisenhower administration allow the fall of the fortress, with its predictable effects on French public opinion? In March 1954, President Eisenhower
told the National Security Council that he would indeed intervene in Viet Nam,
provided such action enjoyed the support of a bipartisan majority in Congress
and the assistance of Western allies (notably Great Britain). The British made
it clear that they were not interested. Even if they had been, leading Republican

senators absolutely opposed any U.S. intervention in Viet Nam; the GOP had successfully branded the Democrats as the war party in the 1952 campaign and prided itself on ending the stalemated Korean War. So Dien Bien Phu fell, a conference of the Great Powers opened at Geneva to settle the war, and in June Pierre Mendès-France became French prime minister, pledged to end the war quickly or resign.

THE GENEVA TRUCE

If the Geneva Conference had not met immediately after the fall of Dien Bien Phu, it is more than possible that the Communists would have taken over all of Viet Nam instead of Tonkin and northern Annam only. But with the convening of the conference, some kind of a peace agreement had to be reached.

Almost all the serious fighting by the Viet Minh had taken place in Tonkin. Paradoxically, the Communists had always been far stronger in Tonkin, with its relatively widespread landownership and large Catholic population, than in Cochinchina, where 2 percent of the landowners owned 30 percent of the land. A number of factors contributed to the weak position of the Communists in the south. They had bloodily confronted the popular Trotskyites there in the 1930s. Saigon (like Hanoi) had only a small Communist organization, due to effective police surveillance and the indifference of the relatively sophisticated population.[46] The famine of 1944, which was of such assistance to the Communists in Tonkin, was hardly felt in Cochinchina. When the Japanese surrendered, the Communist Party in the south, unlike its counterpart in the north, had hardly any armed units and thus could not seize Saigon. Tonkin, moreover, had been occupied by the Chinese Nationalist armies until well into the spring of 1946, giving the Communists time to consolidate their position there before the return of French troops, whereas the French were back in Cochinchina in strength as early as October 1945. Most of all, standing in the way of the creation of a powerful Communist organization in the south were the sects, principally the Cao Dai and the Hoa Hao. Between them, these religious-economic formations enrolled what may have been a majority of Cochinchinese. Fighting between the well-armed sects and the southern Communists had broken out very soon after the August Revolution and continued through the spring of 1947, so that the sects became thoroughly alienated from the Viet Minh.

The Americans therefore supported the partition of Viet Nam into a Communist north and a non-Communist south. Ho Chi Minh was naturally opposed to a partition. His Chinese and Soviet mentors at Geneva, however, feared that conservatives might displace the Mendès-France cabinet and, with increased U.S. aid, renew the fighting (Mendès-France himself was already ordering tropical inoculations for two French army divisions stationed in Germany).[47] So partition it was to be. Ho then demanded that the partition line be drawn at the 13th parallel—in effect, the boundary between Cochinchina and Annam. The conference, however, eventually settled on the 17th parallel, considerably farther

to the north. In retrospect, it is tempting to say that the new South Vietnamese
state would have been much better off with the smaller size the Communists
wished it to have. The territory between the 13th and 17th parallels did contain
the ancient and symbolic city of Hue, as well as the home of Viet Nam's prime
minister Diem; but the area was thinly populated, far from Saigon, and bordered
by Laos, through which the notorious Ho Chi Minh Trail would soon penetrate.
Most of the South Vietnamese and almost all the Americans who died in the
subsequent 20-year struggle to preserve the South Vietnamese state died between
those two parallels, and it was in this very area that the South Vietnamese army
would suffer the sudden collapse that brought the final destruction of South Viet
Nam.

A SUMMARY

The fighting in Viet Nam between 1946 and 1954 had cost France 10 times
the value of all its investments there.[48] The cost in blood, just to France and its
Vietnamese allies, was also enormous: 21,000 French, 55,000 French Union,
and 18,000 Vietnamese soldiers killed or missing; French deaths alone would
have been the equivalent, in proportion to population, of 100,000 American
deaths, in comparison to the 50,000 battle deaths the Americans would eventually suffer. Total military casualties approached a quarter of a million, including 78,000 Vietnamese.[49] The cream of the French officer corps was destroyed:
1,300 lieutenants, 4 generals, 21 sons of generals or marshals.[50] By 1953 more
French officers were dying in Viet Nam than were graduating from the national
military academy at St. Cyr. Two thousand women served with the French
ground forces, and another 150 with air and naval units; of these 150 were
killed.[51]

No one, including Hanoi, knows for sure how many Viet Minh fighters died,
but knowledgeable estimates put the number as high as 400,000. The death toll
among innocent civilians will never be known, but it must surely have been in
the hundreds of thousands.

Why, after paying such a price, did the French give up on the war?

In the first place, France was exhausted, morally as well as physically, by the
Second World War, during which it had suffered two invasions, with a cruel
and humiliating Nazi occupation in between. Then, the Vietnamese war got off
to a very bad start, from the French point of view: the extended power vacuum
created by first the Japanese and then the Chinese occupation of Viet Nam, and
then the Communist victory in China, had given General Giap tremendous advantages. Furthermore, for the successive French cabinets directing the war (17
of them), Europe—not Viet Nam on the other side of the world—was the center
of interest and effort, as it was for the Americans. France therefore fought a
quite limited war (no draftees, for example). Thus, although the Viet Minh had
good leadership and many of them were dedicated and brave, the main reason

for the defeat of the French is that they never came close to amassing sufficient forces to fight a proper antiguerrilla war. The French could have overcome this lack of manpower at least to some degree if they had possessed sufficient mobility, but the weakness of their air force meant that the French were utterly lacking such mobility; they never had more than 10 helicopters, for instance.[52] This is the basic reason for the loss of Dien Bien Phu. By then, the war had begun to seem too burdensome, and since everybody knew that despite the rhetoric Viet Nam was not essential to France, the French could and did go home.

There are undoubtedly valuable lessons for everyone in the French failure in Viet Nam. Clearly, however, we ought to approach with much skepticism the assertions of those who profess to see in it some irrefutable confirmation of the universal superiority—even invincibility—of guerrilla fighters over modern armies, especially nonindigenous modern armies, a superiority that is supposed to have profound implications for U.S. foreign policy all over the globe.

And who, in the end, caused the war?

A large part of the blame must of course go to Ho Chi Minh and his disciples. Bao Dai had obtained more than half a loaf from the French in 1948, and full independence could surely have followed in the foreseeable future, peacefully. But Ho insisted that independence be full and immediate, and under the control of his party; this could only be obtained by years of bloody combat. He hoped, by uniting the Vietnamese in a bitter anti-French crusade, to solidify the control of his Viet Minh over them. Counting on the Soviets and Chinese to assist him and on the French public to tire of this distant war, Ho was willing to fight on for whatever length of time and at whatever cost in the blood of his countrymen.

Even then, when the fighting stopped in 1954, and so many were dead or maimed, Ho himself had obtained only half a loaf.

Whatever the blame we might wish to load upon Ho Chi Minh and the other Communists who controlled the Viet Minh, there is plenty left over for the French. The war, and their failure to win it, were rooted in two key decisions: (1) to go back into Viet Nam after World War II as if nothing had happened since 1939, and (2) to deprive the "Bao Dai solution" of the full reality it needed in order to be a compelling alternative to the Viet Minh.

The French refused to see that World War II had finished colonialism in Asia. Even as the British were leaving India and the Dutch Indonesia, the French battened all the tighter on Indochina. They feared what the loss of Indochina would mean to their North African possessions, and their humiliations in World War II made them insensitive and arrogant in dealing with legitimate Vietnamese aspirations for self-government. Thus, although the war eventually came to be seen by many as a conflict between the West (the French supported by the Americans) and international Communism (Ho Chi Minh backed by Stalin and Mao), it did not start out that way. In 1946, it was not anti-Communism but imperialism that fueled the French war machine. "To have underestimated the force of nationalist feeling and to have disregarded all opportunities for genuine compromise may be called the basic French mistakes in Indochina,"[53] mistakes for which, long after the French had departed from Viet Nam, many would continue to pay a truly bitter price.

4

After the Partition

War is the chief promoter of despotism.

—Bertrand Russell

THE FLIGHT FROM THE COMMUNIST NORTH

When the Geneva Conference announced the partition of Viet Nam into a Communist north and a non-Communist south, it further directed that for the period of a year there must be free movement of persons wishing to migrate from one zone to the other. Even the harsh occupation by the Japanese had failed to induce the Vietnamese to flee their ancestral villages and provinces. Yet now, in 1954, appeared one of the most characteristic, significant, and poignant aspects of the 20-year struggle for a free South Viet Nam, an aspect that continued right up until the siege of Saigon in 1975: the massive flight of civilians fleeing ever farther southward, ever away from Communist control.

Estimates of the number of those who fled from Communist North Viet Nam between 1954 and 1956 vary from 800,000 to one million, of whom the majority were Christian Vietnamese. Among those fleeing south was almost the entire student body of the University of Hanoi.[1] If a proportionate exodus took place in the United States, the number of refugees would approach twelve million. The Northern authorities placed many obstacles in the way of those wishing to leave, including murder; the actual number of refugees might have been multiplied several times if there had been that complete freedom of movement called for at Geneva.[2] Nobody can know how many more would have fled if they had had more time to wind up their affairs in the North or had not feared homelessness in the South.

The great exodus from the North had many consequences. It provided South

Viet Nam with some of its most redoubtable supporters; indeed, within a few years of 1954, northern refugees would dominate the southern army and government. It also relieved internal anti-Communist pressure on Ho Chi Minh's regime, thus facilitating the erection of a totalitarian state and setting the stage for calamitous land reform in North Viet Nam.

"LAND REFORM"

A government coming to power in a rural and underdeveloped country may decide to pursue agricultural policies that aim at an increase of food production, or it may attempt to reduce or eliminate perceived social injustice. Leninist regimes in such circumstances, however, invariably imposed collectivization. This involved, first, placing ownership of land and all decisions concerning rural life in the hands of government agents (almost always city men), and second, eliminating landowners, however small their holdings, branding them "class enemies of the revolution." Collectivization of land was not about social justice, and it had even less to do, as much sad experience has proved, with increasing food production. Rather, collectivization was a means for increasing the control of the city-bred, middle-class revolutionary elite over the masses in the countryside. Collectivized equality "is shared poverty by serfs, coupled with the monopolization of both privilege and power by a small (increasingly hereditary) aristocracy."[3] Another purpose of collectivization was to tie large numbers of peasants to the regime through deliberate, state-sponsored criminalization: poorer peasants were encouraged or compelled to testify against landowning peasants, a process that resulted in the death of many of the latter. The fall of the regime would presumably expose those peasants who participated in the collectivization trials to retribution; hence they are its prisoners. From the Leninist point of view, therefore, the bloodier the collectivization campaign against those defined as "class enemies," the better.[4] This was one meaning of the North Vietnamese maxim of those days: "Better to kill ten innocent persons than to let one enemy escape."[5]

During the war with the French, the Viet Minh had promised "land to the tiller." Now the reality of Communist rural policy laid its grip on the villages. The prelude to collectivization was "land reform." Nobody knows how many died during the land-reform drive in North Viet Nam; estimates range from 50,000 to "several hundred thousands."[6] To reach figures like this, it was necessary for the regime to define as "rich landlords" peasants who exceeded the smallest permissible holding by only one-quarter of an acre; many of these so-called class enemies had previously been members of the Viet Minh.[7] Thousands of these unfortunates were executed outright, many by being buried alive.[8] But numerous victims of the land campaign trials met their deaths by suicide or from the effects of "isolation." Relatives of those who had been imprisoned or executed were isolated; utterly shunned by the community under party orders, they could not work, and many starved to death. "Like leprous dogs, they became creatures at whom children were encouraged to throw stones."[9] Young children of parents who had been killed had to beg for food.[10] Few pages in the long and sometimes embarrassing annals of French imperialism can compare to this.

Catholic villages were particularly hard hit by the reforms of 1955–1956. In November 1956 a massive insurrection of Catholic peasants broke out across the North, including Nghe An, home province of Ho Chi Minh; the regime killed or deported thousands.[11] Alarmed at the drop in food production, the party leadership concluded that the bloodletting had gone far enough and called a halt. Regime leaders publicly admitted errors, and the director of the land reform program was dismissed. General Giap revealed perhaps much more than he intended when he observed, "We showed no indulgence towards landlords who had participated in the resistance [Viet Minh], treating their children in the same way we treated the children of other landlords."[12] But why should anybody's children be harshly treated by their own government?

A few years after these events, the regime, having increasingly isolated itself from the West and become totally dependent on the Soviets and the PRC, felt secure enough to hold national elections. There were no voting booths; ballots were marked in the open, in front of election officials. The government announced that its list of candidates had won an overwhelming victory.[13]

THE COMING OF DIEM

By means of two treaties initialed in June 1954, the French recognized the complete independence of the state of Viet Nam under Bao Dai; only the territory south of the 17th parallel, however, would be left to his government. In those same days, Bao Dai appointed as his new prime minister Ngo Dinh Diem. Before accepting the appointment, Diem had demanded full emergency powers, civil and military; Bao Dai granted them, since nobody else of any stature in Viet Nam wanted the thankless job of being prime minister of a war-weary country that was being cut into two parts.[14]

Like Chiang Kai-shek, his neighbor to the north, Ngo Dinh Diem was both a Confucian and a Christian. The Ngos were one of the great families of Viet Nam. Having accepted Catholicism centuries before, they had endured persecution and even death for generations, a legacy of stubborn resistance that showed its influence in Diem. Born in Hue in 1901, the son of a mandarin, Diem graduated first in his class from the French-run School of Law and Public Administration in Hanoi,[15] and he then accepted an appointment to the royal library in Hue. Convinced that an independent Viet Nam would need trained administrators, Diem decided to enter the French government structure, and in 1925, at a remarkably young age, he became governor of Binh Thuan province. Diem got into trouble with the French colonialists from the start. He believed that Viet Nam needed and deserved real powers of self-government; in later years he would insist that the Communists could be fought successfully only through a program of social reform and convincing steps toward real Vietnamese independence. In 1933 Bao Dai appointed Diem to be minister of the interior (an office once held by a relative of Diem). Diem's responsibilities included carrying out certain administrative reforms Bao Dai had promised the previous year. The French blocked these reforms, and so Diem resigned in September 1933. This act overnight made him a symbol of sincere opposition to colonialism. His stature increased when after 1944 he refused overtures from both the Japanese and the French to head Vietnamese governments that in his view lacked sufficient autonomy.[16] "His earlier government career had stamped him as an able administrator; his resignation in 1933 gave him credentials as a principled nationalist, and his subsequent behavior emphasized that he was a man who would not compromise his principles for political gain."[17] Diem's "perfect integrity, his competence, and his intelligence" all enhanced his reputation as a leading nationalist.[18] He preserved this reputation even during the Japanese occupation, when many other Vietnamese nationalists ate the poisoned fruit of collaboration with the conquerors of the French. In March 1945, immediately after they had taken over complete control of Viet Nam, the Japanese (and others) advised Bao Dai to offer the premiership to Diem, which he did not once but twice.[19] Suspicious of the true motives of the Japanese and skeptical of their ability to withstand the Americans, Diem made no reply.

Ho Chi Minh also recognized Diem's prestige as a highminded nationalist. At a meeting at Ho's headquarters in February 1946, Ho offered Diem the post of minister of the interior in his new Viet Minh government.[20] Diem, however, was deeply mistrustful of the Viet Minh's real aims; besides, Communists had murdered one of his brothers in 1945. The two men could reach no understanding, and Ho allowed Diem to depart unmolested from his headquarters.[21] During the subsequent war, the Viet Minh put a price on Diem's head; informed by the unfriendly French authorities that they could not guarantee his safety, Diem left Viet Nam in 1950, traveling first to Rome and later to the United States, Belgium, and France. In the following years, as the Viet Minh war reached its height, Bao Dai three more times asked Diem to return and take over the premiership. Diem each time insisted that the war against the Viet Minh should be run by the Vietnamese, not by the French. Long distrusting Diem for his nationalism, the French would agree to nothing of this nature. Thus Diem continued to refuse Bao Dai's offers. From his resignation as interior minister in 1933 to his final acceptance of the premiership in the summer of 1954, therefore, Diem's mature career had been one long refusal to be anybody's puppet, even at the price of exile both inside and outside Viet Nam. Many decent persons have been unable to resist the offer of political power from the hands of those whom they opposed or despised, on the grounds that power would enable them to accomplish some good, or fend off some greater evil. But Diem distinguished himself from other nationalists in that prior to 1954 he had refused attractive offers to collaborate with the French colonialists, the Japanese conquerors, the Viet Minh, or Bao Dai. His intransigent nationalism, "born of a profound, of an immense nostalgia for the Vietnamese past, of a desperate filial respect for the society of ancient Annam,"[22] his self-conscious rootedness in Vietnamese history, along with his paradoxical but devout adherence to a minority religion— at different times these characteristics would be sources of both strength and weakness to him; but they all marked him out as a man not to be trifled with or to be deflected from his chosen course by mere criticism. Perhaps Bao Dai made his final and successful offer of the premiership to Diem because he believed Diem could get the backing of the Americans; perhaps he hoped that the assumption of high office in such troubled times would finish off Diem politically.[23] Nobody knows. At any rate, on June 18, 1954, the day Pierre Mendès-France took the oath as prime minister of France, Diem announced (in Paris) that he had accepted Bao Dai's offer to become prime minister of Viet Nam.

DIEM'S FIRST DAYS IN POWER

"The overriding need in South Viet Nam was to establish a governmental authority independent of the French and superior to the many centrifugal forces."[24] This was a truly daunting task. Starting from the bottom, Ho Chi Minh had spent 20 years building up the organization through which he now ruled half of Viet Nam. In his capital at Hanoi, Ho was the legatee of both the August Revolution and the victory at Dien Bien Phu. Diem, in contrast, was starting out to build a new state from the top down; he had few resources outside of his own reputation and determination.

While Ho's Democratic Republic of Viet Nam had emerged from the war with a large and experienced army, South Viet Nam's 800 miles of border with Laos and Cambodia were largely defenseless; inside South Viet Nam, moreover, the Viet Minh possessed a good network of fighters and informants. As he looked out, in his first days as prime minister, of his office window at Saigon, one of the loveliest cities in all Asia, Diem knew that his real authority did not extend even as far as his eye could see. The French civil administration was pulling out and taking everything movable; yet 40,000 French troops would remain, menacingly, in South Viet Nam until the end of 1955.[25] The gangster society Binh Xuyen was in control of the police force in Saigon. The armed forces of one religious sect (the Cao Dai) controlled the province west of Saigon, while the troops of another (the Hoa Hao) ruled in the southern Delta area. The Diem government's only link with formal legitimacy, Emperor Bao Dai, was sullenly hostile to his new prime minister. Finally, an inundation of refugees was about to descend from the North.

If Diem were ever to emerge as a serious rival to Ho Chi Minh as a champion of the Vietnamese people and their aspirations, he first had to extricate himself from the debris of the French imperial system and put an end to all vestiges of French control in the South.[26] But the French intended to maintain a "presence" south of the 17th parallel (and perhaps north of it as well); they were therefore determined that Diem had to go. The French had readily at hand an apparently perfect instrument for their policy: General Nguyen Van Hinh, who was not only the chief of staff of Bao Dai's army but also a French citizen and an officer in the French air force. Hinh spoke openly of a coup against Diem. In November 1954, Gen. J. Lawton Collins, President Eisenhower's new special envoy to Saigon, made it clear to Hinh that U.S. aid for the South Vietnamese armed forces would be cut off if Diem were removed by force.[27] Hinh finally ignored these warnings and in April 1955 made a bungled move against Diem, which failed, ending Hinh's career in Vietnamese politics. But the French had not yet played their last anti-Diem card.

Since General Hinh was not the only high-ranking Vietnamese who would conspire against Diem, the prime minister had to try to fill civil offices and military commands with men who were trustworthy as well as competent. This was a major problem. In the first place, hardly anyone expected his government to last more than a few months at best. Even more important, under the French colonial administration native Vietnamese had been prevented from obtaining any experience in important governmental work. Diem also needed persons who were anti-Communist but not tainted by collaboration with the French, whom Diem disliked and who were plotting against him. Later the problem of finding enough leaders would be aggravated by the Communist policy of assassinating local government figures who were too good at their jobs.

All these factors help explain why Diem, from the earliest days of his rule, employed the traditional Vietnamese expedient of filling his administration with family members and close personal friends. Thus one of Diem's brothers, Luyen, went to London as ambassador. Another brother, Can, was in effect the political boss of central Viet Nam. Brother Thuc became archbishop of Hue. Brother Nhu founded and ran the regime's major political vehicle, the Revolutionary Workers Party. Brother Nhu's father-in-law filled the sensitive post of ambassador to Washington. Two other Nhu in-laws were made chief justice and foreign minister, respectively.

Aside from these relatives, Diem forged his government through "personal ties with key lieutenants selected on the basis of individual loyalty to him and his brothers."[28] Diem's "key lieutenants" were most often men of northern birth and Catholic religion. Catholicism had traditionally been stronger in Tonkin than in Cochinchina, where the numerous French colonialists were often anti-clerical or aggressively atheist. In the months after the 1954 partition, nearly three-quarters of a million of these Tonkinese Catholics streamed into South Viet Nam. Once the flow of refugees had been pretty well cut off, native and immigrant Catholics composed about 10 percent of the South's population of about 15 million; in the capital city of Saigon, Catholics may have been as many as one in seven.[29]

Diem looked upon the northern refugees as clearly the most reliably anti-Communist elements in the population, and more and more he made them his political base.[30] Northerners, especially Catholics, seem to have constituted a majority of the members of the Civil Guard, South Viet Nam's first militia.[31]

Not only were northern Catholics reliable supporters of an independent South Viet Nam, but they were also a major source of Western-educated personnel.[32] Understandably then, the Diem administration began to fill up with northern (and mainly Catholic) appointees, even at the local level, where they had no personal ties and often spoke with an irritating accent. Equally understandably, this process caused wide resentment and even hostility in a society characterized by intense regionalism (especially in view of the fact that Diem and his family, while not northern, had their roots outside of Cochinchina, and were demonstratively Catholic).

SOUTH VIETNAMESE SOCIETY

At the Geneva Conference, the southern part of Viet Nam had escaped being handed over to Ho and his Viet Minh mainly because of the relative weakness of the movement there. Ho had often noticed and complained about the individualism of southerners, especially Cochinchinese, their distaste for collectivism and their orientation to a market economy.[33] This infertility of southern soil for the implantation of Communism finds substantiation in the membership figures for the Communist party in the late 1940s, when the Viet Minh war was reaching its height: of 180,000 party members, only 23,000 were to be found in Cochinchina.[34] In northern Viet Nam, the opposition to Ho's regime was largely unorganized and would manifest itself only in emigration or sporadic armed peasant revolts; there was no plausible alternative to the French or the Viet Minh. But in the South, the weakness of the Communist Party was in part a consequence of the presence of well-organized and popular groups that had resisted the Viet Minh during the war.

One of these groups was the religious sect known as the Hoa Hao. Founded in 1939, it soon developed into a sort of mutual protection association; cooperatives offered the peasant some shelter from the demands of landlords, and membership in the growing organization meant a measure of protection from crime in the unsettled "wild west" atmosphere of western Cochinchina.[35] Non-Communist and anti-French, the Hoa Hao enjoyed the favor of the Japanese during World War II and thus had been able to obtain many weapons. Numerous southern Trotskyites sought shelter within the sect when the Viet Minh set out to eliminate them in 1945; two years later, Communists assassinated the sect's founder, Huynh Phu So.

The most powerful organization in the South was probably the Cao Dai, whose founders had consciously modelled their new religion on the Catholic Church. Many of the leaders of Cao Dai were well-educated and worked for the French administration. They were thus in a position to offer relief to peasants hard pressed by landlords. The sect also developed elaborate insurance and welfare systems for its members. Culturally nationalist, Cao Dai's leaders had been on bad terms with the colonial authorities before World War II, but they came to fear the Viet Minh more than the French and had sided with the latter by

1947. In the years before the partition of Viet Nam, Cao Dai held seats in all cabinets, and under Bao Dai and the French the sect had a large measure of territorial autonomy. By the end of the Viet Minh war, Cao Dai was the largest political movement in Cochinchina, deploying from 15,000 to 20,000 armed men and ruling a large area north and west of Saigon.

Home to the powerful Cao Dai and Hoa Hao sects, a native Catholic element, and several middle-class nationalist parties, South Viet Nam also contained ethnic minorities in the mountains and a million resident Chinese (half of them in Saigon), who were notably unenthusiastic about Ho and his Communists. Peasants not belonging to one or another of these groups usually displayed distrust of all political entanglements. It is therefore not difficult to see why the southern Viet Minh had not reached an organizational and military level comparable to that in the North (and soon after partition a flood of anti-Communist refugees arrived). But if the presence of disparate groups and powerful organizations was an obstacle to the domination of southern society by the Communists, it would also prove an obstacle to the effective unification of South Viet Nam, a unification essential if the government was to confront the looming threats of internal subversion and external conquest.

U.S. ASSISTANCE

Faced as they were by so many difficulties and threats, Diem and his southern state were clearly not going to make it without help from the outside. Such assistance was on its way. Col. Edward G. Lansdale had served in the OSS during World War II and had then become special adviser to Philippines president Ramon Magsaysay in the struggle against the Communist Huk guerrillas. Washington would retire him in his fifties (at the rank of major general) for being too outspoken. But in 1954, he arrived in Saigon to help Diem. Lansdale found that Diem's headquarters in Saigon's Independence Palace were so wide open that gunmen might have simply walked in off the streets and killed the prime minister. The first order of business was therefore personal security for Diem and his ministers; Col. Napoleon Valeriano, commander of the Presidential Guard Battalion in Manila, soon came to help Lansdale set it up. In short order a lightly armed guards unit was established next to Independence Palace.[36]

Lansdale was only the harbinger of assistance from the United States, which would eventually reach enormous proportions. U.S. policy toward Indochina since partition had been to "seek an independent non-Communist South Viet Nam."[37] According to the thinking of the Eisenhower administration and its successors, if South Viet Nam fell to the Communists, so would Laos and Cambodia; Burma would be lost to non-Communist influence; Malaya might be taken over by Indonesia, which was itself on the verge of going Communist; the Philippines would become "shaky"; and threats to Australia and New Zealand would "increase."[38] Hence the United States would support South Viet Nam, provided it could locate a reliable leader. After some initial hesitation, the Americans decided that Ngo Dinh Diem was that leader. His unimpeachable personal integrity, his long and clean record as an uncompromising nationalist, and his anti-Communism and pro-Americanism were all very attractive to Washington. He clearly had the backing of the refugees, and besides, the opposition to Diem within South Viet Nam was so fragmented that there was no plausible alternative.[39] Thus the United States helped Diem take over control of the army from the Bao Dai–appointed General Hinh.

But it was not only in the Eisenhower administration that Diem found backing. His brother Bishop Thuc interested the influential archbishop of New York, Cardinal Spellman, in the cause, and Spellman in turn introduced Diem to Cong. Walter Judd and Sens. Mike Mansfield and John F. Kennedy, all of whom became his admirers. In October 1954, Mansfield had become convinced that support for Diem was much in the interest of the United States, and later he wrote that "in the jungle of colonial decay, corruption and military defeat which characterized Saigon in 1954, Diem assumed the [leadership] with few assets other than his nationalism, his personal incorruptibility, and his idealistic determination."[40] In May 1955 Sen. Hubert Humphrey declared that "Premier Diem is the best hope that we have in South Viet Nam; he is the leader of his people."[41] A year later Sen. John F. Kennedy maintained that South Viet Nam was "the cornerstone of the Free World in Southeast Asia" and "an inspiration to those seeking to obtain and maintain their liberty in all parts of Asia—and indeed the world."[42] And in 1957 an influential officer of the Council on Foreign Relations wrote in the prestigious journal *Foreign Affairs* that "history may yet adjudge Diem as one of the great figures of twentieth century Asia."[43]

CONFRONTING THE BINH XUYEN

One of the tactics employed by the French in fighting the Viet Minh, especially in the south, had been to arm the sects and local warlords, conceding to each group what amounted to autonomy within its particular territory. As a consequence of this French policy, Diem faced in his first days in office a breakdown of orderly administration in the countryside, indeed something close to political anarchy. The most immediate threat came from a society known as the Binh Xuyen. Evolving out of a river gang called the Black Flag pirates, the Binh Xuyen by 1954 controlled most of the prostitution, drug, and gambling activities in Saigon. Its members had received training and arms from the Kempeitai, the notorious Japanese military police, and from time to time had worked closely with the Communists. But the Binh Xuyen had also supported Bao Dai in his maneuverings with the French, and in turn Bao Dai, immediately before he left Viet Nam in 1954, "sold" to the Binh Xuyen control of the Saigon police force.[44] This control, plus their private army and the enormous profits they made from vice operations in Saigon, gave the Binh Xuyen leaders something close to absolute authority over Saigon.[45] Now, from his exile, Bao Dai was encouraging the Binh Xuyen to unite with the sects against Diem.[46] But in September

1954, Diem gave the Cao Dai and Hoa Hao seats in his cabinet; he also used some of the money he was getting from the United States to win key sect leaders to his side. Having thus divided the sects from the Binh Xuyen, Diem was ready for a confrontation.

Colonel Lansdale has reported that he convinced the main Binh Xuyen leader, one Bay Vien, to approach Diem with a compromise: the Binh Xuyen would recognize Diem's authority in return for his permitting certain of their more lucrative activities to continue. Diem did not trust Bay Vien and spurned the offer.[47] Binh Xuyen forces thereupon attacked Diem's palace on March 29, 1955. Bao Dai sought to intervene from afar and save the Binh Xuyen. The French authorities still on the scene interfered with fuel supplies for Diem's forces;[48] then, seeing that the fight was going against the Binh Xuyen, the French high command arranged a truce. New fighting broke out on April 28, and within a week Diem's troops drove the Binh Xuyen from Saigon. Surviving elements of this group found their way into the jungles and joined the Communist guerrillas.

Some Americans in later years criticized Diem for the time and energy he spent cleaning out the Binh Xuyen and for spilling blood on the streets of Saigon. The episode allegedly revealed his preference for intransigent authoritarianism over prudent compromise. But, as Diem asked, would Charles de Gaulle, entering liberated Paris in 1944, have shared authority with an organized criminal group that had collaborated with the German occupation? Besides, fighting the Binh Xuyen gained Diem the loyalty of many army officers, the respect of foreign governments, and the gratitude of many ordinary Vietnamese who had long suffered exploitation by the Binh Xuyen and their French colonial accomplices.[49] The defeat of the Binh Xuyen also convinced Cao Dai and Hoa Hao leaders that they should cooperate with Diem, and their armed forces were largely incorporated into the government's Civil Guard militia.

DIEM'S EARLY ACCOMPLISHMENTS

In the aftermath of Geneva, few were predicting the emergence of a relatively stable regime in Saigon. When Diem took over on his first day as prime minister, he actually controlled only a few square blocks of downtown Saigon and confronted the hostility of Bao Dai, the military high command, the French, the armed sects, the Binh Xuyen, the southern Communists, the Hanoi government, and indeed the whole Communist world. Yet by the first anniversary of the Geneva Agreements, the shy, uncharismatic, ascetic Diem had defied Bao Dai's efforts to remove him, thwarted a coup, defeated the Binh Xuyen, brought the army, the police, and the entire city of Saigon under his control, incorporated the sects into his state apparatus, abolished the French-run Bank of Indochina so that South Viet Nam would have full control over its own currency and foreign exchange, and obtained the promise of the French to evacuate their remaining troops.[50] He had also directed the successful settling of almost a million refugees, an enormous accomplishment when one considers that the influx into South Viet Nam was the equivalent of 12,000,000 new arrivals into the United States.

These triumphs would not have been possible without U.S. aid, but they also reflected Diem's devotion to hard work: he usually put in 16- and even 18-hour days, giving up his favorite hobbies of shooting and photography.[51] As the government entered into a period of relative tranquility, Diem sought to enhance the links between the peasantry and the government by touring the country; from mid-1957 to mid-1958 he took 33 separate trips, covering 14,000 miles.[52] These visits to the peasantry appear to have been genuinely well received.[53]

The domestic social and economic picture began to improve significantly. Between 1955 and 1961, the number of South Vietnamese in primary schools doubled, the number of university students increased five-fold, and secondary students increased nine-fold.[54] Economically, the partition was hard on South Viet Nam; the country had no important natural resources; in the pre-partition economic system, the south had sent rice to the north, from which came chemicals, coal, glass, textiles, and other manufactured items.[55] In 1955, out of perhaps 15,000,000 inhabitants, the South had only 50,000 industrial workers. But there was plenty of rice, good fishing, the remains of the French rubber industry, and Saigon's light manufacturing establishments and its good seaport. The government inaugurated a small-scale land reform program, built roads to connect the highlands with the coastal cities and the Delta, and attacked malaria, the principal cause of illness in the country.[56] South Vietnamese economic progress under Diem was not negligible, particularly if we compare it with the North and keep in mind that in the last years of his administration Diem was faced with guerrilla insurgency.[57]

By the fall of 1955, with the most pressing crises solved or contained, Diem was ready to get rid of the anomalous situation in which he was, in legal terms, merely the chief minister of the absent and hostile Bao Dai. In a plebiscite on October 23, 1955, a massive turnout of voters overwhelmingly agreed that South Viet Nam should be a republic, with Diem as first president. An 11-member commission, including well-known French-educated legal experts, along with Filipino and American advisers, set to work to draw up a constitution for the new republic. The document that emerged from this commission in 1956 foreshadowed to a remarkable degree the one Charles de Gaulle promulgated in France a couple of years later. It laid down separation of powers, with a dominant executive, a subordinate legislature, and a judiciary with vague authority. The president and National Assembly were elected to five-year terms by universal suffrage; the president of South Viet Nam (unlike the president of the French Fifth Republic) did not have the right to dissolve the National Assembly, nor could the Assembly overthrow cabinets. In emergencies, the president could rule by decree in the absence of the Assembly and suspend the law in any part of the country. Diem now had a firm legal footing from which to consolidate and expand the power of the new state that had so unexpectedly emerged from the ashes of the French colonial collapse.

THE QUESTION OF THE GENEVA ELECTIONS

One of the documents produced at Geneva provided that general elections were to be held within two years of the partition. The wording on these elections was exceedingly vague with regard to the method for holding them, and even about their exact purpose.[58] Prime Minister Diem made it clear early in his administration that in the existing circumstances he was opposed to the idea of elections on the subject of unification of the two Vietnamese states. He and his supporters on both sides of the Pacific maintained that there could be no free elections as long as North Viet Nam was in the hands of a Communist regime— a position that, to say the least, was based on much concrete experience. The Hanoi leaders would announce that 99 percent of the northern vote had been cast in favor of whatever position they had endorsed, and North Viet Nam had a greater population than the South. Therefore, even if the majority of south-erners should vote against unification—a likely outcome, given the combined strength of the Cao Dai, Hoa Hao, Catholics, northern refugees, Saigon bour-geoisie, Trotskyites, and non-Communist nationalists—the South Vietnamese would nonetheless all be handed over to the control of the northern party-state. Besides, the Bao Dai–Diem government took the position that the French had had no right to partition their country in the first place, or to make any agree-ments with Ho Chi Minh regarding the country's future without its consent. In Diem's view, as a result of their military errors the French had cravenly and illegally handed over half of their country to Ho Chi Minh's armed bands through partition, and were promising to hand over the other half through rigged elections. When the Eisenhower administration became convinced that Diem was able to hold onto power and that he would not cooperate in any rigged election, it backed him in his stance, with bipartisan support: as Sen. John Ken-nedy declared, "Neither the United States nor Free Viet Nam is ever going to be a party to an election obviously stacked and subverted in advance."[59]

During the 1960s Hanoi propagated with much success in the United States the belief that somehow the Viet Nam struggle was connected with or rooted in Diem's refusal to allow his people to participate in an honest election as provided at Geneva. This was a great propaganda victory for the Communist side.[60] But there are reasons to suspect that the leadership of the Hanoi regime, and especially Premier Pham Van Dong, never expected such elections to take place.[61] To have believed that Diem would take all the pains and risks that he did to set up a government in Saigon, only to hand everything over to the Communists in two years, would have been naive, and neither Ho nor any of the other inner leaders in Hanoi were naive.[62] Besides, close to a million north-erners fled from Communist control into the welcoming arms of the Diem government, and many more would have fled if the Hanoi regime had not placed numerous obstacles in their path; all this would be inexplicable and even absurd without a deep-rooted belief on the part of the refugees, and their supporters and enemies, that this escape would be permanent. When, in the summer of 1956 the last possible day to schedule any elections came and went, the Communist world observed this non-event almost without comment, and certainly without action. Indeed, a few months after the election deadline was passed, the Soviet Union proposed that the United Nations admit *both* North and South Viet Nam to membership. The French government from the beginning recognized the Diem government as the only constitutional authority for all Viet Nam, not formally recognizing the existence of North Viet Nam until 1973; the member nations of the Colombo Plan endorsed the legitimacy of the South Vietnamese state when they chose Saigon as the site for their 1957 conference.

Thus, within a few years, against all odds and all obstacles, a republican government in South Viet Nam had taken its place among the nations of the world.

5

The Viet Cong

> One does not establish the dictatorship in order to safeguard the revolution; one makes the revolution in order to establish the dictatorship.
> —George Orwell

A common belief about revolution pervades both the Communist and non-Communist worlds. It is the belief that revolutions occur because a government or a social group is selfishly or stupidly blocking needed and desirable social change. The very willingness of revolutionaries to resort to violence helps to convince us of the necessity of revolution.[1]

Undoubtedly many revolutionary movements, contemporary and historical, can trace their origins to serious social grievances. But as the twenty-first century begins, ascertaining the rights and wrongs of a particular revolution requires not obsolescent formulas but careful, case-by-case analysis. This necessity for caution arises from certain peculiarities of world politics in our own day that can greatly affect the nature of a revolution. These peculiarities include: (1) Leninist doctrine, which finds all non-Communist governments, especially in the Third World, repressive by definition and in need of overthrow; (2) the ability of any Leninist revolutionary movement, no matter how minoritarian, to obtain international support; and (3) the unfortunately very common practice of revolutionaries, Leninist or otherwise, to mobilize an otherwise indifferent population to support the revolution by means of terrorist tactics.[2] Nowhere have these elements come together more powerfully than in the Communist efforts to overthrow the government of South Viet Nam.

THE ORIGINS OF THE INSURGENCY IN SOUTH VIET NAM

The guerrilla insurgency that broke out in South Viet Nam after 1958 had its roots in a number of factors, but the timing of the outbreak, as well as its power and durability, can be explained in terms of only one factor: a decision by Hanoi. Far from being a spontaneous uprising by an exasperated population, the two-decade struggle for South Viet Nam "began by deliberate Communist design."[3] North Vietnamese efforts to depict the southern insurgency as autonomous were very effective but "patently false,"[4] because "from the beginning the movement was organized and directed from the North."[5] Hanoi's decision to take over South Viet Nam by force derived in great part from fear that non-Communist Asia could not fail to draw conclusions from both the Hanoi government's assault on the northern peasantry and the emerging higher standard of living in South Viet Nam.[6]

Acting on the fundamental belief of all Leninists that political power grows out of the barrel of a gun, Hanoi directed the Communists in South Viet Nam to change their tactics from "political struggle" to "armed struggle." The kind of armed campaign most appropriate to their circumstances was systematic terror, the complete erasure of the line between combatant and noncombatant.[7] Terror was aimed above all at local government officials. Local administration was the greatest weakness of the Saigon government, and the Communists understood this. They correctly identified village officials as the key elements in their struggle to take over huge stretches of rural Viet Nam. Communist guerrillas (whom the Saigon government named the "Viet Cong") killed corrupt or oppressive officials to win popularity; they killed hardworking and upright ones to frighten the population by showing that the Saigon government could not protect anybody.[8] Soon they were killing off the very cream of South Viet Nam's middle class: officials, medical personnel, social workers, schoolteachers.[9] Teachers were a special target of Viet Cong assassination; many of them were nationalists, and all of them knew enough about politics to become opinion leaders in the villages.[10] This "campaign of terror in the countryside"[11] took the lives of 20 percent of the village chiefs in South Viet Nam by the end of 1958. In 1960 alone, terrorists killed 1,400 local officials and civilians.[12] By 1965, the total number of civilians killed (excluding battle deaths) or abducted had reached 25,000.[13]

The destruction of personal safety in the villages naturally had a tremendous negative impact on state activities.[14] The government's anti-malaria campaign ground to a halt; many schoolrooms in guerrilla-infested areas were closed.[15] It would be difficult above all to overestimate the psychological impact of the constant terror. Through the most heinous attacks on innocent civilians, the Viet Cong effectively taught the peasants the dangers of associating with the government or resisting the rebels.[16] Caught in the midst of a savage war and unable to practice a prudent neutrality, the peasant was likely to support the side he thought would win;[17] advisers to President Kennedy feared the Viet Cong terror campaign for exactly that reason.[18] The Viet Cong boasted of their terror tactics; when, for example, in 1966, terrorists opened fire with mortars on the main market center of Saigon, killing and maiming many, the Viet Cong radio called the attack "a resounding exploit."[19] Sometimes the Viet Cong would kill the entire family of an official or schoolteacher, just to make their point more effectively;[20] the mass murder of 17 persons in Chau Doc in July 1957 was one of the most grisly examples of these tactics. The details of these attacks on civilians, including women and children, are utterly revolting and therefore will not appear in these pages; if readers insist on knowing to what appalling depths of cruelty human beings could sink in the name of a Communist Viet Nam, they can begin by consulting Dooley's *Deliver Us from Evil*, with the admonition that they will regret their curiosity.[21]

As early as 1957, Saigon newspapers were criticizing the Diem regime's failure to stop the terror in the countryside.[22] As terrorism accelerated into 1958, the government in Saigon began to take the problem seriously and reacted with energy. Government forces attacked Communist base areas in the Plain of Reeds and elsewhere; they killed 2,000 Communists and arrested 65,000 Communist sympathizers and suspects. Southern party membership plummeted; party historians identify the years 1958–59 as "the darkest period."[23] In 1959, recognizing that the Diem government was too strong to be overthrown by propaganda, subversion, and assassination alone, the Central Committee of the Communist Party in Hanoi decided that the South must become the scene of full-scale armed struggle, but that northern involvement must be disguised.[24]

The first fighting troops began to slip into the South around May 1959; these were mostly southern Viet Minh who had been evacuated to North Viet Nam in 1954–55 and whose infiltration back into their native provinces was fairly easy.[25] On July 9, 1959, Viet Cong units attacked the U.S. Army detachment advising the 7th Vietnamese Infantry Division at Bien Hoa while the Americans were watching a movie, killing two and wounding one. These were the first American advisers to die by enemy action. This attack signaled that the campaign of violence against South Viet Nam had moved into a new phase, a change confirmed on January 26, 1960, when heavily armed Viet Cong units overran an Army of the Republic of Viet Nam (ARVN) regimental headquarters in Tay Ninh province, killing many and capturing 500 weapons.

WHY DID THEY JOIN?

With Hanoi's overall direction of the southern insurgency hidden from the view of all but a select inner circle, on what basis were the leaders of the Viet Cong able to recruit members for their guerrilla organization? The themes that perhaps jump to many readers' minds, whatever their other views on the Viet Cong, would be those of national unification and redistribution of wealth. Surprisingly, the unification of North and South seems to have played little part in either Viet Cong recruitment propaganda or peasant response to it.[26] And although the Viet Cong leadership promised "a better life" after the war, those Americans who wish to identify poverty, or rather a profound revolt against economic inequality, as the root of the Viet Cong encounter some serious difficulties. In a South Vietnamese village class differences were small, especially by Western standards, and the gradations between classes were subtle.[27] Most often "what the preasant may really want is not that the landlord disappear but that he be good."[28] Besides, if the basis of Vietnamese Communism were indeed discontent with the rural class structure, it should always have been, as Bernard Fall pointed out, strongest in the south and weakest in the north, which is the exact opposite of the actual situation. In any event, while the class-struggle aspects of the insurgency were undoubtedly important to many, studies of Viet Cong prisoners fail to uncover revolt against rural poverty and inequality as the primary motivating force.[29]

Available evidence suggests that instead of a popular revolt against partition and poverty, the engine of Viet Cong rebellion derived its power first of all from serious and repeated errors on the part of the South Vietnamese government, and secondly from effective recruitment methods on the part of the insurgents.

GOVERNMENT ERRORS

Many Communist agents—perhaps as many as 10,000—remained behind in South Viet Nam after the 1954 partition. Such persons were certainly a legitimate object of government anxiety and attention. But the Diem government from its earliest days tended to view all former Viet Minh as Communists or potential Communists, and it subjected many thousands of them to surveillance and other forms of harassment and intimidation.[30] Such actions smoothed the way for insurgent recruitment.[31]

Official corruption also fed the ranks of the guerrillas. Far too often officials of the Saigon government sought to use their authority for personal financial gain. This was certainly nothing new in Viet Nam, and the Viet Cong itself practiced extortion on a big scale. But the contrast between the officials, who extorted for personal gain, and the insurgents, who demanded money and goods for the movement, was damning.[32]

Cultural factors also weakened the southern government. The republican administration in Saigon rested mainly on the country's urban middle classes and made little effort to broaden the base of its supporters in the countryside. Hence, many of those whom Saigon sent out to administer rural provinces and districts were city men, who all too frequently displayed a disdainful ignorance of peasant ways and susceptibilities.[33] This disdain resulted in personal slights on the part of officials to individuals or to peasant communities as a whole, and it was a real burden to the governmental side in the war. When the Viet Cong drafted an inhabitant of a village, or even when it carried out abductions, it usually took pains to explain to everybody involved why it was thought necessary to do this. Government officials, on the other hand, would just round up conscripts, with no attempt to explain what the government was doing or why the people should support it; on top of that, draftees were often treated with harshness.

Peasants complained that government officials would often hand out punishments without deigning to offer a single word of explanation, whereas the Viet Cong almost always provided an elaborate rationale for why it was going to punish or kill some person or family.[34] The Viet Cong would often induce nature, or even the Saigon government, to do its punishing for it. A guilty person, for example, would be given physically dangerous work to do or be sent into areas where government troops were active; sometimes, to punish a whole village, the Viet Cong would fire at a passing ARVN unit and then run away while the soldiers poured return fire into the village.[35] (This sort of thing was quite apart from those numerous situations in which ARVN, carrying out a sweep of an area and failing to uncover any guerrillas, would visit indiscriminate retribution on a village; see chapter 6.) And because the Viet Cong often possessed better intelligence than the government, it would inflict accidental damage on villages much less frequently than ARVN (and later U.S.) forces.[36]

Thus Viet Cong punishments and exactions, often indirect and almost always explained, could be forgiven, while government officials stirred up much needless resentment by failing to explain the law and how a given action was in accordance with it. The Viet Cong cadres naturally capitalized on the often stupid errors of the government.

The Viet Cong of course did not rely only on government mistakes to do their recruiting for them but employed many themes and stratagems to obtain support and members. After the partition at Geneva and the massive movement of population which followed it, many Communist cadres remained behind in the South. These agents, seeking to undermine and eventually overthrow Diem, worked to win over non-Communist elements in the old Viet Minh to the new revolutionary organization. They tried to link their new movement with the heroic image of the Viet Minh, fighting bravely against foreign oppression. Before 1965, the U.S. presence in the South was not large, numbering only 10,000 advisers as late as 1962, and these were "an elite of unprecedented quality and dedication."[37] Nevertheless, from its earliest days the presence of U.S. military and civilian advisers lent at least some credence to Viet Cong charges of neocolonialism against the government in Saigon, and many Viet Cong saw themselves as fighting to rid their country of the foreigner.[38] Even more importantly, the massive infusion of U.S. troops into South Viet Nam after 1965 helped Hanoi to convince a whole generation of North Vietnamese that their sufferings were necessary to liberate the South from the barbarous Americans.[39] (This Communist emphasis on driving the Americans out of South Viet Nam is more than a little ironic, since had it not been for the Viet Cong the Americans would not have been there in any appreciable numbers.)

The weapon of anti-Americanism, however, was not terribly effective in

South Viet Nam in the days of relative peace (1955–58) and low American presence (to 1965). Hence Viet Cong recruiters had to supplement appeals to patriotism with appeals to self-interest, including opportunities for more schooling, professional advancement, or promotion in either the Viet Cong political or military hierarchies:

> The revolution also offered an avenue of social advancement more exciting than anything the government could propose. The insurgents would after all become the leaders of the new Viet Nam. The Party offered young men and women a powerful vision of the future. In return, it asked absolute political dedication, obedience, and a willingness to face the very real prospect of death. . . . *So it did not really matter whether or not the Front had the support of a majority of the peasantry.* . . . [T]he Party had what it needed, the support of the most politically aware and most determined segment of the peasantry.[40]

Thus, joining the Viet Cong (or VC) often meant an escape from the drudgery of peasant life and a real chance to step up in the world; at the same time, widespread ignorance among the southern peasantry about what was going on in the North preserved the VC from the kind of damage that knowledge about life in the eastern zone did to the Communist cause in West Germany.[41]

The guerrillas found it easy to recruit young boys; how many 15-year-olds could resist the offer of a real gun and the opportunity to fire it in the direction of wicked men? The Viet Cong emphasis on good cooking no doubt reinforced this kind of appeal. Often the Viet Cong would simply abduct a youngster and then force him to participate in some outrage against helpless peasants; the ties of that youth with normal civil life would thus be broken, and he would henceforth belong to the VC. When the South Vietnamese government instituted conscription, the Viet Cong obtained many recruits by promising young men who were likely to be drafted by the government that if they joined the VC they would face shorter enlistment periods and receive assignment nearer their homes. Older or less adventurous elements in the population would sometimes offer a little help to the Viet Cong without making a sharp break with the government, as a sort of insurance policy; such persons could later be forced to join the guerrillas through blackmail.

The Viet Cong, in marked contrast to ARVN, frequently made prisoners join their ranks. This practice arose from the traditional Communist belief that the circumstances of one's life shaped one's attitudes ("environment determines consciousness") and thus that even a former foe, compelled to live as a Communist insurgent, would eventually become one.[42] The VC method of coercion-indoctrination-conversion seems to have worked in numerous instances, especially when the prisoner or draftee or kidnap victim found himself far from home and without friends.[43]

Once a person became a member, by whatever route, of a Viet Cong unit, the leadership devoted a great deal of energy to indoctrinating him. Viet Cong pronouncements constantly stressed the inevitability of final victory. They also provided a convenient vocabulary of political heroism to those who originally had joined for more selfish motives. Viet Cong cadres strove to instill in their units a powerful "spirit of righteousness"—as in Cromwell's army, right belief and right behavior would guarantee victory.[44] This righteousness of the insurgent appeared in many forms: the VC organization urged its cadres to avoid cursing and foul language, and to speak always in a soft voice; its propaganda equated the liberty of South Vietnamese society with "sinful indulgence."[45] But the essence of Viet Cong indoctrination seems to have been the inculcation of hatred of the enemy; it was this unrelenting exposure to efforts to motivate through hatred that most distinguished the insurgents from government forces.[46] And just in case all the indoctrination were unsuccessful, the welfare of the Communist soldier's family was explicitly tied to his conduct.

NORTHERNIZATION OF THE INSURGENCY

No method of indoctrination, however, could eliminate the hardships of guerrilla life, and these took a toll among the Viet Cong. This was especially the case among those for whom service in the insurgency was more a matter of emotional rather than economic needs, and for those who were serving unwillingly. Besides the rigors of climate, battle, and outdoor living, Communist jungle fighters had from the beginning to contend with malaria and poisonous snakes. Then, after 1965, the growing U.S. intervention seriously damaged the insurgency, psychologically as well as militarily. Almost everyone understood that as long as large U.S. combat forces remained in South Viet Nam, victory for the Communists was impossible. But in later years the greatest fear among the Viet Cong guerrillas was the American B-52, whose bombs would begin exploding around a guerrilla unit before anybody had heard the engines.[47]

Beginning in 1965, therefore, morale within the Viet Cong began to decline, while the number of volunteers decreased and desertions rose. It became more and more necessary to employ conscription and abduction to meet minimal quotas. The general rule once had been to send volunteers to main-force units while keeping conscripts and abductees at lower levels, often in noncombat roles; as the war heated up, however, there were more and more exceptions to this practice. Before 1962, the Viet Cong normally accepted recruits only between the ages of 17 and 30. With the growing severity of the war, more and more peasants dodged the Viet Cong draft or deserted guerrilla units (apparently almost always for personal and hardly ever for ideological reasons);[48] thus the Viet Cong not only took younger and younger recruits but sent them much more frequently than before into what had previously been elite main-force units.[49] It also became increasingly necessary to employ terror tactics to get the peasants to pay guerrilla-imposed taxes. Thus, in dramatic contrast to the practice of Maoist revolutionaries in China, Viet Cong atrocities against civilians became more frequent, always a sign of poor morale in any army.[50]

The Viet Cong never gained many adherents among the educated and technically skilled elements of South Vietnamese society, and so this type of person was numerically prominent among the first infiltrators from the North.[51] Eventually all kinds of personnel had to be brought down, and by late 1966 the infiltration rate had reached 5,000 a month.[52] North Vietnamese Army personnel who went south were told that southerners lived in poverty and squalor. As late as 1975, the victorious NVA units marching into South Viet Nam's capital carried wooden rice bowls as gifts for the allegedly starving millions of Saigonese. Many northern fighting men were deeply disappointed at the apathetic or even hostile greeting they received in the South. More southerners wanted peace than desired "liberation," and they tended to blame northern infiltrators for the continuation and escalation of the war.[53] But the infiltration continued and grew until northerners came to dominate the war effort: by late 1968, fully two-thirds of mainforce Communist units in South Viet Nam (about 125,000 troops) were composed of northerners.[54] Without this infusion of northern fighting men, the insurgency could not have been sustained.

6

Fighting Guerrillas

> He who controls the countryside controls the country.
> —Samuel P. Huntington
> *Political Order in Changing Societies*

HOW GUERRILLAS FIGHT

Thick clouds of romance surround the guerrilla, who has become a metaphor for heroic struggle against oppression. It is therefore worthwhile to reflect that those who fight as guerrillas do not do so by choice; rather, they are forced into this status because of a complete and manifest inferiority, in numbers, training, and weapons, to the armed forces of the enemy, whether this is one's own government or a foreign occupation. Guerrilla tactics are a set of operational principles to guide those who would fight against a greatly superior enemy. In essence, guerrillas seek to fight very limited actions in which they possess numerical superiority at the scene, thus defeating the enemy or at least inflicting maximum damage upon him while sustaining only limited losses themselves. In the words of Mao Zedong, one of the most influential writers on the subject: "The strategy of guerrilla warfare is to pit one man against ten, but the tactics are to pit ten men against one."

Guerrilla tactics require maximum deception: the guerrillas conceal themselves most of the time, emerging suddenly, usually at night, to launch surprise attacks on small outposts or convoys, rapidly withdrawing before the enemy can send reinforcements. The guerrillas thus begin to acquire, in their own eyes and those of the government's or occupation's soldiers, an air of invincibility.

The successful practice of these tactics, especially in the beginning stages, will usually require the guerrillas to operate in remote areas that are relatively unimportant or inaccessible to the enemy, establishing base areas for training, stockpiling, and rest. Success—in fact, survival—also requires the guerrillas to have good intelligence: they must know where the enemy is, what his strength is, what he is likely to do, and what he thinks about the guerrillas. This kind of information can only come to the guerrillas from contacts in civilian society; the guerrillas must therefore have the cooperation of the rural population among which they move. Sometimes this civilian support comes for the asking, as when Mao's guerrillas were fighting a cruel and destructive Japanese occupation. Sometimes guerrillas receive support because they have an attractive program, such as "Land to the tiller" or "Expel the foreigner [or infidel, or tax collector]." At other times the guerrillas will have to extract intelligence from the civilians through vivid demonstrations of the harsh punishments that await those who do not cooperate.[1]

Up to 1968, guerrilla strategy in South Viet Nam reflected Hanoi's adaptation of Mao's three-stage scenario for revolution. In this scheme: (1) the revolutionary nucleus builds up an organization within civilian society and carries out terrorist attacks against selected government officials and other targets; (2) the revolutionary organization begins guerrilla operations; these gradually increase in magnitude and scope as the government becomes less and less able to control or even respond effectively to them; (3) the revolutionary forces eventually grow to such size and power that they can abandon guerrilla tactics, field regular military units, and defeat the enemy in conventional warfare.

In Maoist strategy, these stages are not mutually exclusive; one shades into another. Nor is progress from one stage to another inexorable and irreversible: revolutionaries may find it prudent or necessary to revert to a previous stage for a while, they may never get out of the first (or second) stage, or they may suffer defeat in the conventional-war stage (but this is unlikely).

The study of Maoist-style guerrilla movements since World War II suggests the following propositions. First, serious guerrilla activity emerges only after a revolutionary organization is already in place; it is the blossom of a deeply rooted plant, and its appearance should therefore be an alarming indicator that something is very wrong with the government's intelligence, police, and social services. Second, time works for the guerrillas; its passage enables them to prune and develop their leadership cadres, while it frustrates the government's forces, who cannot get the guerrillas to stand and fight on their terms; indeed, the true target of the guerrilla is the morale of the enemy. Third, while since the Second World War numerous guerrilla insurgencies have failed, not one has succeeded without considerable assistance from outside the country, and in no instance was outside help of greater importance than to the Viet Cong insurgency (which also, in military terms, failed).[2] Fourth, for the guerrillas to control an area, they do not have to occupy it in force; guerrilla control of a village or district means that they can obtain from it the intelligence, supplies, and recruits they need. Even if government troops are present, therefore, the guerrillas can be in control, through the operation of their political infrastructure. It is around this fourth point that the following discussion revolves.

HOW TO FIGHT GUERRILLAS

In general, four responses are available to governments confronted by guerrillas. The first response is surrender, the option of the French in 1954. The second response is for government forces to kill everything that moves in an area where guerrillas are operating; this was the policy of the Japanese in China in the early 1940s, and the Soviets in parts of Afghanistan in the 1980s. The third is to try to kill as many guerrillas as possible while limiting damage to the surrounding civilian society; this was the essence of the American operations in South Viet Nam from 1965 to 1968. The fourth is to try to break the link between the guerrillas and the civilians from whom they obtain what they need. This link is the revolutionaries' political infrastructure: the agents of the revolution who live not among the guerrillas but inside the villages. The political infrastructure of the Viet Cong was the principal source of the intelligence without which the guerrilla units would simply have been unable to operate for long. The infrastructure also channeled supplies and new recruits to guerrilla units; that is why the guerrillas could suffer the massive losses they did in South Viet Nam for years and still survive and even increase in number. The reinforcements that the Viet Cong constantly obtained from North Viet Nam would have done relatively little good if there had not been an organization in the South to receive, absorb, conceal, and deploy these professional soldier-infiltrators.[3] The infrastructure could function in and thus "control" an area even when government troops had temporarily chased guerrilla units away. It is not difficult to understand why many students of guerrilla war in general and of Viet Nam in particular—however their views may otherwise differ—are agreed that "the most important element in a guerrilla campaign is the *underground political structure*."[4]

Sometimes there is an opportunity or a need to destroy a particular guerrilla unit; on rare occasions big sweep operations (see below) may be justified. But killing guerrillas or temporarily sweeping them out of a particular area both fail to get at the political infrastructure. Besides, a serious guerrilla insurgency is almost always a sign that the army has been penetrated by agents of the revolution; hence over-reliance by the government on military means to combat the guerrillas may actually aggravate the problem. Guerrilla warfare is primarily a political phenomenon; the government must therefore give priority to the political defeat of the guerrillas. It accomplishes this not by killing guerrillas (easier said than done), who can be replaced, but by identifying and removing the agents of the revolution among the civilian population and consequently drying up the flow of intelligence, supplies, and recruits from the villages to the guerrillas.[5] Even highly motivated troops employing good battle tactics will probably fail to destroy a guerrilla movement if the infrastructure that nourishes it is not broken up.

The Diem government defined the essential task of its struggle against the Viet Cong as protection of the village from outside attack, while it practically ignored the protection of the individual person from violence from within the village (see chapter 7).[6] This fundamental error (later compounded by the Americans) of course meant that the government failed to get at the Viet Cong infrastructure. This failure was the root of the almost complete collapse of personal security in vast areas of rural South Viet Nam. Between 1956 and 1965, the Viet Cong murdered or abducted 25,000 civilians.[7] Schoolteachers were a special target of Viet Cong assassination.[8] But almost anybody could be the object of a savage attack to impress upon others the grave dangers of sympathizing with the government and resisting the rebels.[9] The massive assassination campaign of the Viet Cong, in which the political infrastructure played a major role, had many destructive effects. It became very difficult merely to maintain a government presence in many villages. The blatant inability of the government to protect even its own employees from guerrilla reprisals deeply impressed the peasants, many of whom quite understandably displayed a marked reluctance to incur even the suspicion of friendliness toward the government or the Americans. On the other hand, the manifest power of the infrastructure to work its will even under the very noses of government troops gave the revolutionaries the nimbus of eventual victory. This greatly enhanced their ability to obtain recruits for guerrilla units and to conceal infiltrators from the North.[10] Insecurity even aggravated governmental corruption, a cancerous growth in South Viet Nam; many officials, such as district chiefs, thought that their jobs were so dangerous that they were entitled to supplement their meager salaries through graft, a condition that undermined the authority of the government and played into the hands of the guerrillas.[11] (Incidentally, government officials in dangerous areas who take no precautions against kidnapping or assassination are probably in league with the guerrillas; interrogation of such persons should prove to be a source of much interesting information.)

How can a government eradicate, or at least reduce, a revolutionary infrastructure?

The beginning of an answer is: *not* by relying totally, or even primarily, on the army.

The main mission of an army is to fight other armies. In counter-guerrilla warfare, the army is best employed in support of a well-organized police force with local intelligence sources. If such a police force does not exist and the army has to take on the burden of directly engaging the guerrillas, the result is that most of the army must go onto the permanent defensive: protecting cities and towns, holding outposts, guarding bridges, patrolling roads, and so on.[12] The effects of such a posture on the morale and efficiency of regular troops over the long term are destructive.[13] The army, moreover, will predictably view its primary job as destroying the military units of the enemy; the basis of the guerrilla war, the revolutionary political infrastructure, will therefore escape attack.

Meanwhile, through a curious and fateful symbiosis, the more money and attention lavished on the army's war against the guerrillas, the more militarily powerful the guerrilla movement may become. There are many examples of such a process. The increase in U.S. aid to the ARVN meant a corresponding increase in the number of weapons captured or stolen by the Viet Cong. The increase of U.S. goods in the essentially insecure countryside meant an increase in the ability of the VC to build up their own forces through extortion. The vast increase in the U.S. military presence after 1964 gave more credibility to Communist propaganda attacks on the Saigon government as the puppet of foreigners. The more effective application of the draft by the South Vietnamese government after 1963 meant that the Viet Cong felt able to raise their own manpower demands on the peasantry.[14]

When regular troops try to escape from the defensive posture into which fighting guerrillas forces them, the usual result is the so-called sweep operation. The purpose of a sweep is to catch guerrillas and infrastructure members by a sudden descent upon a village (or district) in which they are thought to be located. Sweeps were usually unsuccessful in Viet Nam, as they had been in Malaya, but lack of success is by no means the principal objection to such operations.

"Competing with a vigorous rebellion, a precarious authority should be concerned with respect for the people's dignity at least as much as with [raising] the level of their income."[15] The guerrillas always claim to be morally superior to the government. When government troops fail to distinguish the innocent civilians from the guilty, when they try to force information out of terrorized peasants, when they beat, rape, or steal, they reinforce these claims. The government must cloak itself in legality and traditional procedures, protecting all citizens regardless of their circumstances.[16] Ramon Magsaysay, the Philippine president who defeated the Communist Huk rebels in the 1950s, maintained that government troops should never enter a village in a posture of hostility unless they were certain that active guerrillas were present. Otherwise they should behave as if they were going among friends. Magsaysay even provided antiguerrilla troops with candy to hand out to village children, in conscious imitation of U.S. troops in World War II.[17]

Sweep operations many times provided the circumstances, or the excuse, for the flagrant violation of these principles. The ARVN would occupy a hamlet where enemies were supposed to be; because the movement of even fairly small numbers of troops can be heard a long way off, or because the troops had faulty information, or perhaps because Communist agents within the ARVN had tipped off the objects of the sweep, usually no enemies would be present.[18] The soldiers might nevertheless discover unmistakable evidence of a recent guerrilla visitation. Painfully aware that the ARVN would soon leave and the guerrillas would return, the villagers would decline to give any information to the soldiers, who would then often vent their frustration on them.[19] Sometimes the Viet Cong would take up positions in a hamlet, open fire on an approaching government patrol, then secretly withdraw, their intention being to provoke the soldiers into calling down artillery or aerial bombardment on the helpless villagers. The predictable results were that "all too often the GVN [government of (South) Viet Nam] appear[ed] in the countryside in the form of an alien army," and terrorist attacks were less damaging to rural security than the misconduct of local officials and soldiers.[20] Such behavior is worth more than gold to the rebels, since they are judged by their promises, while the government is judged by its deeds. It would be impossible to overstress the principle that in areas that are securely in government hands, government troops are free to deal severely with rebel supporters, but they must under no circumstances punish such persons in contested or insecure areas, where the peasants are at the mercy of the guerrillas.[21] The use of artillery against insurgents, moreover, is almost always a sure sign the government is losing; political isolation, not government firepower, is the best weapon against guerrillas. Since artillery (and jet aircraft) cannot discriminate between innocent and guilty, the less sophisticated and destructive the army's weapons, the better.[22] The French had learned, painfully, that "all ground combat operations should have a political purpose," but the government of South Viet Nam and its U.S. allies frequently acted as if they did not understand these things.[23]

In summary, placing the burden of the anti-guerrilla effort onto the army produces a combination of defensive occupation and periodic sweeps. These tactics are inadequate and even self-destructive. But there is a proven alternative method.

CLEARING AND HOLDING

Generations ago, the great French colonial strategist Marshal Louis Lyautey, a veteran of wars and politics in Indochina, Algeria, Morocco, and Madagascar, laid down the principle that the key to defeating guerrillas is to establish security in rural areas. Security means that the guerrillas cannot make sustained contact with civilians. Lyautey established security by the "oil patch" method: from areas already firmly under their control, government forces took over adjoining districts piecemeal. (Lyautey sagely suggests that the commander in charge of a clear-and-hold operation should be designated the future governor of the pacified area, so that he will conduct his conquest with an eye to economic and social life after the fighting is over.)[24]

A prolific contemporary exponent of this strategy has been Robert Thompson, who served as Permanent Secretary of Defense in Malaya during that country's long guerrilla war. For Thompson, as for Lyautey, the essence of anti-guerrilla strategy is not to kill guerrillas but to cut off the guerrillas from intelligence, supplies, and recruits by winning the loyalty of the civilian population. To this end he urges the government side to discard search-and-destroy and sweep operations and to concentrate on clearing and holding one section of territory after another. This is a long-term, low-casualty strategy.

The first step is for the government to establish firm security in its own natural base area, which will normally consist of the urban centers of a country. Clearing a district requires saturating it with troops and police; the point is to render the free movement of guerrillas literally impossible, forcing them to abandon the area. Saturation also impresses the local civilians with the power and permanency of government control. Then begins the attack on the political infrastructure of the area, which almost always consists of local people who have relatives and friends in the village. The best method for rooting them out is routine police procedure, based on information provided by friendly civilians. These may be political sympathizers or seekers of rewards or vengeance; in the days of the Emergency Laws in Malaya, a civilian caught in possession of a gun in a cleared area was automatically under the sentence of death, to be commuted if he gave evidence. Meanwhile, once it is obvious to the civilian population that the government has effectively removed armed guerrilla units from the saturated area, the next step is to set up a militia, backed by some mobile regular units, sufficient to prevent the reinfiltration of the now-secure area by guerrillas. To establish security in its base area, the government must use whatever resources may be necessary, even at the cost of letting the control of more remote rural areas go by default to the guerrillas for the time being. Once the base area has been thoroughly secured (and this may require a long time, perhaps as much as two years), most of the troops can leave it and saturate an adjoining insecure area, pushing the armed guerrilla bands away and rooting out the infrastructure, carrying on the process until ultimately nothing remains for the guerrillas but jungles or other inhospitable and sparsely populated sections of the country.

The French ignored this rule of first securing one's own base area, to their great cost.[25] And like Chiang Kai-shek in the Chinese civil war, the South Vietnamese tried to hold onto everything at once instead of attempting to move out from areas of natural strength; such over-extension and the consequent lack of reserve troops was a main factor in the country's final collapse.

In graphic terms, a country undergoing clear-and-hold operations consists of three parts (from the government's viewpoint): the secure base area, cleared of the enemy and controlled by police and militia; around this core, other districts under thick occupation by regular troops; and beyond these occupied areas, the disputed or "reconnaissance" territories. In the latter areas, government forces hold only the administrative centers and perhaps a few villages close to them, while the guerrillas operate more or less freely in the countryside. Only the best officers and the best-disciplined troops should be assigned to disputed areas. To avoid ambush, the soldiers should move around only a little, and should themselves employ the ambush as their main weapon, in order both to impede easy contact between the guerrillas and their civilian infrastructure, and to intercept couriers. The British in Malaya constantly harassed guerrilla encampments with small attacks. This tactic kept the guerrillas on the move, so that messages were lost, supplies became hard to accumulate, and coordination between rebel bands deteriorated.[26] Government troops may move in force into a rebel-held district at food-harvesting time, or just to show the flag and keep the guerrillas off balance. Since, however, civilians who live in unsecured areas have no choice but to cooperate with the guerrillas, the soldiers who participate in these expeditions must never consider their purpose to be punitive. Nor should government forces raiding a guerrilla-controlled zone ever attempt to rally the inhabitants to the government, for the area will quickly be abandoned, and the guerrillas will return.

Clear-and-hold is the exact opposite of guerrilla warfare. The guerrillas care nothing about holding territory; they move by stealth and employ small numbers to inflict great damage. In contrast, the government wants its occupation of a given area to be permanent, makes its presence as open and impressive as possible, and uses great numbers of troops while seeking to inflict minimal damage. Since World War II, successful campaigns against guerrillas in Greece, Malaya, the Philippines, South Korea, and Algeria all involved the combination of mobile strike forces and territorial control, which is the essence of the clear-and-hold strategy.[27] The *Pentagon Papers* made it clear that many policy makers and planners understood proper methods of pacification and guerrilla fighting but that allied forces in the field preferred massive airmobile operations and big sweeps. Few soldiers and little attention remained for clearing and holding— that is, protecting the civilian population—and this was the root of the allied failure to deal effectively with the insurgency.[28]

STRATEGIC HAMLETS

The "strategic hamlet program" of 1962–63 represented a variation of the clear-and-hold strategy. The rise and fall of this effort provides many revealing glimpses into the essential weaknesses of the counter-guerrilla effort in South Viet Nam.

A subdivision of a village, the hamlet is the smallest organized community in rural Vietnamese life. "Strategic hamlet" was a new name for a very old idea: the inhabitants of Annam had lived for centuries in stockaded villages, and strategic hamlets had played an important role during the conquest of the southernmost areas of their country.

In February 1962, close advisers of President Kennedy concluded that personal security in the villages of South Viet Nam was the key to winning the war against the guerrillas.[29] The strategic hamlet campaign was the centerpiece in this view. A well-set-up strategic hamlet program serves several purposes, including (1) separating the armed guerrilla bands from sympathizers inside the hamlet (the revolutionary infrastructure) who previously supplied them with recruits, food, and intelligence, (2) providing the opportunity to root out this infrastructure, and (3) organizing the peasants into self-defense units to resist demands or attacks by the guerrillas.

In the late 1950s, the Diem government had launched a forerunner of this program, the so-called *agrovilles*. The central idea was the removal of peasant communities from exposed areas into new and more secure locations. Most of those peasants involved were loath to leave their ancestral homes, graves, and gardens, and resented having to contribute their labor, free, to the construction of the *agrovilles*. Government financial assistance to this program was inadequate, and the Communists did all they could to disrupt it. Hence by 1961 the government, having constructed only 22 *agrovilles*, abandoned the program.

But late that same year, the strategic hamlet campaign got started, under the direction of President Diem's brother Ngo Dinh Nhu. In contrast to the failed *agrovilles*, the new program did not normally require the peasants to move into another settlement. Instead, existing hamlets were to be fortified. This would require much less expenditure and bureaucratic involvement, while keeping peasant resentment to a minimum. Local Catholic organizations had already launched some unofficial strategic hamlets, and they were quite successful.[30]

The strategic hamlet program of the Diem government was sound enough in concept. As with so many other things in South Viet Nam, it was the execution of the plan that was inadequate. Robert Thompson, among others, had urged Diem to follow the tactics of the British in their successful war against Communist guerrillas in Malaya. This would have meant building the strategic hamlets slowly and steadily, first solidifying the "white" areas around Saigon, then moving into contested zones, and leaving penetration of "red" zones to the last. But Diem did not listen: he moved ahead quickly and massively.[31] The program began officially in January 1962; in three years the British in Malaya had constructed 500 strategic hamlets; in two years, the Diem government set up 12,000.[32] Diem thrust fortified hamlets deep into contested territory, filling them with northern refugees, southern Catholics, or army veterans. Their location was often haphazard, in places of no strategic value, with large gaps between them so that they could not support one another and the Viet Cong could move easily around them.

The defense of these strategic hamlets required first of all the participation of the inhabitants themselves, with sufficient training and arms to be able to beat off attacks by small guerrilla bands. If the guerrillas attacked in numbers too great for the hamlet itself to handle, either ARVN or Regional Forces would intervene. Such a system requires a determined defense of the hamlet until an efficient communications system brings relief by mobile reserves. Strategic hamlets worked best when they were located close to an intervention force—near a military base, for instance, or a large town. But even when there were sufficient troops nearby to come to the rescue, the besieged hamlet might lack a radio with which to call for help, or the radio might be useless for want of replacement parts, or the would-be rescuers might not have adequate transportation.[33] Support units, furthermore, would often hesitate to go to the aid of a hamlet under attack at night because experience had taught them to fear ambush and resulting high casualties. Helicopters could have overcome this problem, carrying rescuing troops high above ambushes and boobytraps, but there were not anything like enough of them to take care of all the strategic hamlets.[34] The ARVN did not believe in the strategic hamlet program: it wanted money and attention spent on conventional military operations, not on support of armed civilians.[35] The Viet Cong, for their part, were quick to point out to the peasants the ultimate vulnerability of the hamlets under these conditions.

There were other problems besides lack of security. In some of the newly created hamlets, preparation of the sites had been inadequate, often due to the incompetence or corruption of local officials. The government had promised the peasants in these hamlets improved social services, but in many instances the peasants received only exhortation and rhetoric. Nevertheless, with all its shortcomings, the hastily launched and inadequately supported strategic hamlet program caused a lot of problems for the Communists. Radio Hanoi launched a furious and prolonged campaign of denunciation of the strategic hamlets, and captured documents indicate that the Communists were greatly preoccupied with finding the right way to deal with them.[36] Many groups in South Viet Nam took to the program with enthusiasm, including hill tribesmen in Annam, the Cao Dai sect in Cochinchina, and numerous Catholic parishes.[37] Many of the hamlets gave very good accounts of themselves against guerrilla attacks.

The strategic hamlet campaign was, in the words of a major U.S. Defense Department study, "the unifying concept of [South Viet Nam's] pacification and counterinsurgency effort."[38] A few years before that analysis, an informed observer of the South Vietnamese situation declared, "It is no exaggeration to say that the survival of non-Communist Viet Nam depends upon the success of its strategic hamlets."[39] Secretary of Defense Robert McNamara and General Maxwell Taylor stated in their report to the president of October 2, 1963, that "we found unanimous agreement that the strategic hamlet program is sound in concept, and generally effective in execution although it has been overextended in some areas of the Delta."[40]

A month after that report, President Diem and his brother were murdered. The strategic hamlet program was closely identified with the Ngo brothers; when they went, its days were numbered. Caught up in the post-coup purges and changes, the territorial forces could no longer effectively protect the hamlets; most of the weaker ones began to fall to the Communists or just fall apart. Only the very best organized hamlets with the most determined defenders were able to hang on.

ADDITIONAL ANTI-GUERRILLA TACTICS

The infiltration of guerrillas and supplies into South Viet Nam was made enormously easier by the country's long coastline and the jungle and mountain frontiers with Cambodia and Laos. Attempts to seal off any long jungle border are a waste of time and troops. But the government can drastically cut down on the utility of such areas to the guerrillas. One way is for its agents to buy up all surplus food available in the general vicinity.[41] Another is to deprive the guerrillas of easy movement (one of their principal advantages) by sending small numbers of specially trained fighters into the jungle to set up ambushes. Such tactics do not involve grave risks for the government soldiers; in jungle fighting very few combatants ever engage or even see one another, and the movement of large numbers of men is audible a long way off.[42] Under President Magsaysay the Filipino army organized units with the very specialized purpose of eliminating Huk leaders.[43] President Diem long wished to set up Ranger battalions for real counter-guerrilla work and place less emphasis on the Korean War–type army the United States insisted on creating for him.

The government may attack the guerrillas in ways that do not involve actual fighting. One of these is offering handsome rewards for the capture of guerrilla leaders. In Malaya, the British offered cash awards, graded according to the rank of the prisoner, that were fabulous in comparison to the annual income of an average peasant. Under Magsaysay, great publicity surrounded such captures, to spread suspicion between peasant and guerrilla (and among the guerrillas themselves). Magsaysay developed a clever twist to the reward system: the government identified individual Huk leaders whom it accused not of being rebels but of having committed specific crimes (murder, arson, robbery, rape) at specific times and places. This policy helped reduce the image of the Huks from rough Robin Hoods to mere (dangerous) criminals, and it sowed dissension within Huk ranks, because the most aggressive guerrilla leaders would feel themselves the most vulnerable to betrayal.

But by far the easiest, cheapest, and most humane way to beat guerrillas is to overcome their will to fight and thus get them to surrender. Amnesty has often been a very effective counter-guerrilla weapon. In Malaya, many guerrillas took advantage of amnesty once it became clear that their initial hopes of easy victory were unrealistic. These surrendered fighters provided much valuable information to the armed forces and were effectively used in pro-government propaganda.[44] In seeking to persuade guerrillas to turn themselves in, the government should avoid the pejorative term "surrender" and substitute euphemisms such as "coming in" or "returning to normal life." Prisoners who take advantage of amnesty must be rigorously segregated from those captured in battle. Finally, in order to further spread dissension within rebel ranks, amnesty should not apply to truly criminal acts.[45]

The South Vietnamese government offered huge rewards to anyone who uncovered a guerrilla weapons cache and to those who deserted the enemy ranks with their weapons. But the actual enforcement of the amnesty policy under Diem left much to be desired, owing to the strong opposition from within ARVN.[46] Army officers deeply distrusted surrendered guerrillas ("ralliers"), because in their eyes one who had fought against the government and then turned himself in had already been a traitor two times.[47] Although prisoners and ralliers usually provided excellent intelligence, ARVN often killed guerrillas captured with weapons even before interrogating them. Nevertheless, the *Chieu Hoi* ("Open Arms") program began in 1963; between 1966 and 1975, 194,000 Viet Cong (and some NVA) came in, mainly in the Fourth Military Region, the Mekong Delta. Most of these surrendered personnel were of low rank, and undoubtedly some of them were repeaters. But the loss of such a large number of men severely pinched the Communist side, and it represented a grave propaganda defeat as well. The Communists loathed the *Chieu Hoi* program: they imposed the death penalty on the relatives of ralliers and declared the killing of one rallier to be the equivalent of killing ten enemy soldiers. But there is no recorded instance of any rallier going back to the other side, even during the Tet Offensive.[48]

POLICE AND TERRITORIAL FORCES

Protecting base areas, occupying areas to be cleared, and contesting the other parts of the country require a substantial number of troops, police, and militia. The guerrillas, in contrast, do not have a defense and occupation mission like the government, and it takes only a small amount of energy to blow up a bridge compared with the energy expended on protecting it night and day for weeks or even years.[49] Besides, in South Viet Nam many guerrilla units engaged in combat very seldom, perhaps only twice a year, while government forces had to be on the alert everywhere all the time. Thus any government facing a serious guerrilla insurgency is going to need a considerable advantage in the ratio of its manpower to that of the rebels. Controversy surrounds the question of exactly what that ratio should be. The standard formula is that the government needs to have 10 persons active on its side for every guerrilla.[50] Yet Thompson maintains that it is not the ratio but in whose direction the ratio is moving that is the key to forecasting victory; ten-to-one is not much good for the government side if last year its advantage was fifteen-to-one (or if the ten-to-one ratio is maintained by the presence of foreign troops).[51]

Whatever the proper ratio may be, it is clear that for the last ten years of its existence, South Viet Nam was supporting a regular army much too big for its economy. Maintaining such a force made conscription necessary, which was in turn directly related to the high desertion rate. A further deleterious effect of such a large army was the diversion of manpower, money, and attention away from the police and the territorial forces (militia).

If the first reaction to guerrilla warfare should be the protection and control of the civil population, "the key [to peasant security] is the survival of the village police posts."[52] One authority estimates that in the early stages of an insurgency the government needs five policemen for every two soldiers and that a well-armed, well-trained, and sufficiently large police force would have been quite sufficient at one point to stop the spread of the Viet Cong.[53] Even after the insurgency had become a major national problem, years of patient police work in the secure areas and in districts being cleared would have been infinitely more effective than periodic army sweeps, especially by Americans. But President Diem neglected the police forces. Until at least the 1970s they were small in numbers, poorly trained, badly paid, split into several commands, and openly despised by the ARVN. The officer corps of the ARVN attracted most of South Viet Nam's elite manpower.[54] Police protection hardly existed outside the larger towns,[55] and Saigon policemen who misbehaved would be sent out to the villages as punishment.[56] Their reputation was quite bad; many believed that the Viet Cong bribed police not to interfere with the transshipment of supplies bought in Saigon.[57] The handling of prisoners by Saigon police often left a great deal to be desired.[58] Far from being the cutting edge of the anti-guerrilla effort, the police were the weakest of all the South Vietnamese forces.

From the very beginning, South Viet Nam's territorial (militia) forces had serious security responsibilities. They were originally called the Civil Guard and the Self-Defense Corps, and their mission was to protect the local civilian population, freeing the regular army for active campaigning. But Diem gave these forces little money or attention. With sketchy formal training and less indoctrination, lacking good leadership, carrying castoff weapons, and shrunken by 1959 to about 86,000, the territorial forces "had very limited combat capabilities."[59]

This disastrous condition of the territorial forces resulted in large part from U.S. strategy. Dictated by U.S. weapons systems and combat doctrine, this strategy, like the French one before it, emphasized forcing the enemy into set battles. Hence the United States built up a Korean War–style army for South Viet Nam to resist a conventional invasion from the North, and it almost completely neglected, especially between 1955 and 1960, the militia forces on which a successful population security strategy ultimately depended.[60] South Vietnamese territorial forces did not receive U.S. aid until the early 1960s, when it was in many senses too late.[61]

After 1964, the government integrated the territorial forces into the overall military command system. The Civil Guards were renamed the Regional Forces (RF), and the Self-Defense Corps became the Popular Forces (PF). Each Regional Forces unit was recruited from a specific province and ordinarily was not sent outside provincial boundaries (the average province was roughly 1,200 square miles in area, equivalent to a circle with a radius of 20 miles); Popular Forces served in their own villages.

Little improvement in the security picture followed this reorganization. The guerrillas rested by day and operated at night, and only occasionally; the territorials were peasants working hard by day and thus not very good for fighting or even patrolling at night. Formal training was close to nonexistent. The Popular Forces, moreover, had no system of ranks; no member could achieve promotion, and thus a major incentive for initiative and bravery was lacking.[62]

The main reason, however, why security did not significantly improve after the reorganization of the territorial forces in the mid-1960s was the fundamental weakness of the overall defense system. Territorial troops are best employed in areas cleared of active guerrilla units, but allied strategy neglected clear-and-hold in favor of big-unit operations. Hence population security fell by default to static defense, a series of outposts that were supposed to "show the flag" among the peasantry and hamper any large-scale movements of the enemy. Deployed in prolonged and exhausting defensive duties, the poorly trained territorials fell victim to routinization that undermined their initiative and morale and permitted small parties of guerrillas to circumvent most of their outposts at will.[63] Besides, village forces under attack very often lacked radios that worked, and Regional Forces frequently lacked the mobility to respond in time. Above all, the Communists soon learned how to undermine the relationship between territorials and regulars on which the system relied. They would stage a fake raid on a village at night; the Popular Forces would summon the nearest ARVN units. The roadbound ARVN rescuers would then fall into neatly arranged ambushes, suffer serious casualties, and arrive at the village to find no attack going on. At the next summons, the ARVN would respond very slowly, often refusing to answer calls for help until daylight.[64] Territorials in fixed outposts thus became sitting ducks for the basic guerrilla tactic of employing numerical superiority in small-scale attacks. As a result of all these depressing factors, RF/PF and the Communist guerrillas in the area often worked out arrangements to live in mutual tolerance.[65]

In October 1967, Gen. Creighton Abrams, deputy commander, MACV, directed a study on upgrading the territorial forces. But it was the Tet Offensive, galvanizing South Vietnamese society into an anti-northern effort, that breathed new life into the Regional and Popular Forces (see chapter 9, below). Between January 1968 and December 1972, the number of 100-man RF companies doubled to 1,800. At the same time the 30-man PF platoons numbered around 7,500.[66] The Saigon government gave them quantities of good weapons. Those too old or too young to join the RF/PF could enroll in the People's Self-Defense Force (PSDF), serving without pay in relatively secure areas when RF/PF had been temporarily redeployed.[67] After Tet, RF/PF continued to receive inadequate training and were subject to local political interference. Perhaps worst of all, they received no recognition: "Their virtues were seldom extolled and their accomplishments usually slighted."[68] Yet in spite of all this neglect and incomprehension, territorial forces succeeded in making an enormous contribution to the struggle. The war effort throughout the populous Mekong Delta rested primarily on territorial forces, and in the 1972 Easter Offensive some RF units not only had to fight outside their home provinces but also to face regular North Vietnamese troops, against whom they did very well.[69] Between 1968 and 1972, the ARVN lost 36,932 men; the RF/PF lost 69,291.[70] Indeed, "The RF/PF took the brunt of the war, more than any other South Vietnamese armed force."[71] Inferior in weapons, leadership, and training to both the Viet Cong and the NVA, the territorials took heavier casualties than they inflicted. Yet, receiving only 2–4 percent of the war budget, the Regional and Popular Forces accounted for roughly 30 percent of all VC/NVA combat deaths, making them clearly "the most cost-effective military forces employed on the allied side."[72] One can only speculate on the fate of South Viet Nam if more attention and a little more money had been devoted to the territorial forces.

The Overthrow of President Diem

The History of man is the history of the continuous rise and fall of elites.
—Vilfredo Pareto

Power creates its own legitimacy.

—Henry Kissinger

DIEM'S LEGITIMACY PROBLEM

In his struggle to create and sustain an independent South Viet Nam, Ngo Dinh Diem labored under the weight of enormous burdens.

First of all, Diem had less than perfectly solid claims to being the legitimate head of a legitimate government. Ho Chi Minh ruled as the undisputed leader of a revolutionary movement victorious in battle over a foreign enemy. Diem, in contrast, had built up his own power through a series of maneuvers that, in effect, were coups: against the army high command, against the French, against the sects, against Bao Dai, and against the expectations of some of the Geneva Powers.[1] His open dependence on the Catholic minority, increasing reliance upon the Americans, and continuing inability to defeat the guerrillas further undermined his claim to be the authentic representative of a traditionalist Vietnamese polity.

Like other Southeast Asian leaders, Diem sought to build his authority on the bedrock of nationalism. This was no easier for him than for them. In peasant societies, the concept and passion of nationalism are of concern almost exclusively to the middle class, and especially the urban intelligentsia; among the peasant majority in South Viet Nam its appeal was esoteric and limited, especially since millions of southerners gave their supreme loyalty not to the nation but to religious sects, such as the Cao Dai. In addition, those groups that were most willing to serve an independent South Viet Nam undercut the credibility of Diem's nationalism: "[His] administration had been staffed, down to the lowest level, with officials who served the colonialists prior to independence."[2] No key commanders in the ARVN had opposed the French; indeed, most of them had fought on the side of the French forces, several held French citizenship, and others were much more at ease speaking French than colloquial Vietnamese.[3] U.S. support for Diem, while essential, further blunted his appeal to nationalist sentiment: after all, the United States, for whatever reasons, had for several years helped the discredited French.

But the most serious reason why South Vietnamese nationalism was such an unsteady support was that it was directed not at some alien enemy but against the Hanoi regime and its southern collaborators. However distasteful millions of southerners found the prospect of a Communist regime, and whatever the historical and regional bases for a southern separatism, in the last analysis the North Vietnamese and Viet Cong were not aliens but compatriots. At the same time, Diem failed to make sufficient propaganda use of the fact that behind the vaunted nationalism of Hanoi stood the Chinese, the detested ancestral enemy.

Associated to a large degree with the French occupation (Diem himself being a notable exception), disproportionately northern and Catholic in background, the political and military leadership of South Viet Nam was also well educated and overwhelmingly urban. These characteristics were a considerable handicap in confronting a rural insurgency in a predominantly peasant society; they lay, for instance, behind the disastrous policy of requiring that only high-school graduates hold military commissions (see chapter 8). The urban frame of reference of the Saigon regime manifested itself in two key decisions regarding peasant society. In the first instance, Diem decided that village chiefs would no longer be locally elected but appointed from Saigon. There was justification for this move, in that the old system had already broken down, the Viet Cong were dominating the selection of leaders in many villages, and Diem was sincerely seeking (though he would fail) to build up an effective and honest rural administration. Whatever the rationale, the decision to centralize the selection of village heads was an unpopular mistake.[4] On the land question, the city-bred character of the Saigon administration caused even more damage. During the French war, the Communists had seized a good deal of land from the landlords and distributed it to the local population. Diem insisted that the new owners pay the former owners for this land, through a series of small installments over many years. This undoubtedly satisfied the urbane predilection of government bureaucrats for order and legality, but it was immensely unpopular with many villagers, who resented having to pay for land that as far as they were concerned had already been given to them for nothing. There were, of course, many in rural South Viet Nam whose dislike of Diem was more than balanced by a fear and distrust of the Communists. Prominent among these were members of the southern religious sects and Catholic refugees from the north. But in the end, the

Saigon government found it very difficult to broaden significantly its base of support beyond the overlapping groups of the army officer corps, Catholics, northerners, and the urban middle class.

THE ADMINISTRATIVE FAILURE

"The real fault of Ngo Dinh Diem was not that he was tyrannical but that he did not know how to administer. The misjudgment of the United States was to decide that Diem's greatest needs were money and a big army, when what he really required was an effective civil service."[5] There is no doubt that the lack of good grassroots government helped the guerrillas.[6] The Saigon government produced a number of well-conceived projects for rural betterment, including land reform, but one after another these endeavors came to little, mainly because of the absence of well-motivated and well-supervised administration. The strategic hamlet program is an example of really poor administration (see chapter 6). One of the ways Diem sought to safeguard himself from a coup d'état was by crossing lines of authority and keeping his ministers isolated from one another. This same sort of weakness showed up in the crucial area of military security. South Viet Nam had no less than 10 different intelligence services, badly coordinated.[7] Personal loyalty to Diem was more important in the promotion of army officers than professional competence.[8] Diem's efforts to prevent a coup ultimately failed, but not before they had ruined the chances of defeating the guerrillas through effective, honest administration.

In his first year in office Diem had overcome tremendous obstacles. These experiences had convinced him of his own good judgment, and perhaps of his luck. Less and less willing to accept criticism or even advice, Diem grew increasingly isolated. He seemed to pay attention only to secret reports by toadies and yes-men. Serious troubles within ARVN escaped his attention, because no one was willing to brave the presidential wrath that erupted when he was presented with bad news. "Diem talks but never listens; he looks but never sees."[9]

Diem was as far as can be imagined from the stereotype of the bloodthirsty tyrant: in all his years in power, most of which were dominated by insurrection and invasion, the number of nonjudicial executions amounted to only 33, including some Viet Cong shot during a prison-camp riot.[10] His weakness lay elsewhere. To the Viet Cong, noted for "ruthless discipline and monolithic policymaking," Diem opposed a government that was factionalized and inefficient.[11] A gray, totalitarian, and militarized North confronted not a free and burgeoning South but a kind of Latin American dictatorship, arbitrary without being effective.[12] This was a pitifully thin barrier to erect against an externally supported and self-confident revolutionary movement promising national unification and land to the tiller.

And here we have the real key to all Diem's troubles. Just as the weaknesses of the South Vietnamese state protracted the war, so the war exposed and exacerbated the state's weaknesses. The questionable legitimacy and inadequate performance of the Saigon regime would not have appeared as anything like so serious matters in time of peace. It was in fact the determination of Hanoi to conquer the South and the consequent power of the Viet Cong movement that made Diem's government seem much worse than it actually was. It is hard to imagine another Vietnamese acting much differently from Diem in similar circumstances, and probably none would have done much better.[13] Diem's regime "was as good as most Asian governments at the time and better than some";[14] it could certainly stand comparison with those of Sukarno and Marcos—let alone Pol Pot. Despite his policy errors and isolation, Diem was able to hold on because of the open support of the Americans and because many in the South knew something about the nature of the northern alternative.[15] The Viet Cong were never able to expand their following from the countryside into the cities; on the other hand, Diem was not afraid to distribute arms to hundreds of thousands of peasants through the Self-Defense Corps. An attempted coup against Diem failed to elicit any civilian support; the *New York Times* attributed Diem's reelection in 1961 not to coercion or fraud but to growing prosperity and widespread anti-Communism.[16] In December 1961, President Kennedy assured Diem of U.S. support for his government, with South Viet Nam receiving highest priority in terms of increased aid.[17]

In spite of many difficulties, expert observers believed in late 1962 and early 1963 that the South Vietnamese government, backed by numerous anti-northern and anti-Communist elements and receiving copious assistance from the Americans, had begun to win the war against the guerrillas.[18] But in the spring of 1963 a series of disasters erupted that within a few months swept Ngo Dinh Diem completely away and set the stage for what looked like an imminent Communist conquest of the South.

THE BUDDHIST TROUBLES

In April 1963, Monsignor Ngo Dinh Thuc, archbishop of Hue and brother of the president, celebrated the jubilee of his ordination to the priesthood. For a week, bunting hung from churches in the old capital, the white-and-yellow papal flag flew everywhere, and schoolchildren received a holiday, as if this anniversary were some sort of national fête.

Buddha's birthday fell on May 8. Monks in Hue urged their followers, in imitation of the recent Catholic celebration, to display Buddhist flags. On May 6, local officials incomprehensibly decided to enforce an old law prohibiting the flying of any flag unless the national flag was also displayed. A delegation of monks protested to the province chief, a Catholic. The minister of the interior, also a Catholic, happened to be in Hue at that time. He gave his permission for the flying of Buddhist flags, and the monks expressed satisfaction. Nevertheless, the Hue events had aroused long-simmering resentments and ambitions. A Buddhist leader named Thich Tri Quang and his monkish accomplices, some of whom were almost certainly Viet Cong, were determined to bring down the

Diem government. An increasingly sophisticated manipulation of the U.S. visual media would be one of their principal weapons.[19]

On May 8, a riot was breaking out in Hue when a bomb exploded, producing a stampede that resulted in several deaths. Diem dismissed the Hue province chief and received a delegation of monks from the city, with whom he exchanged peaceable sentiments; still, Tri Quang declared that he would not rest until Diem had been overthrown. On June 11 occurred the first self-immolation: in a downtown plaza a Buddhist monk had himself doused with gasoline, and an assistant set him on fire. The foreign press was standing by, duly alerted for a shocking incident. Grisly pictures of the suicide appeared all over the world the next day, including on President Kennedy's Oval Office desk. The American public was advised that the persecution of the Buddhists by the Catholic Diem regime must be savage indeed if despairing and anguished monks were willing to take their own lives in protest. (This, of course, was a grossly ethnocentric distortion of reality. Buddhist attitudes toward suicide are quite different from those of most Westerners, and self-immolation in honor of Buddha was a Vietnamese tradition, with no necessarily political implications.[20]) The media further explained to the Americans that since everybody in Southeast Asia had a religion, and since Catholics were less than a fifth of the South Vietnamese population, then the Buddhists must be at least four-fifths, and therefore Diem had aroused the overwhelming majority of the population against himself. (The CIA estimated that of South Viet Nam's population of about 16 million, only 3–4 million were more than nominally Buddhist and that the followers of the anti-government militant monks amounted to about one million, almost all townsmen. Notably, government relations with rural monks remained generally amicable.[21])

The U.S. media were deeply involved in these events. Members of the American press corps in Saigon detested Diem, seeing no connection between his problems and the long and complex history of Viet Nam. In their eyes, everything was Diem's fault; the United States would lose South Viet Nam to the Communists if something were not done about Diem and his family. President Kennedy's press chief, Pierre Salinger, later testified to the hostility of American correspondents toward Diem. Ambassador (and General) Taylor wrote of their "full-scale vendetta" against the South Vietnamese president. "To me, it was a sobering spectacle of the power of a few relatively young and inexperienced newsmen who, openly committed to 'getting' Diem, . . . were not satisfied to report the events of foreign policy but undertook to shape them." Ambassador Frederick Nolting wrote that "our media and our government were incredibly gullible" during the Buddhist crisis and that "I have no doubt that the American media played a major role in undermining US confidence in the Diem government."[22]

Contrary to government hopes, the crisis failed to die down; indeed, it worsened as the summer wore on. Anti-government elements, including Communist agents, used the Buddhist troubles as an opportunity for the expression of various demands. Some student groups joined the growing chorus of dissatisfaction; the demonstrations became increasingly violent. On August 18, 10 senior army generals asked Diem to proclaim martial law in Saigon, so that they could send back to their home provinces the hundreds of Buddhist monks who had come pouring into the city; on the 20th Diem agreed. It is not clear whether Diem was then aware of what was to happen next. On August 22, special forces under his brother Nhu's own command carried out raids on four Saigon pagodas that had been used as headquarters for various anti-government groups and for stock-piling weapons.[23] After these arrests calm returned to the capital for a while, and pro-government monks took responsibility for the care of the pagodas. But a chain of events was about to unfold with the most severe consequences. The agitator Thich Tri Quang requested and received sanctuary at the U.S. embassy. Foreign Secretary Vu Van Mau used the pagoda raids as the occasion for his resignation, calling upon students to continue to "fight for their rights"; South Viet Nam's ambassador to the UN also resigned. Under the prodding of several Southeast Asian states, the UN decided to send a "fact-finding mission" to in-vestigate persecution of Buddhists in South Viet Nam.

The open defiance of the regime by urban Buddhist elements began to con-vince members of the Kennedy administration that Diem no longer had sufficient popular support to fight the Communists effectively.[24] Ambassador Nolting, sympathetic to President Diem, was replaced by Henry Cabot Lodge, Richard Nixon's 1960 running mate. While the Buddhist troubles were uppermost in the administration's mind, certain trends within the inner circle of the Saigon gov-ernment also increased Washington's anxiety. Diem had always employed a number of ex-Communists in his government, and his fervent nationalism oc-casionally expressed itself in a display of mild irritation toward American of-ficials who thought they knew more about his country than he did. In addition, Diem had made it clear that he did not wish his country to be flooded with American military units. In the fall of 1963, Diem's brother and closest adviser, Nhu, began making increasingly critical statements about American conceptions of the war. Then, rumors surfaced concerning tentative talks between Nhu and Hanoi.[25] These rumors of a possible peace in Viet Nam negotiated behind Wash-ington's back heavily tipped the American scales against the Diem government, especially in light of Ambassador Lodge's increasingly open hostility toward Diem.[26] An anti-Diem group inside the administration was led by Averell Har-riman, who had engineered the disastrous "neutralization" of Laos (see below). This group effectively bypassed sound decision-making procedures in Washing-ton and directed Lodge to encourage an army coup to remove Diem.[27]

As Diem's stock fell precipitously in Washington, he rapidly lost support in Saigon as well. Within the ARVN, dissatisfaction centered on the distrust Diem displayed toward certain generals, and on Ngo family interference in internal army affairs. Many generals also liked to tell Americans that the failure to defeat the guerrillas was Diem's fault. The government's confrontation with Buddhist elements and the resulting bad publicity in the United States summoned up doubts about the regime's viability, and many officers resented attempts to iden-tify the army with the pagoda raids.[28]

So it was that a conspiracy developed within the army to overthrow President Diem. Gens. Duong Van Minh and Tran Van Don, the main leaders, were southern and Buddhist, in contrast to the central Annamese and Catholic flavor[29] of the Diem government, but some Catholic officers, such as Colonel Thieu (later president of South Viet Nam) were also involved. (General Don, born in France, had volunteered for the Viet Minh in 1945 but had been rejected.) Within Saigon, elite marine and airborne battalions were sympathetic to a move against Diem, as were certain air force elements.[30]

THE COUP

Of course Diem had been taking precautions for many years against an army move against him. In Saigon, the president could count on the Palace Guard, along with some special-forces units, the national police, and paramilitary groups. Military Region IV (south of Saigon) was in the hands of General Cao, who had saved Diem from a coup attempt in 1960. The crucial Military Region III, which contained Saigon, was under General Dinh, a supposed Diem loyalist. Failure to win over General Dinh, in fact, caused the plotters to call off the move against Diem planned for August 31. A few weeks later the Kennedy administration, under prodding from Lodge, announced deep cuts in its aid to the ARVN. The army leadership in Saigon took this as a signal that the over-throw of Diem would be greeted with pleasure in Washington. The plotters then managed to maneuver the vain and naive General Dinh into asking President Diem to make him minister of the interior. Diem refused; now Dinh was sym-pathetic to the coup.

Attending the Vatican Council, Archbishop Thuc told people in Rome that the United States was spending a lot of money in Saigon to promote a coup against his brother.[31] True enough, Ambassador Lodge was clearly supporting a move to oust Diem, in spite of the fact that disagreement over the wisdom of the coup was deeply dividing the counsels of the administration. John McCone, Director of the Central Intelligence Agency, was joined by Vice President Lyn-don Johnson in opposing U.S. approval of a coup.[32] Ambassador Nolting told the president that encouraging the coup was bad policy and bad faith, and would have severely negative consequences.[33] Gen. Paul Harkins, the senior U.S. mil-itary figure in Viet Nam, expressed opposition to the coup to the very last hour.[34] In the week before the coup, National Security Adviser McGeorge Bundy wrote to Kennedy: "Should we not cool off the whole enterprise?"[35] On October 29, only hours before the event, Attorney General Robert Kennedy, the president's brother and close adviser, declared that "to support a coup would be putting the future of Viet Nam and in fact all of Southeast Asia in the hands of one man not now known to us." Maxwell Taylor and John McCone supported him in this view.[36]

But Henry Cabot Lodge, supremely confident of his ability to comprehend and manipulate the complexities of South Vietnamese politics, was determined to have his way and rode roughshod over all qualms inside the embassy and back in Washington.

Accordingly, despite all the misgivings among the Americans, in the late morning of November 1 the first units supporting the coup deployed around Saigon. At 1:45 P.M., General Don called General Harkins to inform him that the coup was proceeding. By that time the coup makers were taking over the airport, the post office, and the radio stations, and they were blocking off exits from the city. At 4:00 P.M. they launched the first attack against the Presidential Palace. From inside, Diem tried to telephone commanders of outlying garrisons to come to his aid. He had a difficult time getting through to several units; when he did make contact, his interlocutors one after another told the president that they were supporting the coup and that he should surrender. Diem telephoned the U.S. embassy; Ambassador Lodge was icy, expressing polite concern for Diem's safety. No one came to Diem's assistance. The men upon whom he had counted to control the army had all turned away from him, even the commander of Military Region IV, his own godson, while the cadres of both the government-sponsored Can Lao party and the Republican Youth remained inactive. At 5:00 P.M. the leaders of the coup called upon Diem to surrender. Instead, around 8:00 P.M. Diem and his brother Nhu escaped from the palace. The originally reported version of this event had the brothers leaving the palace area through an underground tunnel, but actually they just walked off the grounds, a fact of which those attacking the palace were ignorant until the coup was over.[37] (In a similar manner, in October 1917 Alexander Kerensky escaped from the Winter Palace by calmly driving his car past the lines of besieging Bolsheviks.)

At 9:00 P.M. a bombardment of the palace began, and around 3:30 the next morning tanks and infantry joined in the assault. At approximately 6:30 A.M., Diem telephoned the palace from a house in the Chinese suburb of Cholon. He told the defenders to lay down their arms. This telephone call revealed Diem's whereabouts, and twenty minutes later soldiers arrived to arrest him and Nhu. Shortly after, the first president of the Republic of Viet Nam was murdered, along with his brother.

General Don states "without equivocation" that General Minh ("Big Minh") gave the order to kill the Ngo brothers, an accusation that is also leveled by other authoritative sources.[38] Minh, however, never admitted any responsibility for the double murder. Far away in Washington, President Kennedy professed himself shocked by the killing of Diem, as if such an outcome had not been predictable all along: if Diem had lived, he might very well have been able to stage a comeback and punish the coup makers. In any event, the bodies of the president and his brother came to rest in a vacant field inside the security fence at ARVN headquarters in Saigon.[39] When Ngo Dinh Can heard of the murder of his brothers, he appealed to the American consul in Hue for sanctuary. Alas, "different rules applied to him from those applicable to Thich Tri Quang"; the Americans handed Can over to the generals, who executed him.[40]

Not for the last time did the world observe the manner in which the United States treats old friends fallen on hard times.

The decision of Hanoi to support a major guerrilla insurgency in South Viet Nam caused Diem grave problems, some of which his undeniable shortcomings undoubtedly aggravated. But at the beginning of 1963, nobody imagined that his government was particularly shaky or that before the end of the year Diem would have been not only cast out of power but murdered by his own officers. Diem had "presided over almost a decade of impressive economic and educational recovery."[41] He received accredited diplomats from 80 countries.[42] On September 27, elections to the National Assembly had taken place, with a very high turnout and little disruption by the Viet Cong.[43]

As in perhaps many tragedies, the death of President Diem has within it elements that approach the absurd. Consider that the immediate cause of Diem's downfall and all its grim and tearful consequences—the ruin of the strategic hamlet program, the inability to erect a stable civilian government, the flooding of South Viet Nam with U.S. troops—lay in the fact that some Buddhists in Hue may or may not have been allowed to fly the flag of the World Fellowship of Buddhists on Buddha's birthday without the national flag being present as well.[44] As a result of this provincial contretemps the American media and the U.S. ambassador, between them, set the stage for the overthrow of a fundamentally stable, constitutional, and friendly government by military coup. It now seems clear that very few Buddhists, whatever their complaints, wished either a U.S. takeover or a Communist conquest of South Viet Nam, yet both eventually followed and are clearly linked to Diem's downfall. Diem was "the embodiment of his country's soul, for good no less than for ill."[45] In 1963, however, a little group of supremely self-confident American policy makers hardly imagined that their choice lay not between Diem and something better but Diem and something incomparably worse.

A few days after the murder of Diem, Lodge informed the State Department that "the prospects are now for a shorter war, thanks to the fact that there is this new government."[46]

President Kennedy had said numerous times that a fundamental reason why the United States was aiding the South Vietnamese was to reassure its allies all over the world as to the reliability of American guarantees. It is not clear how Kennedy imagined that U.S. participation in the overthrow of President Diem would advance this purpose.

At any rate, "by encouraging the revolt against Ngo Dinh Diem the Kennedy administration set the stage for the tragedy that followed."[47] The Communists received the murder of Diem as "a gift from heaven."[48] In the wake of what Henry Kissinger called "this folly" and "this reckless coup," insurgent attacks, especially against strategic hamlets, noticeably increased, along with infiltration into South Viet Nam by NVA units.[49] The military junta fired 70 percent of the province chiefs; in late December Director of Central Intelligence McCone informed President Johnson that "there is no organized government in South Viet Nam at this time."[50] The killing of Diem and the consequent saddling of the United States with the fate of South Viet Nam led to more coups, followed by more purges, the breakdown of internal order, mounting aggressiveness by the Communists, the dispatch of ultimately two and a half million U.S. troops, the physical and moral devastation of Viet Nam, and grave upheavals within American society. Washington's rejection of Diem had been rooted in his skepticism regarding American omniscience. This approach, "more than any other aspect of the American intervention in Viet Nam, was responsible for the disastrous end of the war."[51]

DETERIORATION AND U.S. INTERVENTION

In the days after the death of Diem, Saigon was notably quiet, as if everyone were waiting to see what the new military rulers of the country would do. These latter soon announced the creation of a body calling itself the Military Revolutionary Council, consisting of General Minh as chairman, along with Don, Dinh, and nine other senior officers, most of whom were Buddhists and native southerners. The MRC set up a cabinet of 15 ministers, of whom 3 were generals and the rest civilians with no popular followings. It became clear soon enough that the ruling generals had no real plans. This increased the burden upon the United States. The Americans had approved of the coup, indeed they had made it possible. Now there was a widespread impression that under the new military government South Viet Nam would be more dependent on the Americans than ever, not only for help in the war effort but "in the practical problems of running the country."[52]

The Kennedy people had turned against Diem because they had identified him as a main cause of corruption, of delay in the effort against the Communist insurgency, and of the apparently widespread unrest of the Buddhists. But these grave problems became not less but more serious after the death of Diem. For instance, despite broad concessions, the Buddhist militants did not become more law abiding and content; there were more self-immolations of monks after than before the coup, reaching a peak in 1966.[53] The Buddhists became an object of intense dislike by the police, in part because of the ease with which Buddhist projects and demonstrations were infiltrated by Communist agents.[54] Indeed, the death of Diem unleashed seething rivalries and factionalism and put the country back in some ways to where Diem had found it in 1954.[55] Instead of having removed the major obstacle to effective action against the Communists, Diem's death had destroyed the source of whatever collaboration and dynamism had existed in the South Vietnamese war effort, just as the opponents of the coup in the U.S. mission in Saigon had feared it would.[56] In January 1964, Gen.

Nguyen Khanh overthrew the council headed by Minh; after this coup, one government after another toppled. These successive coups wrecked the already shaky administration of the country, since each coup in Saigon set off personnel changes all the way down to the village level.[57] The province and district chiefs of the Diem period were all turned out of office, and in many places there were three or four replacements within a single year.[58] The target of increasing Communist terrorism in the cities, the police forces of South Viet Nam continued to deteriorate; the politicization of senior positions meant that continuity of command disappeared, while training often consisted of but three weeks of weapons instruction. The successive coups and threats of coups also wrought havoc with morale in the army, especially among younger officers, who became loud in their disenchantment. Reflecting years later on the meaning and genesis of these events, a senior Vietnamese military officer was moved to confess that the overthrow and death of Diem had indeed been "a great disaster" for South Viet Nam.[59]

The immediate post-Diem military governments were utterly unable to stem the rising tide of Communist insurgency. This failure, of course, had many causes, but two were primary. The army was, at one and the same time, trying to fight a war and run a country; the resulting politicization of the officer corps surpassed anything known under Diem. Simultaneously, the North was heating up the war; in December 1963, a few weeks after the killing of Diem, the Ninth Plenum of the Communist Party Central Committee convened in Hanoi and decided on a major escalation of the struggle.[60] By the end of 1964, regular North Vietnamese Army (NVA) elements had been introduced into the South, and large Viet Cong units were maneuvering near the capital.[61] At the end of the winter of 1964–65, almost half the population and nearly two-thirds of the territory of South Viet Nam were in Communist hands. The southern republic seemed on the verge of extinction. It was in this context of emergency that the Johnson administration began a rapid buildup of U.S. ground forces in the country, at first concentrated into coastal enclaves. Serious defeats suffered by the ARVN seemed to demonstrate that merely deploying U.S. forces in enclaves would not be enough, and General William Westmoreland was thus given permission to maneuver his 75,000 U.S. troops over wider areas. Half a year after these decisions, Sen. Michael J. Mansfield returned from a personal inspection tour of South Viet Nam to inform president Johnson that the U.S. military effort had saved the country but that the end of major fighting was not in sight.[62]

THE ELECTION OF PRESIDENT THIEU

Students of politics in third-world societies consider political leadership to be primary and decisive in the successful functioning of new states. Diem was by no means the epitome of the ideal leader for a country with the problems of South Viet Nam. Nevertheless, with all his faults, Diem came from an ancient and distinguished family and had a long record as a fervent and austere nationalist. Those who succeeded him in the leadership of South Viet Nam could not begin to match his credentials or prestige at home or abroad.

The successive military regimes following the murder of Diem failed to give the country charismatic or even dignified leadership. But at least governmental stability eventually returned, in the person of Gen. Nguyen Van Thieu. Born in 1923 near Phan Rang, a descendant of army officers and farmers, Thieu had engaged in some sort of flirtation with the Viet Minh during the Second World War but had then turned against it. He had graduated from the military academy at Dalat in 1948, achieved the rank of major by the time of partition in 1954, and received further training in France and the United States in later years. He was a convert to Catholicism through marriage, although he seems to have postponed his baptism for years in order to avoid the appearance of trying to curry favor with President Diem.[63] By 1965 he held the rank of lieutenant general and, as chairman of the last military junta, he was nominally head of state, although real power was temporarily in the hands of Prime Minister Nguyen Cao Ky. For years, especially in the period just before the fall of South Viet Nam, Thieu was the object of accusations that he condoned the corruption that was poisoning the life of the republic, but evidence that he himself profited from this corruption is only circumstantial.[64] Whether or not, or to what extent, Thieu was venal is, in the circumstances of war-torn Southeast Asia, beside the point. It was to be his level of leadership and political judgment that would in the end help decide the fate of his countrymen. Maxwell Taylor thought Thieu was a man of "considerable poise and judgment."[65] This may well have been the case. Nevertheless, this observation of Taylor unwittingly highlights the fact that Thieu had risen so high in ARVN not because of a talent for success on the battlefield but because he was essentially a skillful political operator in an army uniform.

All during World War II, the British postponed national elections in the United Kingdom, in spite of the fact that there were no enemy troops on British soil and that after 1940 there was no danger of invasion. South Viet Nam—a poor, rural, third-world country just emerged from a century of authoritarian colonial rule and racked by a cruel, externally supported insurgency and a foreign invasion—had no tradition of national elections, honest or otherwise. Nevertheless, the Johnson administration was eager to establish South Viet Nam's credentials as a democratic society and thus a worthy recipient of U.S. assistance. Hence Washington insisted on "meaningful" elections as soon as the military situation stabilized.[66] The people of South Viet Nam had to choose an assembly to produce a new constitution, leading to the election of a new president and national legislature. Elections to a constituent assembly were duly conducted in 1966, and an impressive 81 percent of the eligible voters turned out.

Drafted largely by politicians who had led the opposition to Diem, the new Vietnamese constitution, like its predecessor (and like that of the French Fifth

Republic and most Latin American states), established a centralized system with a dominant presidency.[67] Elections for this new presidential office took place in September 1967. Twenty-two candidates competed for the offices of president and vice president. With 84 percent of the voters participating, the ticket of General Thieu and air force commander and prime minister Nguyen Cao Ky came in first with 35 percent of the total, the remainder divided among the other tickets.[68] A year later, 1,206 candidates competed for 137 seats in the new National Assembly; in that contest, turnout reached 73 percent of the eligibles.

How valid were these elections? There was a good deal of criticism, especially in the United States, of the presidential victory of Thieu. This criticism can be summarized in two somewhat contradictory propositions: that (1) Thieu rigged the vote in his own favor, and (2) his low percentage showed his lack of popular support.[69] On the other hand, the large number of candidates in the congressional elections would be difficult to explain unless most of these men and women believed that they were participating in a worthwhile contest. In the populous Mekong Delta, the Cao Dai and Hoa Hao sects, cowed and sullen since the early days of the Diem regime, returned to active politics in strength and elected many of their candidates to the new legislature.[70] A well-known journalist long familiar with Southeast Asia wrote that the constituent assembly elections (which failed utterly to produce an openly pro–Viet Cong or pro-Hanoi element) were the fairest ever conducted in Viet Nam.[71] Finally, a leading academic authority in the field of comparative elections pronounced the electoral contests in the 1960s and 1970s in South Viet Nam to have been real tests of public opinion and major steps on the road to true democracy.[72]

8

The ARVN from Dien Bien Phu to Tet

The foundation of states is a good military organization.

—Machiavelli

THE SOUTH VIETNAMESE ARMY

In 1948, the French faced both an increasing need for troops to fight the Viet Minh and a rising opposition to the draft in metropolitan France. The response of the French government was to create the force that after partition became the Army of the Republic of Viet Nam, or ARVN. By 1953 this force numbered 200,000 men, and by the end of the Viet Minh war (July 1954) a total of 400,000 Vietnamese were serving either in the future ARVN or in French army units. Only about 1 percent of these Vietnamese were officers.[1]

These Vietnamese who fought beside the French against their fellow countrymen of the Viet Minh—were they traitors? Or perhaps merely mercenaries? It is true that pay rates in the Vietnamese army were on the French scale—that is, they were very high for an Asian country. But surely more than monetary considerations must have entered into the decisions of so many Vietnamese to take sides against the Viet Minh and to keep up the struggle for so many years at the cost of so much bloodshed, danger, and suffering.

For generations French civilization attracted both admiration and loyalty from many inhabitants of non-European areas—and still does. It should present no great puzzle or scandal that millions of Vietnamese, especially Catholics but also members of other, more indigenous religions, saw temporary cooperation with France as at the very minimum the lesser of evils compared with the permanent triumph of the local representatives of Stalinist totalitarianism. France had, after all, recognized the independence of the Vietnamese state under Em peror Bao Dai; legally, therefore, the French forces in Viet Nam were fighting alongside Bao Dai's army to preserve his sovereign government. No less than 35 foreign countries maintained diplomatic relations with Bao Dai. For many, it was clearly more patriotic—more Vietnamese—to prefer Bao Dai and his traditionalist nationalism to Ho Chi Minh and his Euro-Leninism.[2]

A general staff for the Vietnamese national army began operating in 1952; Nguyen Van Hinh, a lieutenant colonel in the French air force and a son of the prime minister of Viet Nam at the time, became chief of staff, with the rank of major general. Development of the Vietnamese army (as opposed to simple increase in size) had not made much progress by the time the First Indochina War ended; in 1954, there was besides General Hinh himself hardly any general staff, no artillery, no heavy armor, no engineering or communications capability, and most of the officers, especially above the rank of lieutenant, were French. For a time after partition, training of the ARVN was in the hands of both French officers and Americans (Military Assistance and Advisory Group Viet Nam, or MAAG-V). When the French left South Viet Nam for good in 1956, the Americans remained to train an expanding southern army.

The army of independent India did not reject its British antecedents and traditions, nor did the army of the Philippine Republic reject its American ones. The departing French were therefore surprised and offended when ARVN shed the uniforms and insignia of the French past to adopt those of the Americans.[3] But it casts a revealing light on the pragmatic motivation of many Vietnamese who had fought on the side of the French against the Viet Minh that the ARVN dated its foundation not from 1948 but from 1955.

THE ARVN OFFICER CORPS

The ARVN always seemed to be short of officers (especially good ones), and the training of many of them was sketchy at best.[4] In the 1950s even most South Vietnamese generals were only recently elevated from the ranks of noncommissioned officers. The Vietnamese National Military Academy, founded in 1948 at Hue and then moved to Dalat, did not graduate its first four-year class until 1969. Several hundred ARVN officers attended various courses at U.S. military schools in the Phillipines, Japan, and the United States, but language was a barrier even for the most conscientious, while sightseeing and shopping consumed a great deal of time.[5]

Most ARVN officers entered the service right after graduation from high school or university. Many of those with civilian work experience before joining ARVN had been teachers.[6] The commissioning system for ARVN officers placed exceedingly heavy stress on formal education. One result of such policies was that the ARVN had one of the most degree-laden officer corps in the world: in the mid-1960s, 5 percent of its generals, over 13 percent of its colonels, and nearly 15 percent of its field-grade officers held doctoral degrees.[7] Another consequence of the stress on formal schooling was that, since Western-style education was available almost exclusively in cities, and mainly for the middle classes, the ARVN possessed an officer corps almost totally unfamiliar with and unsympathetic to the country's peasant majority, among whom and over whom the war was being fought.[8] Beginning in 1966, steps were taken to open up the officer corps, including the promotion of NCOs, commissions for battlefield heroism, and the establishment of training schools for enlisted officer-candidates.[9] But no one will ever be able to calculate the amount of injury the ARVN inflicted on its own cause by years of restrictive officer-recruitment policies; not only did these restrictions create severe difficulties in winning over or even understanding the peasantry, but very often those who had leadership ambitions and natural abilities but lacked the formal schooling necessary for advancement in the ARVN joined the Viet Cong.[10]

The artificial limitation of recruitment to the urban middle classes was not the only, nor the worst, problem afflicting the ARVN officer corps: in too many cases, assignments and promotions depended more on political considerations than on military competence. In the words of one observer, "political loyalty, rather than battlefield performance, has long dominated the promotion system in the officer corps, with the result that there is often an inverse relationship between rank and military skill."[11] This deplorable situation was deeply rooted in the history of the South Vietnamese state. President Diem's experience with the attempted Hinh coup in 1955 (see chapter 4) taught him to value political loyalty above all other virtues, and he took an active personal role in officer promotions with that consideration in mind. Diem was especially partial to fellow Catholics, believing them to be more fervently anti-communist, and to northerners, believing them to be more efficient, than other Vietnamese. Even after Diem's departure, these patterns of promotion and favoritism remained quite salient: in 1967, out of 25,000 ARVN officers, fully one-fourth had been born in the North, and the Catholic proportion was twice that of the nation as a whole: 19.4 percent of officers as compared with 10.4 percent of all South Vietnamese. (Buddhists made up 59 percent of the population and 62 percent of the officer corps.)[12] Those who were both northern and Catholic usually marched along a smooth path to preferment and higher rank. Of course one cannot automatically assume that Catholic or northern-born officers were not qualified for the posts they held, but the known favoritism of the Diem government toward these categories was extremely annoying to non-Catholic and southern-born officers, and it must have been especially galling in instances where Catholics and northerners were in fact more competent.

While vigorously enforcing religious and regional criteria in promotions, Diem was anything but vigorous in rooting out corruption among ARVN officers. The opportunity to engage in racketeering was omnipresent in a war-torn country with a large army to whose hands more and more normally civilian administrative posts were entrusted. Yet neither incompetence nor corruption on the part of an officer offended Diem per se, because he and his brother Nhu sought to make use of such failings to pressure the guilty officer into becoming a fervent Ngo family supporter. In many Far Eastern officer corps, superiors are hesitant to inflict loss of face through reprimands to subordinates;[13] in the ARVN, this tendency to overlook inadequate performance was magnified because commanders were often reluctant to punish subordinates who might have political connections.[14] For much the same cause, superior officers frequently saw their orders evaded or disobeyed. This morale-breaking favoritism and its accompanying back-biting, sycophancy, and corruption were epidemic throughout Diem's officer corps, hobbling the efforts of thousands of officers who were doing their best to save their country. The politicization of the ARVN would have many grave consequences, including the assassination of President Diem and the seizure of the state by the army intended to protect it. Reflection on the grave consequences political favoritism had for the efficiency of the ARVN provides a powerful argument in favor of strict adherence to seniority in the matter of promotions, a practice favored by the highly efficient pre–World War II Imperial Japanese Navy, among others.[15]

The problems within the officer corps did not end with the death of Diem—far from it. Under Thieu, family and political ties often interfered with the disciplining or removal of officers who did not perform adequately.[16] This was a very serious shortcoming, since most ARVN commanders, inexperienced and poorly trained as they often were, pursued very conservative battlefield tactics in order not to be singled out for criticism later.[17] As a general rule, good field commanders were the least favored for promotion.[18]

It is precisely for these reasons that some American critics of the war insist that it would have been much better to have had a unified command under a U.S. officer, as in the Korean conflict. Under that system, General Matthew Ridgway rooted out incompetent Korean commanders as soon as he discovered them, replacing them with the best he could find, neither knowing nor caring who anybody's relatives or friends might be.[19]

THE AMERICANS BUILD UP THE ARVN

In the 1950s, Col. Edward Lansdale, a close personal adviser to President Diem, argued that since armed opponents of the South Vietnamese state were few in number at that time, the ARVN should be lightly armed and well trained in anti-guerrilla tactics. Small, elite, self-confident and highly mobile forces would pursue the scattered rebel bands, while paramilitary units maintained security in the cities and villages.[20] The U.S. role would have consisted primarily in supplying these forces, backing them up with air and naval power, and shielding the South from an invasion across the DMZ.[21] A U.S.-backed ARVN built on these lines would have profited from expensive lessons learned in counter-guerrilla warfare in Malaya and the Philippines.

Unfortunately, it was not from these conflicts that the U.S. Army drew its inspiration for training the ARVN but from the recently ended Korean War. The Americans decided to construct a Vietnamese army that would be able to repel a massive, conventional invasion from the North. Laboring under their Korean concepts, the Americans built a force that was cumbersome and road-bound, like the French one before it. The leaders of this new conventional army had, of necessity, been rapidly advanced from much lower ranks and were not experienced at this type of command. Under them, the ARVN developed very bad habits. It relied on massive firepower as a substitute for flanking movements on the ground.[22] Forays into the countryside never lasted longer than seven days, so the ARVN inflicted only minimal damage to Viet Cong bases and rest areas and learned relatively little about jungle fighting.[23] This reluctance of the South Vietnamese army to get out, find, and grapple with the enemy was really a reluctance to fight a kind of war for which it had neither been trained nor equipped. (Besides, Viet Nam had been at war for most of the time since 1941, and many ARVN officers took a very long-range and hence non-urgent view of this particular phase of the conflict.[24])

The U.S.-model army carried with it other major costs as well. The rapidly expanding officer corps took all the country's best young men, leaving rather unimpressive material for staffing the all-important police and the civilian administrations.[25] Funds and attention were diverted from police and low-level self-defense efforts that, especially in the early years of the republic, would have been the cheapest and most effective way to checkmate the guerrillas.

But probably the most serious long-term damage to South Viet Nam from the ill-conceived construction of a conventional ARVN was erosion of support in the United States. Some maintain that the conventional strength of the ARVN prevented Hanoi from launching an over-the-border assault. This may well be true, and if so it was very unfortunate for the South Vietnamese, for U.S. support would have been much easier to muster and sustain in the face of a classic invasion. What is certain, however, is that the sheer size and budget of this conventional army and the consequent neglect of state-building made the army by far the most cohesive force in the country; thus political power came to mean control of the ARVN, and vice versa. Under both Diem and Thieu, generals were named more for their political loyalty to the government than for their military distinction, or even competence, and they in turn appointed subordinate officers according to the same criteria all the way down the line.[26] With all the coups and attempted coups of the 1960s, and with the ARVN administering most of the country and supplying its most visible leaders, leaders who could not seem to win, it was easy to present to the American public a picture of South Viet Nam as nothing more than a military dictatorship, and an inefficient one at that. Partly because of its size and training, partly because of its politicization, the ARVN never learned how to combat the Viet Cong with lasting effect, so that the fighting got beyond its ability to control. The Americans therefore took up the burden of the war, for which they too were unprepared. Predictably, this regrettable situation came to be attributed to South Vietnamese corruption and cowardice. Equally predictable was the erosion of support within the United States for its ever more massive, ever more bloody involvement in

Southeast Asia. In a word, the Americans first mistrained the ARVN, then became exasperated when the ARVN did not win, and finally decided to abandon its allies to "the inevitable."

TRAINING AND EQUIPMENT

The ARVN had a well-educated officer corps, but it was not a well-trained army. Programs and projects to overcome training deficiencies arose from time to time, often under U.S. prodding and guidance, but little came of them. When President Diem, for example, created ranger units, U.S. Special Forces advisers arrived to train them. Ranger training in the United States required nine weeks; the advisers suggested at least seven weeks, but in the end ARVN rangers received only a four-week course.[27] Throughout the 1950s and 1960s, systematic training was often interrupted or postponed because of the demands of combat operations, guard duty, and similar requirements. Even after the beginning of "Vietnamization," one-third of the ARVN battalions did no training at all, less than half trained for two hours a week, about one-fifth of all ARVN units trained only 20 minutes a week, and much of this training was ineffective or of only marginal benefit.[28] It was not only duty demands that interfered with serious training; when forced to supply cadres for training centers and programs, military commanders, being naturally unwilling to lose any of their good officers, made a practice of sending inferior ones.[29] "The greatest obstacle in improving and training the armed forces was the lack of qualified leadership at all levels, both officers and noncommissioned officers."[30]

The ARVN's inadequate combat training (which undoubtedly caused many needless casualties over the long years of the war) was matched by a deficiency in political training. The tendency to downplay or ignore completely the importance of political education of the armed forces is a grave weakness of all Western and Western-trained armed forces, and the ARVN was no exception. In contrast with Communist armies, including the Viet Cong and the NVA, where no one is ever permitted to lose sight of the central fact that a war is being fought to achieve some political aim, Western armies normally separate military operations from political goals. Indeed, the former often run counter to the latter, and nowhere was this truer than in South Viet Nam. The most visible result of the failure to educate the ARVN about what the war was being waged for was the ARVN's poor and sometimes disgraceful treatment of the peasantry. Especially when the ARVN was operating in contested areas, its units behaved more like an army of foreign occupation than a national army whose purpose was to protect and elevate the civilian population among whom it moved.[31] Thus it was not uncommon for U.S. advisers to be eyewitnesses to the looting of southern villages by ARVN units.[32]

While the training and indoctrination of the ARVN stayed at low levels, the size of the army increased inexorably. By 1972, the ARVN alone enrolled over 400,000 men; there were another 100,000 in other regular South Vietnamese military services, as well as over half a million in the territorial forces (Regional and Popular Forces, or "Ruff-Puffs").[33] Even with U.S. aid, maintaining all these men in service was an extremely heavy burden for the country, one that deeply distorted the entire economy.

Machiavelli praised the Greeks and Romans for making war with armies that were small in number but excellent in training.[34] South Viet Nam sought to protect its independence with exactly the opposite kind of army. Smaller armed forces—less expensive, more disciplined, and better trained—would have served South Viet Nam much more effectively than greater and greater numbers. In the rueful reflection on the French experience in Viet Nam, it needed "fewer battalions but better battalions."[35] A more compact army would have increased the proportion of volunteers to conscripts, thus making it easier to imitate the Roman practice of strict discipline and constant training, and facilitating an improvement in the political awareness of the troops as well. The money and effort saved by keeping the numbers in the ARVN within bounds could have been spent on improving security for the civilian population, especially through the buildup of the very inexpensive but not ineffective territorial forces. In a smaller, better army devoting greater attention to local security and self-defense, the degree of politicization, or at least the consequences of it, might also have decreased.

Almost totally dependent on the United States for armaments, ARVN had problems in this area as well. The United States supplied ARVN with the World War II–vintage M-1 rifle; this weapon, good in itself, was much too heavy and clumsy for the slim and compact Vietnamese soldier. On the other hand, by 1965 the Viet Cong possessed the excellent Russian-made AK-47 assault rifle, to which the M-1 was manifestly inferior.[36] But 1965 was also the year of the great buildup of American forces in Viet Nam, and Secretary of Defense McNamara was opposed to diverting any M-16 rifles, which were more than a match for the AK-47, or much of any other first-class equipment, to America's beleaguered ally. The ARVN therefore did not begin obtaining the M-16 until the spring of 1967, and it was in short supply for years.[37] Needless to say, nobody wanted to waste good M-16s on the hapless Ruff-Puffs, who did not receive them in numbers until 1970, an example of a persistent, costly, inexcusable error on the part of both the Americans and the ARVN.[38]

THE ROLE OF U.S. ADVISERS

In the early 1960s, in part because it was the wrong kind of army for the country it was supposed to protect, ARVN was visibly suffering from inadequate leadership, questionable morale, and an inability to guarantee security for an increasingly large percentage of the South Vietnamese people.[39] The army, that is, resembled the government it was supposed to be defending. How did ARVN's U.S. advisers respond to this lamentable and dangerous situation? The notorious "can do" attitude of most U.S. Army advisers meant that all problems were seen as correctable, and this contributed to many over-optimistic reports. Feeling (rightly) that there was very little they could do to affect the general political situation in the country, advisers concentrated on teaching the Vietnamese about what they knew best: the weapons and tactics of a conventional army. Reflecting a serious general weakness of American society then and now, the U.S. Army at the beginning of its involvement in Southeast Asia had no Vietnamese-language training program, and the number of U.S. officers who could speak and understand Vietnamese always remained grotesquely inadequate. Consequently, U.S. advisers tended to like and trust a South Vietnamese officer if he could speak decent English (if he drank bourbon, so much the better).[40] The South Vietnamese had been taking orders from white men for an awfully long time; U.S. advisers were therefore urged by their superiors to establish "rapport" with ARVN officers, and confrontation would seem to indicate its absence. U.S. advisers, therefore, often failed to demand the removal of even a clearly ineffective ARVN commander, because they feared it would look bad on their own records. Thus "rapport" became a dangerous concept.[41] More unfortunately, most U.S. advisers served for only one year. Just as he was getting to know the ARVN commander whom he was advising, the American officer would have to leave and be replaced by a new one who probably knew nothing of the language or what was really going on and who could thus be manipulated or circumvented by the local ARVN leaders.[42] The U.S. policy of short terms of service in South Viet Nam meant that, in general, the Americans never learned anything about the unhappy country. As one acute and devastating observation had it, the Americans did not fight a ten-year war in South Viet Nam; they fought a one-year war ten times.

THE PROBLEM OF DESERTION

In spite of all these difficulties, by the end of 1962 the campaign against the guerrillas was going reasonably well, and there was very little danger that the northern-inspired insurrection would shatter the ARVN or overthrow the Diem government. Then in 1963 came the Buddhist riots and the killing of Diem, events that struck the ARVN like a typhoon. After the murder of Diem, ARVN morale, discipline, and performance really deteriorated, the Communists undertook operations in main-force units, and South Viet Nam's republican experiment seemed perilously close to collapse. The Johnson administration decided in the spring of 1965 to insert massive numbers of U.S. troops into South Viet Nam. This decision meant that assistance to the ARVN would be deemphasized, and thus the South Vietnamese army was reduced to the status of an auxiliary force in its own country. Saigon was saved, for the time being, but the root problems afflicting the ARVN remained unsolved. The assumption of the burden of the war by the Americans meant that they would begin to suffer large numbers of casualties, something no democracy can sustain over an extended period of time without visible progress toward victory, and the Americans did not know with what yardstick progress in a guerrilla war could be measured. Protracted large-scale U.S. participation in the war also presented the Communists with a valuable opportunity to attack the nationalist credentials of the South Vietnamese government. Finally, although ARVN forces were consigned to smaller and less glamorous operations, they consistently suffered more casualties than the Americans (in proportion to population, the ARVN lost 40 men killed to every one American; see chapter 12), a fact that U.S. troops were disinclined to acknowledge and the American media completely ignored—if they even knew about it.

In light of all the problems confronting the young republic and its equally young army, that the ARVN suffered from high desertion rates is no surprise. The monthly gross desertion rate reached an all-time peak in the fall of 1968, at 17.2 per thousand; it eventually leveled off at 12 per thousand, but desertion was always higher in combat infantry units.[43]

Naturally, desertion had many causes. Citizens were drafted for the duration of the war, and leave policies were very stringent.[44] The pain of family separation, low pay, poor housing, an inadequate promotion schedule, the indifference of many officers to the condition and problems of their men all contributed their share.[45] Desertion rates were highest among first-year servicemen, during the Tet holidays, at harvest time, and in units with poor commanders—indicating that personal rather than political reasons were uppermost in the minds of those who left ARVN unlawfully. Vietnamese society did not view desertion as a serious moral failing, and the Saigon government made only haphazard efforts to discover and punish deserters.[46] A general amnesty for desertion in 1964 both expressed the government's less-than-stringent attitude toward the problem and taught future deserters to expect similar forgiveness.[47]

There can be no doubt that desertion gravely interfered with the combat readiness of the ARVN; it also supplied much ammunition to critics of U.S. involvement in the war on the side of an ally whose moral and political shortcomings were symbolized for them by these egregious desertion rates. One must, however, take note of several other interesting aspects of this question. First of all, the Viet Cong suffered desertion rates comparable to those of the ARVN.[48] Second, desertion in the Regional Forces, who served in their home provinces, was significantly lower than in the ARVN, whose units often lived and fought far from home.[49] Third, thousands of deserters from the ARVN eventually returned to their original units, or joined ARVN units closer to home, or entered the Ruff-Puffs, thus increasing the combat effectiveness of the territorial defense forces;[50] gross desertion rates did not reflect this. Finally, and perhaps most significantly, desertion from ARVN hardly ever turned into defection to the enemy. During the Chinese civil war of the 1940s, whole units, even whole divisions, of Chiang Kai-shek's nationalist armies would change sides; in Viet Nam, such a thing never happened at the big-unit level, and hardly ever even at the platoon level. Compared with the number of deserters, defectors from the Saigon government side to the Communists were very few, a fact attested to by numerous trained observers.[51] On the other hand, 200,000 Viet Cong and NVA not only deserted their cause but defected to the Saigon side between 1963 and 1972.[52]

Desertion rates in the ARVN were high partly because desertion was easy: the South Vietnamese soldier was fighting in his own country. It may be instructive to examine desertion figures from another civil war, that of the Americans. In June 1863, on the eve of Gettysburg, the Army of the Potomac was down to an effective strength of only 75,000, because over 85,000 of its men had deserted.[53] During the last two years of the conflict, desertion in the Federal forces approached 330 per thousand. As for the Confederates, the total authorized strength of their armies in December 1864 was 465,000; of that number 187,000 (400 per thousand) were listed as absent without leave.[54]

ON THE EVE OF TET

When Viet Cong insurgents became a serious problem in the late 1950s, local self-defense forces had not been prepared to meet the challenge, and so the ARVN, originally set up to fight a Korea-style war, was thrown into a conflict for which it too was ill prepared. Rampant politicization of the higher officer levels, thorough penetration by Viet Cong agents, low technical and tactical proficiency of both soldiers and officers due to poor training, overlapping responsibility and divided authority deliberately fostered by President Diem to protect himself from a possible coup—all these factors prevented the ARVN from rooting out the southern insurgency before it reached the proportions of an emergent civil war. By 1968. Diem was gone, and the generals were in control; many of the old problems had become predictably worse, while newer ones were added. A persistent shortage of commissioned and noncommissioned officers was aggravated by the practice of sending the best people to headquarters. Orders often went unobeyed, the training problem remained unsolved, political education was insufficient. U.S. advisers found their Vietnamese counterparts always willing to listen but seldom willing to change.[55] As a result of the coup of 1963, the ARVN had to administer the country as well as defend it. The generals in command of country and army were, with very few exceptions, in power because they had distinguished themselves not in battle but in political intrigue. They possessed neither the technical ability to command large numbers of armed men nor the political talents to ameliorate the problems of a war-torn and underdeveloped country. Indeed, by 1968 ARVN resembled less a national army than a feudal alliance of local armies. Political power rested on command of troops. The movement of a division out of one command area into another therefore became a major political problem, and flexibility in the deployment of ARVN units was consequently almost nil. The Communists were aware of this weakness and often took advantage of it by conducting their operations on the boundaries between two military regions, or by running across the boundaries of one region into another.[56]

By the end of 1967, Hanoi's leaders had come to two conclusions: (1) they could not defeat the Americans militarily; (2) they could still win the war politically, if they could convince the Americans that the South Vietnamese were not viable long-term allies. The easiest way to accomplish this would be to cause the ARVN to break apart. It had long been the Communist strategy to avoid U.S. forces and concentrate on the South Vietnamese. Now, as the New Year holidays of 1968 approached, Hanoi prepared to administer a masterstroke against the ARVN, a blow that it hoped would precipitate the departure of the Americans and thus open the road to the conquest of the South.

9

The Great Tet Offensive

History is like a picture gallery in which there are few originals and many copies.

—Tocqueville

TOWARD AN OFFENSIVE

In the waning days of 1967, the Hanoi leadership was poised on the brink of its greatest gamble: to convince the Americans, with one tremendous blow, that the war was lost.

Two powerful factors had converged to produce the decision for such an effort. The first was the enormous cost of the war to Hanoi, both in absolute terms and relative to what it was costing the Americans. Only 3 percent of the American GNP was devoted to the war. From 1965 to 1967, only one eligible American male in 50 was drafted; only half of these went to Viet Nam; one in 50 who went to Viet Nam died there. Between 1960 and the summer of 1967, 13,000 Americans had been killed in action, less than the number of Americans who had died in the United States during those same years as the result of accidental falls.[1] For the Communists the war was a much different story. North Vietnamese casualties were five times as great as allied casualties.[2] North Vietnamese deaths were almost 10 times American deaths.[3] The Hanoi regime was in fact requiring its own people to endure a casualty rate nearly twice as high as that suffered by the Japanese in World War II. In 1969 General Giap told a European interviewer that between 1965 and 1968 alone, Communist military losses totaled 600,000.[4] The lack of real progress against the Americans and the ARVN, despite these vast sacrifices, was seriously hurting morale.[5] While it was clear that support for the war was waning among the American public and inside the Johnson administration, the Hanoi leaders knew that they could not hope to win the war as it was presently being fought. They needed some great, shocking triumph. They needed a second Dien Bien Phu. The Tet Offensive was thus Hanoi's acknowledgement that its campaign of insurgency against the South had failed.

This leads to the second factor behind the Tet Offensive of 1968: Communist insight into the psychology of the Americans. In 1962, Premier Pham Van Dong had said to Bernard Fall, "Americans do not like long, inconclusive wars."[6] In his book *Big Victory, Great Task* General Giap had predicted that the United States could not and would not maintain large numbers of troops in South Viet Nam for long. Thus Hanoi needed to convince the Americans that the war was indeed going to be protracted and costly, with victory not easy to foresee.

Accordingly, as early as the spring of 1967, meticulous preparations began in Hanoi for an offensive in 1968.[7] The campaign would have two major objectives. The first was to crumple up main ARVN units. The second was to capture the great cities of South Viet Nam, with the aid of a mass civilian uprising against the Thieu government. "The primary objective of the Tet Offensive was to win the war by instigating a general uprising"; indeed, this concept of an end to the war in a general uprising "represents the major Vietnamese contribution to the theory of people's war."[8] In this way the state of South Viet Nam would come perilously close to paralysis, and the Americans, disillusioned and disheartened, would go home. Thus General Giap would have his latter-day Dien Bien Phu; as in 1954 one spectacular battle had destroyed the will of the French to continue the war, so 14 years later another spectacular battle would surely shake the resolve of the Americans.

The Tet Offensive took the Americans, in Viet Nam and at home, by surprise. This is not as mysterious as it might seem. Surprise is an integral part of warfare. Recall for example the fall of France, the Nazi invasion of the USSR, Pearl Harbor, the Normandy landings, the Battle of the Bulge, the North Korean attack in 1950, the Chinese intervention in Korea, Dien Bien Phu, President Johnson's sending large numbers of ground troops to Viet Nam in 1965, and the Egyptian assault on Israel in 1973. Hanoi itself would receive some very unpleasant surprises during its well-planned Tet Offensive.

The Tet surprise resulted first of all from deliberate Communist tactics. Hanoi took great pains to keep the plans for the offensive secret, even to the point that secrecy interfered with coordination of the coming attacks. Besides, the Tet New Year holidays constituted the most significant religious and family event of the Vietnamese calendar, and official Tet truces had occurred in previous years. In 1968, the Communists went all out to puff up the idea of a Tet truce, to last from January 27 to February 3. In addition, on January 21, 1968, the Communists launched a major assault against the American base at Khe Sanh. The attention of the media, and especially of the Johnson White House, was riveted on the beleaguered outpost, where 6,000 U.S. and ARVN troops held off over 20,000 North Vietnamese regulars.[9] Analogies to Dien Bien Phu reverberated in Washington. Proposals for negotiations by Hanoi's foreign minister Trinh further muddied the waters, along with the crisis resulting from the North Korean seizure of the USS *Pueblo* on January 23.

Nevertheless, as Tet drew near, allied intelligence was picking up a great deal of suggestive evidence. Captured documents, monitored enemy movements and communications, and testimony from prisoners of war, defectors, and allied agents all indicated that some sort of big enemy effort was close at hand.

But American analysts knew that the Viet Cong were not strong enough to defeat the allies without a massive civilian uprising; they also knew that such an uprising was simply not in the cards.[10] Thus, despite mounting evidence, the Americans found the idea that the Viet Cong would actually try to seize the big cities totally incredible; such an attempt would amount to suicide.[11] The South Vietnamese government, well aware of the very low level of support for the Viet Cong inside Saigon and the other major cities, was as skeptical as the Americans that the Communists were actually going to mount a major effort in these areas.[12] (Many local Communist cadres also knew that no uprising was going to happen in their areas.)[13]

Information suggesting that the Viet Cong were going to throw away their advantages of guerrilla war and expose themselves in large numbers in the cities seemed to contradict common sense; it was too good to be true. "For the allies to predict the Tet Offensive, they would have [had] to overcome probably the toughest problem that can confront intelligence analysts: they would have [had] to recognize that the plan for the Tet Offensive rested on a communist mistake."[14] Or, in the words of one U.S. intelligence officer, "even if we had [had] the whole plan, it would not have been credible to us."[15] Nevertheless, in a speech to the Detroit Economic Club on December 18, 1967, Gen. Earle Wheeler, chairman of the Joint Chiefs of Staff, warned that a latter-day Battle of the Bulge—a desperate throw of the dice—might be approaching in Viet Nam.[16] The speech was ignored by the media. On January 20, 1968, almost two weeks before the offensive broke out, General Westmoreland cabled the Joint Chiefs that some major move by the Communists was definitely coming. U.S. battalions that had been sent outside the Saigon area returned to the city. The CIA had also been warning about an enemy surprise. President Johnson later admitted that he should have prepared the American people for a major enemy move in his 1968 State of the Union address.[17] His failure to do so was crucial for subsequent events, because more than anything else it was the *surprise* of Tet that so upset domestic opinion.[18]

Throughout January, Communist troops, NVA as well as main-force Viet Cong, drifted singly and in small groups into the major towns and cities, disguised as simple peasants intent on holiday revels. (This freedom for its enemies to move about was only a small part of the price South Viet Nam paid for being a relatively open society.) At the same time, most ARVN units were only at half strength, owing to holiday leaves. President Thieu himself was out of the capital, visiting his wife's relatives in the Mekong Delta.

THE EXPLOSION

In the early hours of January 30, the Tet Offensive erupted all over South Viet Nam, like a series of volcanoes. Communist forces launched infantry and mortar attacks on dozens of provincial capitals and other towns. In and around Saigon itself, 15 Viet Cong battalions struck Independence Palace, the general staff headquarters, the naval ministry, the national broadcasting station, Ton Son Nhut airport, and the U.S. and Philippines embassies.

Viet Cong in ARVN uniforms attacked the presidential palace but were quickly driven off. Other units managed to break into the main radio station and to hold it for six hours. Had the Communists been able to broadcast their prerecorded messages that the Saigon government had surrendered, real chaos might have resulted. The government, however, had set up a pre-arranged signal whereby the station could be shut down in case of attack, and the Viet Cong thus found themselves trapped inside a useless facility. Fifteen suicide volunteers penetrated the grounds of the U.S. embassy compound (not the embassy itself, as much of the American media reported); within hours all 15 of those men were dead.

The main purpose of Tet was to smash the ARVN. During the offensive the Associated Press quoted John Kenneth Galbraith, President Kennedy's former ambassador to India, as saying that there would soon be massive defections of ARVN units.[19] Nothing of the sort happened. The Communists had attacked during the solemn Tet holiday truce, when much of ARVN was away on leave. The AK-47 weapon carried by many Viet Cong was manifestly superior to the U.S. Army–surplus rifles of the ARVN.[20] Yet the ARVN performed well above expectations; "Even though most ARVN units were at half strength, they did not desert to the communists. Instead, they fought valiantly and ultimately drove the VC out of dozens of cities and towns."[21] The ARVN "came of age during the 1968 fighting."[22] The despised and neglected Ruff-Puffs also held their own against the well-equipped and well-planned Communist sneak attack.[23] Also, almost everywhere, especially in the capital, the much-maligned and deeply troubled police forces stood up to the onslaught.[24]

The Viet Cong were stunned all the more so when the vaunted popular uprising failed to materialize.[25] "The communists soon discovered that they were not welcomed as liberators. Civilians ignored the call to stage a general uprising and largely failed to cooperate with the communists. Some civilians even jumped at the first opportunity to inform the authorities of the whereabouts of VC units or to volunteer information about VC plans."[26] The Communist leaders had "wildly miscalculated the mood and the will of the people of South Viet Nam."[27] The Viet Cong did not urge civilians to "join Communism" but merely to repudiate the Thieu government in favor of "neutrality, democracy and peace"; hence the Communist failure to rally the urban masses was all the more revealing. Most Saigonese saw Viet Cong soldiers for the first time in their lives during Tet; they could not believe that these naive peasant boys (Hanoi was mobilizing thirteen-year-olds) could possibly defeat the Americans and the U.S.-armed South Vietnamese rangers and marines. In short, "the people did not join the Viet Cong attackers; they did not revolt against the Thieu government; and they did not turn against the Americans."[28]

Southern steadfastness, both military and civilian, was one side of the coin; on the other side were enormous Viet Cong casualties. No one, even in Hanoi, knows for sure how many men the Communists lost; estimates of killed, defectors, and deserters range from 30,000 to 92,000.[29] The disaster was even worse than the numbers indicate, because Tet destroyed not only quantity but quality; "For [the Viet Cong's] greatest toll of dead was among its most experienced southern political and military cadres, both urban and rural."[30] Thus, "in truth, the Tet Offensive for all practical purposes destroyed the Viet Cong."[31]

This debacle—both the huge casualty rates and the utter failure of the uprising—prompted some Viet Cong to charge in its aftermath that the Tet Offensive had been a plot by Hanoi not only to destabilize and discredit ARVN but also to engineer a massacre of the Viet Cong, "killing two birds with one stone," thus removing all obstacles to Hanoi's eventual takeover of the South.[32] Whatever the truth of these accusations, desertions from the Viet Cong, and also from regular North Vietnamese units in the South, reached a peak in 1969, especially in the populous and rice-rich Mekong Delta.[33]

The failure of Tet, and specifically the death of so many Viet Cong, ultimately delivered much of the countryside into the hands of the Saigon government, as official Communist sources admit.[34] In the major cities, the Offensive forced critics and fence-sitters to choose sides, and overwhelmingly they chose the government.[35] Buoyed up by the rally of public opinion in and after its hour of peril, the government substantially increased the size of its armed forces. Washington soon began supplying ARVN with M-16 rifles, a match for the Viet Cong AK-47 and much superior to the vintage weapons ARVN had hitherto been forced to use.

Beyond the complete military failure of Tet, Communist terror tactics during the battle strengthened the hands of the GVN in Saigon. Most of the Viet Cong attacks on cities were beaten off in two or three days, but one of the longest and bloodiest actions of the entire second Viet Nam war raged in the ancient capital of Hue. Before and during the allied counterattack on the city, the Communists rounded up many hundreds of civilians—known anti-communists, students, Catholic priests, low-level government employees and their relatives. Perhaps as many as 2,800 of these were shot, bludgeoned to death, or buried alive.[36] Some American apologists for the Communists would try to excuse these atrocities as merely the nervous vengeance of a defeated army or as justified retaliation against "enemies of the people." Yet, in the words of a distinguished American journalist, these mass murders were clearly "a deliberate slaughter, ordered from on high for plain and specific purposes."[37] The grisly deeds at Hue received little attention in the American press, especially compared to its later fascination with the details of My Lai.[38] But there is no disputing that the bloodbath at Hue played a significant role in the popular backlash against the Viet Cong and the resulting rally to the GVN:

Before the Tet Offensive, 18-year-old villagers would lie and say they were 13 to get out of the draft; after the Tet Offensive, 13- and 14-year-olds would lie and say they were 18 to get into the draft before the Communists got to them. The perception of the craziness of what the Communists were doing was increased, and the idea that they were inevitable winners was so deflated that people changed very much how they felt.[39]

In terms of military equipment, territorial control, popular support, and general self-confidence, the republic of South Viet Nam was much stronger after Tet than before. The Communists had begun their long-planned offensive against an unprepared and dispersed enemy by violating a sacred holiday truce. They had expected the disintegration of the ARVN and massive upheavals in the cities. Instead, the Viet Cong suffered irreparable losses. Tet was so costly to the Viet Cong that they had to regress to mainly small-unit actions; it would be years before Hanoi felt able to launch another major offensive. In summary, "the Tet Offensive was the most disastrous defeat North Viet Nam suffered in the long war."[40] Truly, "had the Viet Nam war been another conventional war, had it been decided on the basis of past wars, it would have been over by mid-1968 with the defeat of the Communist forces."[41] And it was in fact the end of *one kind* of war. "More than just dealing a sharp military defeat to communist forces, [Tet] destroyed an entire political-military strategy, a revolution of Marxist people's war."[42] For the Communist side, Tet "was the end of People's War, and essentially, of any strategy built on guerrilla warfare and a politically inspired insurgency."[43] Henceforth regular North Vietnamese troops would have to assume an ever-increasing share of the war's burden.

Thus Hanoi's hopes for a popular uprising and the breakup of the ARVN met with disastrous disappointment. Yet on another front the Offensive met with great and unpredicted success: public opinion in the United States.[44] Polls in late 1967 found a majority of Americans believing that "progress" was being made in the war in Viet Nam; in June 1968, a few months after Tet, less than one in five expressed that belief.[45] Bobby Kennedy, campaigning for the Democratic presidential nomination, openly ridiculed the idea that Tet had been a setback for the Communists. Even Sen. John Stennis, hitherto a strong supporter of President Johnson, stated that he could no longer back the same old policies in Viet Nam. Perhaps the greatest casualty of all in the Tet Offensive was President Johnson himself. Within a few weeks of the opening of Tet, his standing in the polls had sunk to such a level that his advisers seriously doubted his ability to win the nomination of his party for another term. Indeed in March he stunned the nation with a television address in which he irrevocably took himself out of the presidential contest.

How did it happen? The Communists emerged from the Tet Offensive of 1968 with their hopes dashed and their guerrilla apparatus wrecked, while the

Saigon government emerged (no doubt to the surprise even of its well-wishers) bloodied but stronger. How did what today is universally understood to have been a Communist military debacle turn into a Communist political triumph that forced first Lyndon Johnson out of the White House and then the Americans out of Viet Nam? One part of the answer to this extraordinary puzzle lies in the way the news media presented Tet to the American people.

TET, THE MEDIA, AND THE WAR

The fundamental aim of Tet had been to break up the ARVN. The responses of South Vietnamese units varied widely, but overall "their stout performance was an essential factor in Hanoi's military failure."[46] Yet during and after Tet, neither *Newsweek* nor *Time* published a single article on the ARVN, and apparently no newspaper in the United States ever ran even one positive story on the fighting qualities of a single ARVN unit.[47] The unprecedented mass arming of the civilian population by Saigon after Tet was a very big story indeed, but the U.S. media never got it. The only Pulitzer Prize in the Viet Nam War went to photographer Eddie Adams, for his picture of Gen. Nguyen Ngoc Loan executing a Viet Cong prisoner on the streets of Saigon at the height of the Tet Offensive. This graphic illustration of the ugliness of irregular warfare understandably shocked and troubled millions of Americans; it was seldom explained to them that throughout Tet, especially in Saigon, Viet Cong terrorists carried out deliberate attacks on the wives and children of ARVN officers, and that shortly before the picture was taken Loan had viewed the bodies of a family of six children whom the Viet Cong prisoner had massacred.[48]

To be sure, some of the reporting of the war in South Viet Nam, and of Tet in particular, was of good quality. One of the most trenchant critics of the media states that "those few TV newsmen who actually covered ARVN troops in combat were a good deal less disparaging in their broadcasts than their colleagues who did not."[49] The universally respected dean of American journalists, Walter Cronkite, actually flew to Viet Nam at the height of the raging Tet Offensive to try to see for himself what was going on. He reported to the American people that ARVN had fought well, with no defections, and that the Viet Cong had suffered "a military defeat."[50] But these instances were unfortunately not typical. On the whole, the media, especially television, presented the Tet Offensive as an unprecedented catastrophe for U.S. forces, a totally unexpected, nearly complete, and probably irredeemable breakdown of security all over South Viet Nam.[51] Few viewers of the nightly network news could escape the suggestion that the United States was bogged down in a dirty war against invincible enemies for the sake of feckless allies who could not or would not fight.

Some reporters no doubt consciously allowed their political views to override their professional responsibilities. Others were probably just naive. But part of the failure of the enormously expensive and prestigious (in those days) U.S.

news media to get the real story to the American people was rooted in the nature of the news industry. The very immediacy and vividness of television news-casting worked against the Americans and their Vietnamese allies. In the words of one veteran newsman, television has "increased the power and velocity of fragments of experience, with no increase in the power and velocity of reasoned judgment."[52] Regular viewers of the Cronkite or the Chet Huntley–David Brinkley newscasts saw more infantry action during Tet than most U.S. soldiers in Viet Nam did at the time.[53] This "nightly portrayal of violence and gore and of American soldiers seemingly on the brink of disaster contributed significantly to disillusionment with the war."[54]

Few reporters on hand in Saigon during the Tet Offensive had seen the terrific destruction of cities that occurred in World War II or Korea. Many of them were therefore profoundly shocked and frightened at the violence they saw or heard around them, especially in their formerly pleasant Saigon. The isolation and inexperience of many journalists stimulated "the media's penchant for self-projection and instant analysis," so that major network "specials" on Tet "assumed [that] average South Vietnamese reactions were [similar to] those of American commentators,"[55] and therefore that everybody in Saigon was as overwhelmed by the Offensive as the newsmen were. Thus the coverage of Tet "cannot be treated as a triumph for American journalism."[56]

The editor's injunction to his reporters is "Keep it simple," and many reporters in Viet Nam apparently had no trouble at all in following this directive.[57] Like the intelligence and academic communities, American journalism was woefully short of people knowledgeable about Southeast Asia, especially about the complexities of the struggle in South Viet Nam. With only a sketchy idea of the country's recent history and none at all of its distant past, unfamiliar with military strategy in general and guerrilla warfare in particular, unacquainted with Leninist political tactics, lacking command of any of the languages of South Viet Nam, even French, many journalists were remote from how and why things were happening in Viet Nam. Under increasing pressure to file stories that would "grab attention," they thus drew false conclusions from false premises.[58] To an ever-increasing degree, the media portrayed South Viet Nam as a land of corruption, criminality, cowardice, and cruelty, in part because all these elements were found there, but in part because it was a wartime society open to scrutiny by the press, whereas North Viet Nam was not. Very few journalists seemed to appreciate the profound importance of this asymmetry; at any rate the closed nature of the North magnified the scars and blemishes of the South.[59] Sometimes reporters saved themselves the discomfort and danger of gathering news on their own by purchasing stories from helpful Vietnamese, who too often were agents of Hanoi. For instance, *Time* magazine's principal Vietnamese news supplier was an officer in the People's Army of Viet Nam.[60] The influential Harrison Salisbury of the *New York Times* flew to Hanoi and sent back to the United States searing stories of American bombing atrocities, using material supplied to him by the government of North Viet Nam.[61]

These and other failures of journalistic coverage of the war eventually provoked scathing criticism, not only from experts on Viet Nam but also from the
ranks of professional journalists themselves. One veteran newsman wrote that
Newsweek's editors had "a penchant for sweeping generalizations" and "did not
separate but closely welded fact and opinion," and that during Tet "drama was
perpetuated at the expense of information."[62] Another journalist stated, "The
New York Times and many others had succeeded in creating an image of South
Viet Nam that was so distant from the truth as not even to be good caricature."[63]
Robert Elegant, former editor of *Newsweek*, charged that "Viet Nam was covered by a press corps that was bitterly distrustful of Washington and harshly
antagonistic toward Saigon. The press consistently magnified the allies' deficiencies, and displayed almost saintly tolerance of those misdeeds of Hanoi it
could neither disregard nor deny."[64] *The Economist* noted that many journalists
believed nothing said by Washington or Saigon and everything claimed by the
National Liberation Front or Hanoi.[65] North Vietnamese propaganda had "turned
skeptical newsmen credulous, careful scholars indifferent to data, honorable men
blind to immorality."[66]

The cause of South Vietnamese independence suffered serious damage from
all this journalistic naïveté, prejudice, and ignorance. Indeed, the eventual abandonment of the South Vietnamese to whatever fate might await them dates from
the time of Tet.

Yet clearly, blame for the allied failure in Viet Nam cannot be placed on the
shoulders of the media alone—far from it. After the Tet Offensive, the Communists were exhausted and confused. The right kind of increased U.S. effort
might have changed the entire course of the war. Lyndon Johnson, however,
did not know how to rally his people. No Churchill and no FDR, Johnson failed
to speak to the Americans in an effective way, so that the opportunities presented
by the Communist failure could be grasped. The combination of wrong strategy
(search and destroy, leaving the Ho Chi Minh Trail and the port of Haiphong
open, bombing pauses, body counts, etc.) with an insistence on allowing the
Great Society to proceed undisturbed, as if the war in Viet Nam hardly existed—
all this was the creation of the Johnson administration, not the media.

In February 1968, during a battle around the Mekong Delta town of Ben Tre,
a U.S. Army major told the press, "It became necessary to destroy the town in
order to save it." This sensationally obtuse remark was just the kind of thing
the media delighted in, and it was splashed all over the newspapers and television screens. Yet the incident did point up an important truth, that U.S. tactics
in Viet Nam depended on the far-too-lavish use of destructive firepower, even
to the point of damaging the political aims of the war. Few if any Americans
would ever want their houses or their home towns "liberated" in the manner of
the U.S. Army in Viet Nam. (When Creighton Abrams became commander in
Viet Nam, he successfully strove to decrease the use of excessive force.[67])

The war as the administration was waging it was inflating the economy and
undercutting U.S. commitments to NATO and South Korea. Nevertheless,

shortly after Tet, General Westmoreland asked for 200,000 more troops. This turned out to be perhaps the greatest public-relations blunder of the war, because congressmen and cabinet members found it hard to understand why, if Tet had indeed been a grave defeat for the Communists, such a great augmentation of U.S. forces was necessary. (Westmoreland and his superiors might have foreseen that result: after Hannibal had won his great victory over the Romans at Cannae, he sent to Carthage asking for more men and supplies. His political enemies there mocked him, saying, "If this is what he asks for after a so-called victory, what would he ask after a defeat?")

None of this, alas, was the invention of the media. If television viewers had demanded sophisticated analysis of the war rather than news "capsules" sandwiched between scandal and sport, the media would have found ways to provide it. The weaknesses of the news industry intermeshed to a discouraging extent with the weaknesses of American culture. There is little to suggest that the situation has since improved.[68]

While the Americans at home tried to come to grips with the meaning of Tet, in South Viet Nam the physical and moral strength of the Viet Cong had suffered a tremendous blow, whereas the Saigon government emerged with new vigor and confidence. The conflict in Viet Nam would from now on become much less a guerrilla war and much more a conventional conflict between North and South, exactly the kind of conflict the Americans were good at and for which they had been equipping the ARVN all along.

Vietnamization: From the Parrot's Beak to the Easter Offensive

Everything in war is simple, but the simplest thing is difficult.

—Clausewitz

INTO CAMBODIA

The year 1968 had been momentous indeed: the great Tet Offensive, the withdrawal of Lyndon Johnson from the presidential race, the election of former vice president Richard Nixon. But as this year of turmoil and upheaval began to wind down, so did the war. The carnage of the Tet Offensive had wrecked both the structure and the morale of the Viet Cong. The death of Ho Chi Minh the following year was a further blow to the Communists; his successors, although experienced revolutionaries and clever propagandists, lacked Ho's prestige and charisma. The radically changed political and military scene thus provided breathing space for the development of "Vietnamization."

Vietnamization is a term and process associated with the Nixon administration, which took office in January 1969. But in fact, General Westmoreland's newly appointed deputy commander, General Creighton Abrams, had received the assignment of upgrading the ARVN in 1967. In March of 1968, General Matthew Ridgway proposed the essence of Vietnamization to President Johnson: build up the South Vietnamese armed forces over the next two years to the level that would permit the withdrawal of U.S. combat troops. It fell, however, to the Nixon administration to carry out the general plan. The widely employed term "Vietnamization" was a very poor one. It implied that hitherto the South Vietnamese had been bearing little or no burden in the war—which was, of course, utterly false. However unfortunate the name, the success of the program—in essence building up the ARVN's capabilities and cohesiveness—would be put to the test in three major challenges: the Cambodian incursion in 1970, Operation Lam Son 719 in 1971, and above all the great Easter Offensive of 1972.

Cambodia, especially those areas bordering Vietnam, had for years been full of sanctuaries for the Viet Cong and the North Vietnamese regular army: training camps, rest and staging areas, food and ammunition dumps. Not until 1966 did Cambodian premier Sihanouk admit that the Communists had been systematically violating the neutrality of his country. As the size and elaborateness of these operations in Cambodia increased, however, Sihanouk's attitude hardened. In December 1967 he announced to the world that he did not approve of the use of his country's territory for Vietnamese Communist bases and operations and therefore had no objection if U.S. forces crossed into Cambodian border areas in "hot pursuit." Seeking help in getting rid of the Vietnamese Communists, who had actually set up their command post for South Vietnam (COSVN) in his country, Sihanouk journeyed to Moscow in March 1970. While Sihanouk was outside Cambodia, the head of the army, General Lon Nol, declared him deposed (March 18) and closed Cambodian seaports to shipments of supplies to the Viet Cong. By the beginning of April, Cambodia was the scene of full-scale fighting between Lon Nol's small Cambodian army and the Communists: before the end of the month it was clear that the NVA/VC forces would soon conquer Cambodia if something drastic was not done quickly.

The Nixon administration viewed the Communist sanctuaries inside Cambodia as threats to the continuing evacuation of U.S. forces from South Viet Nam and as almost a guarantee that there would be a massive attack on Saigon from Cambodian territory as soon as this withdrawal was completed.[1] A serious effort to break up these sanctuaries would relieve present and future pressures on the allies, bolster Lon Nol's beleaguered regime, and not incidentally provide a good test of how Vietnamization was working. Thus on April 29, 1970, 12,000 South Vietnamese troops with U.S. advisers struck the principal sanctuary, the Parrot's Beak. In the following days the ARVN made additional border crossings, from the Mekong Delta to Pleiku. Eventually 50,000 ARVN and 30,000 U.S. troops participated in these Cambodian operations. President Nixon later asserted that "our Cambodian incursion was the most successful military operation of the entire Vietnam war."[2] That statement contains a good deal of truth. The invasion was a real boost for ARVN morale. At last they were on the offensive, and they did well, scattering VC forces and seizing over a million and a half rounds of small arms ammunition, 300 vehicles, 30 tons of rice, and much else. But Hanoi immediately began to devote a lot of effort to improving the Laotian segments of the Ho Chi Minh Trail; in time, the VC was able to replace all the captured supplies. Most disappointingly, the COSVN entirely escaped. Nevertheless, at the minimum the South Vietnamese action had purchased more time to continue Vietnamization, because "enemy pressure was for all intents and purposes removed from the III and IV Corps area [Saigon and the Delta]."[3]

There were also serious negative effects from the Cambodian affair for South

Viet Nam; these, however, did not derive from military maneuvers in Asia but from political maneuvers in Washington. The clumsy secrecy and prevarication with which the administration sought to shroud the Cambodian incursions further eroded already diminishing support in Congress for the war.[4] As violence again convulsed American campuses, congressional opponents of U.S. involvement in Viet Nam achieved the repeal of the Gulf of Tonkin Resolution of 1964, the charter by which Lyndon Johnson had led his countrymen into their perplexity.

LAM SON 719

In the latter half of 1970 it became apparent that Hanoi was carrying out a major buildup of troops and bases inside Laos. This could only be the prelude to another major attack against South Viet Nam. Saigon decided on a preemptive strike, an operation known as "Lam Son 719."

Lam Son 719 was the second major offensive operation of the ARVN outside the borders of the republic. But Lam Son was also a first of its kind: ARVN was going to take on the NVA not only without the support of U.S. combat troops but even U.S. advisers. The incursion into Laos was to be strictly a South Vietnamese show, and therefore it was an even more important test of Vietnamization than the operation into Cambodia had been the year before.

On February 8, 1971, 5,000 ARVN troops crossed into Laos; eventually, 17,000 ARVN soldiers would participate. On the South Vietnamese side of the border, 10,000 U.S. combat troops stood close by in support. Once again, the ARVN discovered great quantities of rice and weapons. But as the days passed, Communist resistance rapidly escalated. With the closure of the port of Sihanoukville in Cambodia and the success of allied pacification in the Vietnamese countryside, the Ho Chi Minh Trail was the only supply route left for Communist forces in the South; hence the NVA reacted ferociously to this mortal threat to its lifeline. "The enemy understood that we were after his jugular. . . . [H]e threw in almost all his readily available reserves."[5] ARVN troops began recrossing the border around March 18. Some units, under heavy NVA pressure, fell into panic. The American media showed films of helicopters flying home with ARVN soldiers desperately clinging to their landing gear. Such scenes reinforced the growing conviction in the U.S. that despite Vietnamization, the ARVN was not really much good.

The tally sheet of the operation showed pluses and minuses. Some ARVN units had suffered heavy losses, perhaps as high as 50 percent killed, wounded, or missing; ominously, the ARVN showed a tendency to over-rely on U.S. air support and across-the-border heavy-artillery fire. Northern troops and supplies soon resumed their massive movements down the Ho Chi Minh Trail. On the other hand, the incursion into Laos had been so disruptive for the NVA that, in spite of the ever-increasing influx of war materiel from its Soviet and Chinese allies, Hanoi remained unwilling to mount a new offensive against the South until another full year had passed.[6] The ultimate test of Vietnamization, therefore, would not occur until the spring of 1972.

THE EASTER OFFENSIVE

Long before 1972, the war had ceased for all important purposes to be a guerrilla struggle and had become instead a classic confrontation of heavily equipped, regular armed forces. Thus, whatever sympathy for the Viet Cong may have still existed in rural areas was largely irrelevant. The outcome of the struggle over Viet Nam now depended on the prowess of the NVA, a "professional army of a Communist state operating outside its borders in conventional style."[7]

The years after the Tet Offensive of 1968 had been good ones for South Viet Nam. Its army was better trained and better equipped, and its militia forces were bigger and gaining self-confidence and skill. If Hanoi did not interrupt this process of gradual consolidation, it might one day be too late.[8] Saigon was expecting a major move by the North in 1972, during Tet; the date was too early, but the suspicion was sound. Hanoi had indeed decided to launch another knock-out effort, along 1968 lines, with the purpose above all of making the United States break its ties with Saigon. Like 1968, 1972 was a presidential election year; perhaps Hanoi could force Richard Nixon out of the White House, as it had forced out Lyndon Johnson.[9] As *The Economist* saw it, "After all, North Viet Nam's leaders know that the election of Mr. McGovern would give them a free hand throughout Indochina."[10]

The 1972 Easter Offensive would indeed be a fearsome and impressive undertaking. The North Vietnamese army was "the most efficient fighting machine in Asia,"[11] and the Hanoi leadership designed an invasion strategy that would best show off its new Russian tanks, surface-to-air missiles, and other sophisticated weaponry.[12] This would definitely be the largest operation the NVA had ever undertaken: well aware that his Communist state was safe from any sort of foreign invasion, General Giap denuded North Viet Nam of troops in order to throw everything possible into his long-sought second Dien Bien Phu. Nothing was left behind in the North except civilian militiamen and two inexperienced regular divisions.[13] At the same time, the number of U.S. military personnel of all types still in South Viet Nam was down to 75,000, and decreasing.

Hanoi's vision of the great Easter campaign had four distinct aspects. First, there would be a furious major attack directly across the Demilitarized Zone, with its objective the city of Quang Tri, less than 20 miles from the North Viet Nam border. Second, a big force would sweep out of Laos toward symbolic Hue. Third, from Cambodia would come a massive assault against the city of An Loc, which was slated to become the capital of the "liberated" areas of South Viet Nam. A fourth and final thrust was aimed against Kontum, in the central highlands, with the objective of eventually cutting South Viet Nam in two.

The offensive began convulsively on March 30, with a powerful attack across the Ben Hai River into Quang Tri Province. Defending that province was the Third ARVN Division, newly formed, untried as a cohesive force, and unprepared to receive a major onslaught. ARVN commanders in this northern danger zone lacked confidence in their ability to contain the NVA without U.S. advisers.[14] After enduring a tremendous pounding from greatly superior NVA forces, the Third Division embarked on a retreat out of Quang Tri City, which the NVA occupied on May 1. A retreat under fire is a most difficult maneuver, even for the most experienced and cohesive and best-led troops. Panic soon afflicted several elements of the Third Division; tanks, trucks, and personal weapons were left behind, and many officers deserted their men. Retreating soldiers and fleeing civilians choked Highway I from Quang Tri to Hue. NVA artillery ceaselessly pounded the defenseless, fleeing columns of refugees, killing or wounding at least 20,000.[15]

The attack against Hue also began on March 30, and NVA units reached the outskirts of that city on May 1, the day Quang Tri City fell. Most civil officials, mindful of the massacres in Hue during the 1968 offensive, and alarmed by reports of mass killings in areas already taken in this Easter Offensive, abandoned the city.[16] Yet, while Hue was only forty miles south of Quang Tri, its fate was to be far different. Not inexperienced troops but the crack Marine Division and the veteran First ARVN Division defended the ancient city, and the area Ruff-Puffs, mobilized under army command, would give a good account of themselves against superior NVA forces. On the second of May, just as the seige of the city was really getting started, President Thieu placed his best fighting general, Ngo Quang Truong, in command of Hue and the whole northern front. Truong stopped the incipient panic, established a new defense line, and held on. Early NVA successes in the Easter Offensive "depended directly on the military hardware donated by the Russians";[17] nevertheless, the defenders of Hue were able to withstand this onslaught, with the indispensable aid of heavy strikes by American B-52s.

An Loc came under attack during the first week of April. Soon NVA and Viet Cong forces had the city completely surrounded; Saigon had to supply the defenders totally by air, despite anti-aircraft fire from Communist forces so murderous that not even helicopters could land. The city took a tremendous pounding from NVA artillery, especially its famous Soviet-designed 130 mm field guns. On May 10, the attack went into a second phase, with seven Communist regiments pitted against 4,000 South Vietnamese defenders. Once again, the awesome B-52s, which the Communists feared above all other weapons in the allied arsenal, mauled the massed NVA units, and the 21st ARVN Division began moving to the relief of the city from the south. The besieging forces began withdrawing on May 15. The failure to take An Loc was "a major military and political setback for the Communists,"[18] a fact recognized by President

Thieu when he promoted by one grade every single soldier who had participated in the defense of the city.

At Kontum, the fourth area of Communist offensive action, real fighting did not begin until May 14. Communist forces were spearheaded by some of the very good T-54 tanks that Hanoi had obtained from the Soviets; nevertheless, fighting in some sectors devolved to savage hand-to-hand combat. The attackers renewed the assault on the 21st of May and again on the 25th. President Thieu visited the battle area on the 30th to confer a promotion on the commanding officer and encourage the defenders. Thanks in part to timely assistance from American B-52s, the attack on Kontum ran out of steam by the end of the month.

Indeed it was clear before the middle of May that the offensive had degenerated into a stalemate. Hanoi had committed everything it had to the great Easter Offensive of 1972 but had attained not a single one of its objectives. Kontum was holding, Saigon was safe, even the vulnerable and exposed Military Region I (the provinces right below the DMZ) was mostly in South Vietnamese hands. An Loc, marked out by the Communists to become the national capital of a southern counter-state, had stood fast. For all its impressive exertions, the NVA had little to show except the city of Quang Tri, but the South Vietnamese opened a counter-offensive on June 28 and retook the city a few weeks later. The Easter Offensive cost the NVA 100,000 casualties, and Giap his command. Not only had the offensive been a vast and costly disappointment militarily, but the myth that a majority of South Vietnamese wanted the North to win had once again been exposed to all who would see.[19] Meanwhile the South was filled with reports of NVA tank crews literally chained inside their vehicles. In contrast, ARVN morale was at probably the highest level in the history of the state;[20] not only had southern forces successfully resisted the NVA onslaught, but in retaliation for the offensive President Nixon had at long last ordered the mining of Haiphong harbor, North Viet Nam's essential reception area for Soviet aid.[21]

In retrospect, the reasons for the failure of the 1972 offensive are not hard to identify. General Giap had made a fatal mistake in trying to do too much; instead of concentrating his resources, perhaps at Quang Tri and An Loc, he sought major victories all over South Vietnam, and he ended by achieving none. For even the most seasoned commanders, the coordination of major movements of infantry, tanks, and artillery is a signal challenge; for Hanoi's relatively inexperienced generals, it was next to an impossibility.[22] Additionally, the South Vietnamese had the inestimable assistance of the mighty B-52s, as well as the services of 25,000 tough South Korean soldiers.

Yet this assistance would have been for nothing, Giap's strategic errors and his commanders' awkwardness at modern conventional war would not have prevented a Communist victory, if the South Vietnamese armed forces, and especially the ARVN, had not withstood the test. It was "the stubborn, even heroic, South Vietnamese defense" in which "ARVN troops and even local forces stood and fought as never before" that stopped the Easter Offensive in its tracks.[23] During the heaviest fighting, General Creighton Abrams exclaimed,

"By God, the South Vietnamese can hack it!"[24] With proper equipment and leadership, South Vietnamese forces were a match for their adversaries.[25]

The euphoria over the performance of southern forces during the offensive unfortunately diverted attention from their faulty strategic deployment. President Thieu's obsession with the necessity to "hold all places" instead of concentrating forces in and around crucial areas left South Viet Nam with very inadequate strategic and tactical reserves. If this shortcoming remained uncorrected, it would have to result eventually in the most disastrous consequences.[26]

Nevertheless, the most undeniable lesson of 1972 was that although it still had some serious weaknesses, the ARVN had developed into a real fighting force—"the South Vietnamese could hack it." Provided with replacement supplies and air support from the United States, they could be counted on to defend the independence of the southern republic indefinitely.

The United States in Viet Nam: Some Reflections

When a president sends American troops to war, a hidden timer starts to run.

—Richard Nixon

There is no such thing as a limited war.

—General Dinh Duc Thien

THE AMERICANS ENTER VIET NAM

Following the Second World War, the United States found itself pursuing, for the first time in its history, an extensive peacetime foreign policy far from its shores.

Resulting partly from the trauma of Pearl Harbor and partly from its total success in the Pacific War, the United States even before 1945 began to consider that its westernmost defenses against future aggression lay in the western Pacific. Immediately after the War, a series of Communist insurgencies erupted in the area—the Philippines, Malaya, French Indochina—soon followed by the unexpectedly complete triumph of Mao's forces in the Chinese civil war and then the invasion of South Korea. All this convinced Washington of the growing importance of Southeast Asia to its defense concerns. American policy makers more and more assumed that forcible extension of Communist control over Southeast Asia would eventually have the gravest consequences in both India and Japan. The Truman administration was achieving remarkable success with the rebuilding of Western Europe in the shadow of a glowering Stalinism. It would therefore have been close to miraculous if it had been able to resist the temptation to aid the French in Indochina, especially after Ho Chi Minh had openly declared himself a loyal adherent of a self-proclaimed monolithic and expansionary world Communist movement. The U.S. government never undertook a really thorough evaluation of the role Viet Nam, or even Southeast Asia, would play in an overall Western defense system. Nevertheless, the United States did not find itself involved in Indochina by accident or inadvertence, as some have alleged; U.S. intervention there was a logical application of basic assumptions that guided the entire foreign policy of the Truman administration.[1]

These assumptions appeared valid to Truman's successors. In a broadcast to the nation in May 1957, President Eisenhower said:

We must realize that whenever any country falls under the domination of Communism, the strength of the Free World—and of America—is by that amount weakened. . . . America cannot exist as an island of freedom in a surrounding sea of Communism.[2]

Later, President Kennedy was more specific:

Viet Nam represents the cornerstone of the Free World in Southeast Asia, the keystone of the arch, the finger in the dike. . . . [If South Viet Nam goes under] our prestige in Asia will fall to a new low.[3]

The passage of the years has made at least two things clear. First, the United States overemphasized the importance of Viet Nam, and of all Indochina, to the security of the United States and its key Asian allies. Second, U.S. policy makers should have been able to foresee the rift between the Soviet Union and China, with all its implications. Yet the dynamics of world politics of the 1950s made it all but impossible for American leaders to stand by and watch self-proclaimed Communists seize control of Viet Nam by armed force. The spectre, in the early 1960s, of an axis between Mao's Peking and Sukarno's Djakarta only accentuated their alarm.

Nor were the Americans the only ones to be transfixed by the importance of Viet Nam. Mao's minister of defense declared in a famous speech that revolutionary guerrilla warfare was the method by which the Communists would "surround" the West;[4] North Viet Nam's General Giap, the victor of Dien Bien Phu, proclaimed that the failure of the United States to defeat this type of warfare would mean that Communism would be invincible all over the globe.

Non-Communist Asian leaders watched events in Viet Nam with great interest. Indira Gandhi told Vice President Hubert Humphrey of her good wishes for the American efforts there.[5] Leaders in Thailand, New Zealand, Australia, Taiwan, Singapore, Cambodia, Malaysia, and South Korea were also supportive; indeed, 70,000 allied troops (chiefly Australian and South Korean) fought beside the South Vietnamese and the Americans.

Today it is fashionable in some circles to ridicule the domino theory of Southeast Asian politics, and the American statesmen who adhered to it, while forgetting that quite a few other world leaders at the time thought the domino theory was a self-evident fact of political life. But the opinion of these leaders, Communist or otherwise, did not *prove* the validity of the domino theory; more importantly, nobody ever offered any proof to the American electorate that averting the potential loss of Southeast Asia—preventing the dominoes from falling—was worth tens of thousands of American lives.

Americans will passionately debate the role of their country in the complex tragedy known to them as the Viet Nam War for decades to come. Whatever the wisdom of initial involvement by the United States in Indochinese politics in the 1950s, there is little dispute that the eventual abandonment of the South Vietnamese to their fate was mainly a consequence of the American electorate's growing disillusionment not with the aims but with the conduct, costs, and length of the war. The following discussion concerns certain features—certain problems—of the U.S. participation in the war that signally contributed to that disenchantment.

PROBLEM ONE: AMERICANIZATION OF THE WAR

The massive buildup of U.S. ground forces in Viet Nam represented a sharp break with the actual containment policies of the Truman and Eisenhower administrations in Southeast Asia. The Americans, moreover, embarked on this new course equipped with very little knowledge of Vietnamese history or culture, or even the major language of the area. Most regrettably, the U.S. forces that went into Viet Nam possessed an inadequate understanding of guerrilla warfare. One can—perhaps—excuse the army officer corps for its unfamiliarity with Roman pacification campaigns in Spain, British experience with rebellion in India, or Russian anti-guerrilla tactics in the Caucasus; but in addition, the leadership of the army knew little of the guerrilla campaigns of the American Revolution or the Civil War, the nineteenth-century conflicts with the Plains Indians, or U.S. Army pacification efforts in the Philippines after 1898. Most difficult of all to understand, the U.S. Army went to battle in 1965 utterly unconcerned with the hard lessons the French had learned in their own eight-year Viet Nam agony.[6]

Under this dark cover of ignorance, the American presence in Viet Nam rapidly mushroomed. When Dwight Eisenhower left the White House, after a decade of concern in Washington with the fate of Southeast Asia, there were only 875 U.S. military personnel in Viet Nam. By the death of John F. Kennedy, that number had grown to 16,000. Two years after Lyndon Johnson's inauguration, 184,000 U.S. troops were in South Viet Nam, and by the end of 1967 the number was half a million. The Americanization of the war was the poisoned fruit of the assassination of Diem. (Even so, at the height of the U.S. commitment, American forces in South Viet Nam equaled about one-third of 1 percent of the total U.S. population.)

In the summer of 1965, when the Americanization of the war had begun in earnest, South Viet Nam was clearly in danger of defeat. President Johnson had to do something drastic, and quickly. But flooding a small, rural Asian country with a half-million culturally and racially alien young men cannot have been the best choice. It was, in fact, a glaring example of the much-criticized American tendency to draw a sharp separation between the military and the political aspects of war. The Americanization of the war deprived the South Vietnamese, the government and the army alike, of initiative, self-reliance, prestige, and even self-respect. It was both an open vote of no confidence in the ARVN and a decision to postpone to an indefinite future the upgrading of Vietnamese forces. Yet, in taking over the major responsibility for the war, the Americans failed to arm themselves with the necessary authority; unlike the Korean conflict, there was never a unitary allied command, with all U.S. and South Vietnamese troops under a single directing hand.

The influx of very young Americans (much younger than the soldiers of World War II) totally disoriented the South Vietnamese. One might ask how American society would stand up to the sudden arrival of 7,000,000 Japanese soldiers. Even that comparison does not begin to approximate what happened in South Viet Nam, because America is a relatively multi-racial and multi-cultural society, affluent and self-confident. In isolated, xenophobic Viet Nam, the arrival of so many inconceivably rich young aliens was in itself a revolution.

To the Vietnamese, we appeared all too often as arrogant, blundering, clumsy, gullible and wasteful. Americans loved dogs, had no respect for the elderly or for ancient things, and insulted everything and everyone around them by boisterous, intemperate conduct and by ungracious displays of wealth. The American ability to acquire Vietnamese women was a deep source of resentment to virtually all Vietnamese men.[7]

The vast American presence provided propaganda fodder for the enemy. There were no foreign troops visible among the Communist ranks, whereas Americans were visible, and audible, all over the place. "Go south and kill fellow Vietnamese" would have been a terrible slogan for the Hanoi leadership, but the United States allowed it to substitute the much more attractive "Go south and kill the American invaders."[8] This was an especially powerful platform in a country that had only recently escaped from 80 years of colonial domination. The Americans had, in a real sense, replaced the French.

A truly prodigal expenditure of treasure accompanied Americanization; indeed, money became a substitute for sound strategy and tactics. Some have estimated that at certain periods it cost about $400,000 to kill a single Communist soldier in South Viet Nam.[9] The Americans also tried to make the Vietnamese conflict a war without war's discomfort: the American presence was luxurious and fat, the most expensive and wasteful war in American history. The Communists benefited enormously from this up-ending of the American cornucopia; the insurgency got its supplies mainly from the same source as the government—namely, the people in the villages. Hence the flooding of South Viet Nam with American money and goods helped arm and feed the Viet Cong.

The confusion of quantity and quality in the American mind helped stir up opposition to the war at home. The rapid escalation of U.S. forces in South Viet Nam stimulated those demonstrations on American campuses that, however minoritarian and even elitist, were soon to become so ugly and destructive. The constant requests for more troops—ever more troops—culminated in Westmoreland's self-destructive request for 200,000 additional men right after the Tet Offensive. Why should the American people have believed that Tet was a great defeat for the enemy when as a consequence of it the U.S. commander was calling for a 40 percent increase in his already huge army?

Perhaps the crowning irony of all this prodigality is that of the half a million men commanded by General Westmoreland in the spring of 1968, less than 100,000 were combat troops.[10] At the cost of weakening NATO defenses and unleashing venomous protests in the United States, South Viet Nam was flooded with American soldiers, the great majority of whom were busy protecting their own installations or talking on radio telephones or compiling questionable statistics or unloading large crates of canned peaches.

PROBLEM TWO: THE WAR OF ATTRITION

The other side of the Americanization coin was the so-called strategy of attrition.

In the summer of 1965, the North Vietnamese state, heir to a centuries-old martial tradition and tightly controlled by a messianic leadership, was determined to conquer South Viet Nam. To this end, General Giap prepared to split South Viet Nam from the Laotian border to Qui Nhon. The Communist summer offensive was inflicting serious defeats on the ARVN, whose casualty rates were unprecedented and desertion rates climbing. In this context the U.S. forces fought the Battle of Ia Drang, in which they confronted for the first time large numbers of first-class North Vietnamese soldiers. The battle ended in the withdrawal of the Communists and the foiling—for the time being—of their attempt to split the territory of South Viet Nam. By the middle of 1966 it was obvious that South Viet Nam was not going to be overrun by the Communists. At that point, at the latest, General Westmoreland could have embarked upon a strategy of security for the civilian population; instead, he chose to continue actively seeking out main-force enemy units, with the aim of inflicting more casualties upon them than North Viet Nam could afford to replace. This was the strategy of attrition, which was no strategy at all.

The concept of attrition, which underlay General Westmoreland's whole view of the war, ignored the determination and ability of the Hanoi regime to make its society suffer any level of losses deemed necessary. It also ignored the fact that the Communists could control the tempo of fighting either by declining combat with the Americans or crossing the borders of Laos and Cambodia. The instrument of attrition was to be the tremendously destructive firepower of the Americans' modern weaponry. Yet Communist "hugging tactics"—sticking very close to American positions—could render American artillery and airpower ineffective. Many of the shells and bombs that the Americans launched against the enemy—perhaps as many as 5 percent—were duds, from which the Communists made thousands of booby-traps and mines. (Up to 1968, an astonishing proportion of Marine casualties—nearly half—were inflicted by such devices.) Guerrilla units, if they chose to fight American troops at all, often operated at night, when tanks and artillery were of reduced effectiveness. Also the root of the Viet Cong insurgency, the political infrastructure inside the villages, was immune to the B-52s. At the same time, American technological power caused tremendous loss of life and property among Vietnamese civilians.

The correct objective in fighting guerrillas is to protect the civilian population and uproot the political infrastructure of the rebellion (see chapter 6). But the strategy of attrition meant that there were no front lines; wherever the enemy could be found or chose to appear, there was the battle zone. Hence the Americans had no incentive to clear and hold territory. Thus the only way for the Americans to measure their progress in such a war was through the notorious "body counts." The number of enemy dead became an obsession, encouraging commanders to shoot first and ignore the political consequences. The Viet Cong encouraged this tendency by entering a village for the express purpose of calling down U.S. firepower upon it; afterwards, every dead Vietnamese on the premises entered the "body count." U.S. commanders who turned in big body counts were considered successful, while those who did not meet their quotas faced replacement.[11] The Americans did indeed kill many, many Communists in Viet Nam, but they rarely succeeded in separating the guerrillas from the peasant population; hence the guerrilla organization survived to fight another day.

Military operations became the heart and soul of U.S. activities in South Viet Nam, to which protection of civilians and building up the South Vietnamese state and army took very subordinate places. Search-and-destroy operations, involving the dispersal of U.S. forces all over the thinly populated areas of South Viet Nam, made the Tet Offensive possible. Thus the attrition strategy produced ever-growing American casualty lists, undermining public support for the war; yet the American people never received, in exchange for the blood and treasure they were pouring out, any firm perception that the area of South Viet Nam securely under allied control was increasing. However large the padding of body counts may have been, there is no doubt that the kill ratio of Communists to Americans ranged between three to one and five to one.[12] The U.S. Army did not lose a single significant battle between 1965 and 1973, "a record unparalleled in the history of modern warfare."[13] From a narrowly military point of view, the American war of attrition worked. Yet the political consequences were disastrous: increasing numbers of Americans at home, and especially their representatives in Congress, turned against the war.

Hand in glove with attrition went the policy of short tours of service for Americans in Viet Nam. The U.S. Army wanted as many of its officers as possible to experience this high-tech, big-unit fighting, excellent training in case of war in Europe. Thus U.S. troops as a rule served only one year in South Viet Nam, and most officers only six months. It is for this reason that it has been said, as observed above, that the Americans did not fight a ten-year war in South Viet Nam but fought a one-year war ten times. Another way of saying this is that by the time an American soldier in Viet Nam learned something about the war, the country, and the people, he was shipped home. The major effect of rapid personnel turnover and the consequent lowering of unit cohesiveness[14] was to boost American casualty rates: 40 percent of Americans killed in Viet Nam died in their first three months of service there, only 6 percent in the last three months.[15]

In summary, the attrition strategy succeeded in killing large numbers of the enemy, but it underestimated the ability of the North both to sustain enormous casualties and to exercise great control over their number by declining to engage. Meanwhile, mounting U.S. casualties and the failure to make visible progress wore down American patience at home.

It is only fair to note that the Johnson administration severely hobbled General Westmoreland: the Joint Chiefs repeatedly requested permission to block the Ho Chi Minh Trail, mine Haiphong harbor, attack across the DMZ, and close the Cambodian port of Sihanoukville (another major entry point for Communist supplies). Washington rebuffed all such requests. In pursuing attrition instead of security, General Westmoreland and his political masters in Washington achieved neither.[16]

PROBLEM THREE: THE HO CHI MINH TRAIL

On the last day of his presidency, Dwight Eisenhower told John F. Kennedy that Laos was the key to Viet Nam and to all Indochina. General Maxwell Taylor concurred in that view.[17] Through Laos ran the main sections of the Ho Chi Minh Trail, begun in 1959. The building of the Trail was in itself an epic. Penetrating some of the most inhospitable terrain on the planet, at a great cost in human life and suffering, the Trail was a victory over debilitating climate, physical exhaustion, disease, insects, and snakes. By the late 1960s an average of 2,000 trucks were on this "trail" every day, carrying 10 thousand tons of supplies each week to Communist forces in South Viet Nam. In 1968 an estimated 100,000 North Vietnamese moved down the Trail. There were also two specially constructed oil pipelines. It all amounted to a sort of slow-motion Schlieffen Plan, by which the allied forces in South Viet Nam were outflanked not just for one battle but throughout almost the entire conflict. Winning the war in South Viet Nam, or preventing a Communist victory, required stopping or at least seriously inhibiting the flow of men and supplies into the South; "It was impossible to defeat North Viet Nam decisively in South Viet Nam without stopping the invasion" via that Trail.[18]

Painfully aware of the Trail's importance, allied military leaders wanted to do something about it for years. In 1965, and again right after the Tet Offensive,

General Westmoreland and other U.S. commanders, supported by South Vietnamese chief of staff Cao Van Vien, urged that a fortified line be erected across southern Laos from the Demilitarized Zone to the border of Thailand.[19] The distance was 120 miles, shorter than that between Washington, D.C., and Philadelphia. The truce line in Korea is 150 miles long; during the Algerian War, the French had erected effective electrified barriers along the 600-mile border with Tunisia; in the 1980s, the Moroccans built the 10-to-12-foot-high, rock-and-sand, anti-guerrilla Hassan Line, equipped with sensors and radar, running hundreds of miles.

Some experts would have vigorously questioned the wisdom of planting a large American force in a Southeast Asian jungle so far from the blue-water navy. Besides, if the allies had effectively barred the Trail, the North Vietnamese might have responded by invading northeast Thailand, with results impossible to foresee. Nevertheless, Gen. Bruce Palmer advocated extending the Demilitarized Zone across to Thailand; three U.S. divisions would hold this line, supported by intensive airpower. The U.S. Navy would blockade North Vietnamese ports and threaten the coast with invasion; there would be no "strategic bombing" of the North. Cut off from replacements and heavy equipment, the Viet Cong would eventually wither. Most of all, "in defending well-prepared positions[,] U.S. troops would suffer fewer casualties."[20]

The Johnson administration, however, forbade any attempt to use ground forces to block the Trail across Laos; it intended to stem the tide of men and supplies by airpower alone. Accordingly, the Americans carried out the most intensive bombing campaign in the history of warfare; some estimate that the United States dropped as many tons of bombs on Laos as it had dropped in all of World War II. North Vietnamese officials later told Robert Shaplen that they had shot down 2,500 U.S. aircraft engaged in bombing the Trail.[21] The air campaign was to no avail; traffic down the Trail was slowed but not stopped. President Johnson later wrote that of course he had been aware that "North Vietnamese and Viet Cong forces were enjoying almost complete sanctuary in Laos and Cambodia."[22] But then why not put a stop to this? The reason was that in July 1962, President Kennedy had agreed to the "neutralization" of Laos negotiated by Averell Harriman. (Hence, later in the war some Americans referred with bitterness to the Trail as the "Averell Harriman Memorial Highway."[23]) In President Johnson's exact words, in May 1967 "we were all concerned that entering Laos with ground forces would *end all hope of reviving the 1962 Laos agreement, fragile though it was, and would greatly increase the forces needed in Southeast Asia* [sic!]."[24]

Leaving open the Ho Chi Minh Trail seemed to allow no alternative to massive bombing of North Viet Nam. In addition, failure both to close the Trail and to adopt an alternative strategy that would have neutralized its effects meant that Hanoi could fight on interior lines, a tremendous advantage. It meant that the enemy was free to invade South Viet Nam continuously: the NVA's colossal 1972 Easter Offensive would have been quite impossible without the Laotian springboard. It meant further that when hard pressed by allied forces the enemy could simply retreat into Laos or Cambodia. This, in turn, meant that attrition—killing large numbers of North Vietnamese who came down the Trail into South Viet Nam—would take longer than key segments of the American public would accept. Both the bombing of the North and attrition itself were forced on the Americans through their failure to interrupt the Ho Chi Minh Trail. Thus the policies of the Johnson administration made a lasting, or even a temporary, American military victory impossible.

Since the fall of Saigon, leaders of Hanoi's war effort have expressed the belief that the Trail was the key to their victory.[25] In this opinion they are not alone. Sir Robert Thompson has written that "if they [the North Vietnamese] had not had this unmolested avenue through Laos, the insurgency in Viet Nam could have been stopped at any time in the early 1960s."[26] Several prominent Johnson administration figures concur. "In retrospect," stated Ambassador Bunker, "I am more certain than I was in 1967 that our failure to cut the Ho Chi Minh Trail was a strategic mistake of the first order."[27] "Surely," wrote William P. Bundy, "we could have held a line across Laos and South Viet Nam with significantly fewer men than we eventually employed within South Viet Nam, far less American casualties, and in the end much greater effect and less bloodshed in the South itself."[28] For Walt Rostow, the 1962 failure to deal realistically with the Ho Chi Minh Trail "may have been the single greatest mistake in United States foreign policy in the 1960s."[29]

The United States paid a very high price for failing to lock the Laotian door, and South Viet Nam paid the highest price possible: extinction.

PROBLEM FOUR: THE BOMBING OF NORTH VIET NAM

The Johnson administration abstained from land operations in North Viet Nam, mainly because it feared a Korea-style Chinese intervention. Besides, even generally successful operations inside North Viet Nam would have cost many American casualties and then exposed the Americans to the kind of guerrilla attacks that had tied down the French. But President Johnson went far beyond mere strategic prudence in dealing with Hanoi. His public and private pledges not to invade the North, his constant refrain that "we seek no wider war," his repeated promises that the survival of the northern regime was never in question, all took the pressure off Hanoi and indeed placed it in a no-lose situation: if the war in the South went poorly, Hanoi had only to pull back, retrench, and await a more favorable opportunity.

Nevertheless, the Johnson administration decided that it could exert powerful pressure on North Viet Nam to call off the war in the South, or at least give up supporting it, through an aerial bombing campaign. The purpose of the bombing was to cause Hanoi to see reason: the Americans were never morally prepared to destroy North Viet Nam. This purpose—to pressure, not to destroy—is the root of the failure of the bombing campaign, because the North Vietnamese leadership could not be "pressured" in any sense that the Johnson administration understood. In the first place, North Viet Nam was a classic Stalinist dictatorship, utterly unprepared to admit even the possibility that there could exist disagreement between the decisions of the Politburo and the wishes of "the people"; Ho Chi Minh and his confederates, moreover, had made it clear that there was no price in blood they would find too high in order to obtain their desires in Viet Nam.[30] Secondly, after more than a decade of Stalinism, all North Viet Nam had to show in the way of economic development was a few bridges, factories, and power stations; the U.S. Air Force could easily knock out these targets without having any appreciable effect on the North's war-making capabilities. The question of exactly what to employ U.S. airpower against was made more acute because for political reasons the Johnson administration ruled out any strikes on the key port of Haiphong, through which flowed vast quantities of Soviet aid, including surface-to-air missiles that that downed hundreds of U.S. aircraft. In addition, for what were called humanitarian reasons, the dikes essential to northern agriculture were never targeted. Thus the United States engaged in protracted bombing of a limited area, leaving the only important targets in the country alone, while North Viet Nam built up an excellent air defense that cost the Americans many expensive aircraft and the crews that flew them. Nevertheless, within these militarily indefensible parameters,[31] the Johnson administration conducted the biggest and most expensive bombing campaign in U.S. history; the futility of the campaign is best illustrated perhaps by the fact that in the end, more American bombs fell on North Viet Nam than on Nazi Germany.

In order to show his "good will" to Hanoi, President Johnson ordered no less than 10 halts to the bombing, including one announced on October 28, 1968, in a blatant effort to influence the presidential election. The enemy, of course, used the halts to rush supplies into the South with which to kill American and allied soldiers and civilians. Johnson later told his successor in the White House that all the bombing pauses had been a mistake.

Unsurprisingly, CIA studies of the effects of the bombing showed that it was having relatively little military effect on Hanoi.[32] Yet in terms of U.S. lives, money, and materiel—2,700 air force personnel killed, captured, or missing, perhaps 2,300 aircraft lost—the bombing was terribly expensive, while in terms of political damage to the United States the bombing approached being an unmitigated catastrophe. The administration's step-by-step escalation in the bombing and its numerous prohibitions as to what could be bombed convinced the Hanoi leadership that it was taking the very worst that the United States could dish out. Thus it felt confirmed in the correctness of its strategy of protracted conflict: Hanoi just had to hold out until the Americans got tired and went home. In addition, the American bombing helped the Communist government rally public support behind it and organize the society down to the last gallon of gasoline.

If, finally, there had been no bombing of the North, if the fighting had been confined totally to South Viet Nam, with protection of the civilian population the main objective, the United States would have been seen as clearly fighting a defensive struggle, and undoubtedly the paroxysms of indignation within certain segments of the American population would have been reduced or contained. Instead, the bombing transformed Hanoi into the underdog. The real aggressor, North Viet Nam, appeared as the small but courageous victim of a gigantic, malevolent Uncle Sam. The Americans had the power to turn Hanoi into a trash heap; although there is no denying that some U.S. planes hit the wrong targets or came too close to forbidden areas, it is painfully obvious that America's destructive power was used with incredible restraint. American bombs never touched the vast majority of buildings in Hanoi, as numerous visitors could plainly see. Yet Hanoi's skillful allegations of wantonness, combined with the eager readiness of many to believe anything the Hanoi leadership cared to say about the war, helped "turn skeptical newsmen credulous, careful scholars indifferent to data, honorable men blind to immorality."[33] Sen. Edward Kennedy, for example, actually described the American air war over North Viet Nam as "a policy of deliberately bombing dikes," a palpable falsehood.[34]

Hanoi fought a total war, with no constraints; Washington fought a limited war, with many self-imposed constraints. Johnson and his advisers robbed the bombing of North Viet Nam of its military potential by imposing a limited and piecemeal approach. Yet these limitations neither spared America's reputation overseas, calmed the increasingly violent protests at home, nor stanched the flow of northern troops and materiel into the South. President Nixon's December 1972 bombing of Hanoi ("the most successful U.S. operation of the war"[35]) shocked the North Vietnamese into a truce and showed what American airpower could have accomplished much earlier and at far less cost to the United States and to the Vietnamese. But by then the Americans were pulling out.

AN ALTERNATIVE: A STRATEGY OF SECURITY

The attrition strategy required a vast American army, one employing tremendously destructive firepower and suffering considerable casualties. The U.S. forces in Viet Nam were much better suited to fighting the Soviets in Europe than guerrillas in Southeast Asia, while the buildup of the ARVN and the territorial forces received inadequate attention. That is mainly why the war ended in bitterness and recrimination.

Attrition had become the U.S. method because the Johnson administration had repeatedly ruled out land attacks on North Viet Nam and—by far the best option—closing the Ho Chi Minh Trail in Laos. The Americans would have to fight, and win, inside South Viet Nam. In these circumstances, to achieve the U.S. aim of an independent South Viet Nam without arousing the notorious impatience of the American electorate, a strategy different from that employed by the Johnson administration was required, a strategy that would have (a) avoided Americanization, (b) denied access to the majority of the population to the VC and NVA, (c) maximized American firepower, (d) minimized American and friendly casualties, (e) diminished the effects of the Ho Chi Minh Trail, and (f) put the responsibility for dealing with guerrillas where it belonged, on the South Vietnamese. A carefully conceived and well-executed shield (or security or demographic frontier) strategy would have fulfilled all these requirements.

The overwhelming majority of South Vietnamese lived in the extreme southern and coastal regions of the country. U.S. troops, supplemented by ARVN units, could have set up a shield defense for the populated areas, protected by elaborate electronic barriers and minefields, and bristling with artillery pointed in the right direction, that is, toward the enemy, away from civilians. Above this shield would loom the awesome power of the U.S. Air Force and naval aviation. Behind the shield the ARVN and territorial forces would carry out classic clear-and-hold operations, along with much-needed training exercises. The well-populated areas of South Viet Nam—mainly the Saigon area and Military Region IV—would become a sort of super-enclave. Such a strategy would have addressed the proper allied objective: not to kill Communists but to stop terror, extortion, and kidnapping, uproot the guerrilla infrastructure, and build an effective government. A secure territorial base in which the great majority of South Vietnamese could live in safety would replace costly search-and-destroy missions and deceptive body counts. The war would assume a territorial nature—a war with front lines—well suited to both American military technology and American public understanding. Equally important, the training and equipping of the Ruff-Puffs, very low in priority given the assumptions behind search-and-destroy, could have received the attention it deserved, so that eventually—sooner rather than later—the ARVN would replace most U.S. forces in the shield, with territorial forces able to back it up.

Additionally, allied forces supported by the U.S. Navy could hold Hue and Da Nang. Both enclaves would serve as potential launching areas for seaborne flank attacks; Da Nang would be the Inchon of Viet Nam (except that the Americans would already be there).

But the supreme and decisive advantage of such a strategy would have been that the disastrous retrenchment of 1975 (see below) would not have been necessary.

The classic objection to this kind of defense is that it yields the initiative to the enemy. This criticism, of course, ignores the fact that the Communists had the initiative all through the war anyway. In any case, it is not a valid argument against a demographic frontier strategy. On one side of the shield ("behind" it), the allies would have been able to take the initiative against the guerrillas, and that was the winning strategy; on the other side of the shield, if Communist main-force units attacked at any particular points, they would have called down upon themselves the Americans' overwhelming naval and air power plus elite mobile reserve units employing airlift and sealift, not to mention artillery. This would have been "attrition" with a vengeance. Frequent patrols and refresher training courses would counter the dangers of developing a garrison mentality.

Not least, such a shield would have rendered the Ho Chi Minh Trail a much less important factor in the conflict.

But there is another objection to the security strategy: the leadership of North Viet Nam would presumably have never given up on its aim of conquest of the South. Therefore, even if ARVN and the territorial forces were eventually well trained and well equipped, a substantial U.S. presence, naval, air, and ground, in support of southern forces might well have been required for many years. This criticism assumes that the Soviet Union and China would have continued massive military assistance to North Viet Nam indefinitely. But even if that assumption had turned out to be true, it would not invalidate a demographic frontier strategy. The United States continues to maintain a substantial military presence in South Korea after five decades, despite the often less than edifying internal political situation in that country and in the teeth of ferocious hostility from the Stalinist North Korean regime.

THE AMERICANS LOSE HEART

Gen. George Marshall once observed, "No democracy can fight a Seven Years' War." One might amend this to read: "No democracy can fight a long war of attrition in an area far from home." Attrition played directly into the hands of the Hanoi leaders and their strategy of outlasting the Americans.

The Americans have historically been a peaceable people. Their traditional isolationism is deeply rooted in a primordial rejection of a militarist Europe, reinforced by a vigorous strain of Protestant pacifism. The most famous (and successful) campaign slogan in U.S. history was "He Kept Us out of War." It requires the pillage of Belgium and the sinking of unarmed merchant vessels, the attack on Pearl Harbor, or the North Korean invasion, to overcome such powerful isolationist tendencies. The American public will support a large military effort overseas only in the case of a clear-cut provocation and for a clear-cut objective; they will not give their lives, or their children's lives, for objectives of limited or cloudy value. The sending of an army of almost 600,000 men to Viet Nam—so far from home—meant that the American people were being asked to sustain an enormous commitment in a country about which most of them had grown to adulthood without ever having heard. There had been no Pearl Harbor to galvanize this commitment, no Korea-style invasion. There were no front lines by which to measure progress, no powerful allies (as in both world wars and Korea), no United Nations mandate, no declaration of war against anybody. Nor did President Johnson subordinate his domestic "Great Society" projects for the purposes of achieving some sort of favorable outcome in Viet Nam. Johnson's unprecedented refusal to call up the reserves resulted in both a dangerous hemorrhage of American troops from NATO and a reliance on a manifestly inequitable draft system that profoundly affected the morale and quality of U.S. troops in Viet Nam. Finally, the president proved utterly incapable of mobilizing American opinion behind the war. Indeed, it is hard to avoid the conclusion that Lyndon Johnson was the worst wartime leader in U.S. history.

To maintain public support for U.S. involvement in the absence of a Pearl Harbor, the limitation of American casualties was essential—but the Americanization of the war and the attrition "strategy" made that impossible. The United States never had a policy for winning the war—or even a real definition of what victory would look like—but only the intention to slug it out with the Communists wherever and for as long as Hanoi wanted to. Thus at one and the same time the Viet Nam War was limited (limited effort implies limited importance), protracted ("Seven Years' War"), and costly (Americanization plus attrition).

Some have said that America's motives in Viet Nam were largely altruistic, that Viet Nam was America's most unselfish war. If that is true, it is indeed the key to why the Americans lost heart: they could see no vital American stake in Viet Nam for which they were spending so much blood and treasure, and they therefore could, in a word, get out.[36] If the Americans had seen some real prospects of victory in terms they could find meaningful, perhaps they would have accepted casualties, taxes, and inflation for a longer period. But year after year of seeing the same news films every night (and hearing the same superficial commentary on these films) made a satisfactory settlement of the conflict seem ever more remote. As one of the most profound students of that dismal conflict has written, "The decisive reason for the growing disaffection of the American people was the conviction that the war was not being won and apparently showed little prospect of coming to a successful conclusion."[37] Both Ho Chi Minh and President Kennedy had said that they were willing to "pay any price" to achieve their ends. But only Ho meant it. The Americans did not reject the end for which the war was fought, only the means; perhaps they were right to do so.

This was all really too bad, because just when the Americans were about to despair of their involvement—after the 1968 Tet Offensive—South Viet Nam had developed a stable government and an army that, given American help, could and would fight well.

NIXON, THE PEACE, AND WATERGATE

A detailed recapitulation of the violence in the streets and the turmoil in the Congress that characterized American politics during the last year of Lyndon Johnson and the first years of Richard Nixon is well beyond the scope of this book, and it is available elsewhere.[38] But the relationship between domestic upheaval and U.S. actions in Viet Nam is so crucial that it deserves to be presented in at least a few broad strokes.

When Richard Nixon became president on January 20, 1969, he could have blamed the whole Vietnamese involvement on his Democratic predecessors and carried off a massive pullout of American troops in his first 12 months in office. Nixon feared, however, the effect on America's friends and enemies of so open a desertion of so major a commitment. So like de Gaulle in Algeria, Nixon actually took four years to extricate the United States finally from South Viet Nam. He began by offering Hanoi, in August 1969, what was in essence the "dove plank" on the war that had been defeated at the cacophonous Democratic convention of 1968.[39] The enunciation of the Nixon Doctrine made the future clear for all who would see: "We shall furnish military and economic assistance when requested in accordance with our treaty commitments. But we shall look to the nation directly threatened to assume the primary responsibility of providing the manpower for its defense."[40] (Of course, that was exactly what the South Vietnamese had been doing for years.) The figures on U.S. troops in South Viet Nam during Nixon's first term tell all the rest: in January 1969, 542,000; in January 1971, 336,000; in January 1972, 133,000. By the end of 1972, all U.S. ground combat troops were out of Viet Nam. Then came the signing of the peace in Paris, whereby the United States withdrew the last of its forces, while permitting scores of thousands of North Vietnamese regulars to remain inside the South. Nixon appears to have believed that the South could be saved for the foreseeable future with large amounts of aid, and he solemnly promised to reinstitute large-scale bombing north and south if Hanoi violated the treaty too blatantly. There is little reason to doubt that Nixon would have been able to carry out this program until the end of his term in 1977; whatever doubts had come to afflict public opinion in the United States, the elections of 1968, and especially those of 1972, had confirmed the definitely minoritarian status of those who wished the immediate repudiation of every U.S. commitment to South Viet Nam.

But by the end of 1973, the furor over Watergate was reaching a crescendo. Nixon's resignation in the summer of 1974 foreshadowed a tremendous Democratic landslide in November; scores of persons were elected to Congress who in normal circumstances would never have got there. Nixon's pledges and the efforts of his successor to help South Viet Nam were gleefully repudiated by this new Congress—whence the widespread belief that "if there had never been a Watergate, there would be a South Viet Nam today."[41] Indeed, Nixon was about to order renewed bombing just as John Dean began testifying before the Senate Watergate committee.[42] As the South Vietnamese began to sink beneath the waves, one could only speculate that it might have been better for them if Hubert Humphrey had won the close election of 1968. Perhaps then the Congress of the United States might not have torn up the nation's pledges to "millions of Vietnamese . . . who depended on American protection against a ruthless and determined enemy."[43]

South Viet Nam on Its Own: 1973–1975

The idea that safety can be purchased by throwing a small state to the
wolves is a fatal delusion.

—Winston Churchill

A PEACE AGREEMENT IN PARIS

In December 1972, as the Paris peace process appeared totally stalled, President
Nixon resumed the bombing of North Viet Nam, striking hard at the hitherto
privileged areas of Hanoi and Haiphong. Although even in these raids there
were many restrictions placed on U.S. airmen, the B-52 missions stunned the
northern regime; East European diplomatic and press sources reported that morale in Hanoi reached a historic low in those December days.[1] Hence the Politburo decided to conclude the negotiations, and a ceasefire was accordingly
proclaimed for January 27, 1973.

Even after the passage of many years, the asymmetries of the Paris agreements
remain impressive. They provided for (1) the withdrawal of all U.S. forces and
the cessation of all U.S. air attacks on the North; (2) the implicit recognition of
Hanoi's right to maintain close to a quarter of a million northern troops in the
South; at the same time, in explicit violation of these agreements, 50,000 North
Vietnamese regulars remained inside Laos; (3) the enforcement of the peace
agreement by an International Control Commission, which included members
from Communist Poland and Hungary and could operate only through unanim-
ity.

Taking all pressure off the North while leaving a whole northern army inside
the South, the Paris peace was a disaster for the Saigon government. As one
observer remarked: "The only part of the Paris agreement that was observed

was the removal of U.S. forces."[2] At first the Thieu government was astounded at the dangerous lack of balance in the agreement and refused to sign. President Nixon recognized that the peace terms were inadequate and unfair. He nevertheless insisted that it was the best his administration could do in the face of a Congress that was ready to legislate the United States out of Viet Nam on any terms whatsoever.[3] (True, Nixon had won reelection in 1972 against an opponent of U.S. support for South Viet Nam by an unprecedented landslide, taking 49 of the 50 states; yet at the same time the new Senate was more hostile to South Viet Nam than ever before.) To persuade the South Vietnamese to go along with the peace agreement, Nixon sent several letters to President Thieu promising that the United States would severely punish any serious violation of the peace by the North. "You have my absolute assurance," Nixon wrote Thieu, "that if Hanoi fails to abide by the terms of this agreement, it is my intention to take swift and severe retaliatory actions."[4] On the other hand, continued South Vietnamese refusal to cooperate would have dire consequences: "You must decide now whether you desire to continue our alliance or whether you want me to seek a settlement with the enemy which serves U.S. interests alone"; in that case, "the result will be an inevitable and immediate termination of U.S. economic and military assistance."[5] Thieu collapsed under this kind of pressure. In return for his acquiescence, the Americans rushed a substantial amount of equipment to South Viet Nam just before the agreement went into effect, to prepare Saigon to deal with minor peace violations while the United States took responsibility for preventing major ones. At the bottom of this approach, of course, were the assumptions that Nixon would be president through the end of 1976 and that his successor could and would honor the publicly and privately pledged word of the president of the United States.

North Viet Nam, meanwhile, remained as determined as ever to conquer the South and hence had no intention of observing the accords. As soon as the last Americans had left, according to General Giap, the North planned "to move forward and topple the puppets" and "liberate South Viet Nam totally."[6]

Hardly had the ceasefire gone into effect when Hanoi launched Operation Landgrab: an effort to increase rapidly the total number of villages and hamlets under Communist control. Landgrab went on for about two weeks, grinding to a halt mainly due to the unexpectedly vigorous resistance by southern forces, especially in Military Region IV (the Delta). The ARVN's reactions to Landgrab showed that it could successfully resist northern forces inside South Viet Nam at that time, and that therefore, with continued U.S. aid and the threat of massive American retaliation for big violations of the peace, South Viet Nam was, for the foreseeable future, safe.[7]

The cessation of U.S. air strikes provided Hanoi with the golden opportunity to improve its illegal highways into the South and greatly increase the traffic on them. Within one year of the Paris accords, the North had infiltrated an additional 100,000 to 120,000 regulars into the South; during 1973 alone, the North Vietnamese army increased its tanks and artillery in the South four-fold.[8]

All of this was completely forbidden by the Paris agreements, and should have been stopped by the International Control Commission, charged with overseeing compliance; yet while the ICC kept careful watch on U.S. supplies to the South, North Viet Nam made it completely clear that under no circumstances would it allow the Commission to impede, or even observe, the enormous flow of men and materiel it was sending into the South. Indeed, the Communists would not even permit ICC members to enter the territories it controlled. In light of this absurd situation, the Canadian members of the Commission announced in May 1973 that they would no longer participate and were in fact leaving Viet Nam.

THIEU'S STRATEGY

In January 1973, the ARVN had 450,000 troops, including the Rangers. The South Vietnamese air force mustered 54,000 and the navy 42,000. Regional and Popular Forces numbered another 525,000.[9] Yet according to General Tran Van Don, of the total of over 1,000,000 men mobilized for the defense of South Viet Nam, only about 100,000 were in combat units.[10] True to its American model, the ARVN had a very big "tail."

President Thieu's strategy after the ceasefire can be described as "hold every-where": every single hamlet, every inch of land, however exposed, must be defended. The reluctance of the Thieu government to desert thousands of peas-ants living in exposed or non-strategic villages was commendable. Nevertheless, the continuing adherence to "hold everywhere" had a number of very negative effects on the war-making capacity of the South Vietnamese. First of all, the ARVN was stretched so thin that it was always on the defensive and could only react to the movements of the enemy, who chose the time and place of battle. The defensive posture of southern forces meant that the Communists were free to use their classic Maoist tactic of achieving numerical superiority at the par-ticular point of attack. As a result, many good southern troops were needlessly lost, and morale began to deteriorate.[11] Second, the ARVN had no strategic reserve; if the enemy achieved a major breakthrough somewhere, there would be no troops available to rush into the gap; even the elite Airborne Division was committed to a static defense role.[12] Third, the ARVN had no troops to spare for interdicting massive enemy staging operations going on in Laos and Cambodia. Fourth and last, too many RF troops were tied down in small out-posts, where they lost their aggressiveness, mobility, and reserves; under these circumstances a serious training program for such units became impossible.[13]

Given the South Vietnamese determination to hold everywhere, the defense of the country demanded mobility; troops had to be able to move quickly to threatened areas. Airlift was the key to the success of this flawed policy, but dramatic cutbacks in U.S. aid (see below) radically diminished the South's abil-ity to transport troops even over land; of course, this lack of mobility gave all the more scope for the Communists to employ their favorite tactic of local preponderance.

INFLATION AND CORRUPTION

At the time of the Paris agreements, economic conditions in South Viet Nam were deteriorating. In 1969, about 160,000 Vietnamese worked directly for the United States; by 1973, after the massive American withdrawal, tens of thousands of these were without jobs. In 1972 and again in 1973, the rice harvests in South Viet Nam were poor; rice had to be imported, and the price rose accordingly. Between 1964 and 1972, officers' pay rose 300 percent, ARVN enlisted pay rose 500 percent, consumer prices rose 850 percent, and rice prices 1400 percent.[14] A colonel in the ARVN, often supporting as many as ten people, would receive about $80 a month, of which half would have to go for rice. A married enlisted man received about one-third of what was necessary to support a family at the minimal level. The ARVN had very few fringe benefits, no post exchanges, little medical care.[15] The poor financial condition in the ARVN was felt throughout South Vietnamese society, since regular army men, with their wives, children, and often dependent parents, made up about 20 percent of southern society in 1968.[16] The ravages of inflation, plus other conditions gathering strength in 1973, naturally undermined ARVN morale: thus one began to hear stories about helicopter pilots charging money for the removal of wounded soldiers from the battlefield. This sort of thing did not happen very often, but it was indicative of a general malaise.[17] Desertion figures began to climb. The writers of the South Vietnamese draft laws had wanted to emphasize the national emergency; hence they made no provision for limited service. Once drafted, a youth was in the army for the duration of the war. The only ways out of military service, therefore, besides old age or death, were self-mutilation or desertion.[18] After the Paris agreements, ARVN desertion amounted to nearly 25 percent of total strength annually, a hemorrhage that replacements could never make up.[19] (After the peace, as before, however, desertion almost never meant defection to the enemy.)

Along with the presence of an enemy army inside its territory and growing inflation and desertion rates, the government in Saigon carried the further burden of a growing reputation, especially among Americans, for corruption. One observer of the scene later wrote that among the South Vietnamese, Communist propaganda was largely ineffective, except on the theme of governmental corruption.[20] It would surely have been miraculous if there had not been corruption in South Viet Nam after years of civil war and foreign invasion, the presence of an enormous number of fabulously rich foreign soldiers, and the lavish expenditure of U.S. government funds. It is very doubtful, however, that corruption in wartime Saigon was worse than that in wartime Naples or Seoul, and overt bribe-taking was probably less than in peacetime India or Thailand.[21] A much more serious problem was the presence, revealed by the Communists after the fall of South Viet Nam, of Viet Cong agents in the government, even in key posts.[22] Nevertheless, the real and alleged corruption in Saigon disenchanted many in Congress—or at least served them as a rationale to abandon South Viet Nam.

In light of all these dire circumstances, what were the prospects for South Viet Nam to survive? More specifically, when the so-called ceasefire went into effect in 1973, how much popular support did the Communists (both Viet Cong and NVA) enjoy, and how much popular support did the cause of an independent South possess?

SOUTHERN SUPPORT FOR THE COMMUNIST CAUSE

By the fall of 1972, out of a population of around 17.5 million, the Communists controlled areas with about 4 million inhabitants; this included both "liberated" and "contested" areas.[23] (A rough definition of a "contested" area would be one in which the government ruled by day and the Communists by night.) The large-scale terrorism and assassination used by the Viet Cong (in relative contrast to the Chinese Communist insurgency) indicates the diminishing level of their popular support.[24] Students of guerrilla war agree that peasants, vulnerable and exposed as they are, will tend to support the side they think will win, or the side that is most likely to harm them if they do not.[25] It is apparent that many southern peasants did not accord the Saigon government legitimacy because the latter had proven time and again that it could not or would not provide them with security from insurgent vengeance. This attitude hardly amounts to an enthusiastic endorsement for the Viet Cong, but rather an elementary form of life insurance.

Government policy in the 1970s was undercutting the appeal of the insurgents. President Thieu returned local government to elected village officials and overhauled existing social programs. Most of all, there was land reform. The domination of South Vietnamese politics by the army, such a burden in so many ways, was a blessing in at least one key area: since most of the officers were urban, they had little sympathy for rural landlords. Hence they were favorable toward serious land reform, indeed "the most extensive land reform program yet undertaken in any non-Communist country in Asia."[26] The program, begun in the spring of 1970, soon reduced tenancy from 60 percent of the rural population to about 34 percent.[27]

In the wake of these programs, it "was clear that support for the insurgents in the Delta was waning in the early 1970s as the whole package of the government's rural development programs was being favorably received."[28] The increasing domination of the war by northerners, even in so-called "VC main force units," underlines the growing difficulty the insurgency had in recruiting among or even drafting the peasantry.

In the urban areas the picture was even bleaker from the Communists' viewpoint. In the early days, they had assumed a priori that the urban masses would be friendly to their cause, but this was an error. Support for either southern

Communism or a northern takeover was never widespread in the cities, and what little there was had diminished over time; nor was the National Liberation Front ever able to absorb the urban opposition to either Diem or Thieu. By 1974, according to one pro-Communist source, party activists in Saigon, a city of over two and a half million, numbered only about 500.[29] The long-expected rising of the oppressed urban masses against the "Saigon puppets and their American masters" never occurred, not during the Tet Offensive, not during the Easter Offensive, not even during the last days of the conquest in 1975. Such incidents as the firing of mortar shells by NVA forces into a crowded schoolyard in the town of Cai Lay on March 9, 1974, reflected the growing knowledge on the Communist side that it had little to lose in terms of urban support ("world public opinion," so vocal in its indignation against any alleged brutality by the allies, retained a composed silence in the face of such atrocities).[30]

The Communists had at first imagined that they could rely on volunteers and food contributions from the peasantry, but they soon had to resort to conscription (of 16-year-olds) and compulsory taxation.

A final indicator of the tenuousness of support for the insurgency is the fact that during and after the fall of Saigon, about 1.5 million people (out of a population of perhaps 17.5 million) fled the country. This was the equivalent of 18 million Americans fleeing the United States—which would amount to one of the greatest migrations on human record. Almost every single one of these refugees had to leave behind all property, usually all money, and often family members. It is not unreasonable to assume that if it had been less difficult to get out of South Viet Nam, and if people knew they had somewhere to go, many, many more would have done so.

That the Viet Cong employed force, including terror, against civilians, to obtain cooperation where necessary is no longer in dispute. Nor, to this author's knowledge, does anybody, in the United States at least, any longer maintain that the Communists had the support of the majority of the population of South Viet Nam. But how many did in fact support them? In 1966, the distinguished East Asian specialist Robert Scalapino offered these rough estimates: for the Communists, 15–20 percent; opposed to the Communists, 35–40 percent; apolitical, 40–50 percent.[31] CBS correspondent Charles Collingwood stated on national television in 1967 that "in secure [allied-controlled] areas there is intense dislike of the Viet Cong" and that the "CBS survey . . . confirms that the Viet Cong does not enjoy mass support outside the areas it controls."[32] An academic source very friendly to the Communists states that the insurgency had the support of about one-third of the peasantry (everyone admits the Communists were infinitely weaker in the cities) in the late 1960s, with about another one-third neutral; Robert Thompson believed that free elections in 1968 would have seen the Communists win about a third of the vote.[33] In 1972, a student of electoral processes around the world wrote that the "vast majority" of South Vietnamese did not wish to see a Communist takeover of their country; in 1975, northern premier Pham Van Dong conceded that from 50 to 70 percent of the southern population would need to be persuaded of the benefits of "reunification."[34]

SUPPORT FOR AN INDEPENDENT SOUTH

Almost all the southern anti-Communist parties and groups were regional or local, divided among themselves and lacking the strong organizational structure the Communists enjoyed. There is no evidence pointing to the existence of a popular majority in favor of the Thieu regime per se; on the contrary, it is clear that most southerners who supported the war were held together more by what they opposed than by what they favored. Yet a southern nationalism, at least in the sense of resisting a northern or northern-dominated takeover, was clearly growing, especially among the peasantry of the populous Mekong Delta region and the middle classes of Saigon.

The great flood of refugees who had come into the South at the time of partition and the scores of thousands of local Vietnamese who had fought against the Viet Minh naturally provided the sturdy bedrock on which to base a popular resistance to a northern conquest. But the numbers of those who would serve the southern cause greatly exceeded these groups. The total armed forces of South Viet Nam grew from 514,000 in 1964 to almost 1,100,000 by 1972.[35] If one allows a very modest four relatives or dependents for every member of the ARVN, the Territorials, the PSDF, and the various police forces, then roughly one-third of the entire population was involved in the war effort. (At the height of its involvement, the United States had one-third of 1 percent of its population in Viet Nam.) True enough, the ARVN relied mainly on conscription. But after the Tet Offensive, the Thieu government distributed 2,000,000 weapons to the civilian population, including 500,000 guns to the PSDF, the lowest level of the popular militia. The 1972 and 1975 offensives provided golden opportunities for the possessors of these arms to turn them against the Thieu government, but nothing of the sort happened—far from it.[36] The elements of the southern armed forces that were most deeply imbedded in the civil population and took the heaviest casualties—the Ruff-Puffs—had the lowest desertion rates.[37] It is not clear how such phenomena can be reasonably explained except in terms of a very widespread determination to prevent a conquest of the South.

One common and decisive indicator that a government lacks wide popular support is that at a time of revolutionary crisis the regime finds its armed forces crumbling away. Consider Russia in 1917, Hungary in 1956, Cuba in 1958, Iran in 1978, the Philippines in 1986. The ARVN—with all its shortcomings— did not collapse. Indeed, it was precisely in the period when South Viet Nam's plight was most desperate that the ARVN began to manifest true fighting qualities. During the battle of Quang Duc, for example, from October 30 to December 10, 1973, the NVA concentrated overwhelming forces against its adversaries; nevertheless, ARVN units held on to the end, showing that "the

South Vietnamese, provided sufficient ammunition, fuel and maintenance support, could overcome the traditional advantages enjoyed by the attacker."[38] Between 1973 and 1975, major battles would take place in Military Region IV (the Delta), and the ARVN would win them all.[39] (Alas, the war was not to be decided in the Delta.) Even as the last hour of a free South Viet Nam was striking, ARVN forces waged a tenacious defense of Xuan Loc against tremendous odds.

The ARVN not only did not disintegrate—even during Tet 1968, even when the Americans went home—but endured incredible punishment. From the time of partition in 1954 to the fall of Saigon in 1975, the ARVN sustained 200,000 killed.[40] (This figure does not include the Ruff-Puffs, whose losses were heavier, or civilian deaths through Communist assassination and terror.) But what does it in fact mean to say that the number of ARVN killed totaled 200,000? Had the American population suffered military deaths in proportion to those of ARVN, the number would be around 2,600,000. The total number of American battle-related deaths in all the wars fought by the United States—the Revolutionary War, the War of 1812, the war with Mexico, the Civil War (including Confederates), the war with Spain, World War I, World War II, Korea, and Viet Nam—amounts to 700,000. In its 20-year defense of the South's right to be independent, the ARVN alone lost proportionately four times the number of soldiers that the Americans had lost in all their wars for nearly two hundred years. Ruff-Puff losses were even heavier.

Yet all this sacrifice was to be for nothing.

THE CUT-OFF OF U.S. AID

When the cease-fire went into effect, the NVA and its Viet Cong auxiliaries had large forces inside South Viet Nam, concentrated around key areas, and the capability for rapid reinforcement of these forces from the North. The ARVN, on the other hand, was stretched thinly around the country and heavily reliant upon the willingness of the Americans to deliver on their promises. The Thieu government apparently never faced up to even the possibility that U.S. aid might be drastically curtailed, let alone be suddenly cut off. Reaction in the United States to Tet 1968, the refusal of General Westmoreland's request for additional troops, and the cutbacks in U.S. presence in South Viet Nam under President Nixon all might have warned Thieu and his advisers just how tenuous their position was—but they did not. In the euphoria following the successful resistance to the Tet Offensive, Thieu could have begun the psychological preparation of the ARVN for a coming U.S. withdrawal; above all, he should have begun to wean the ARVN from the habit of non-conservation of supplies, which it had learned from the Americans. But after Tet, President Thieu returned to "politics as usual" and acted as if American assistance were guaranteed for the indefinite future, as in the case of South Korea.[41] All this meant that when aid was in fact cut off, the Saigon leadership had no real chance to think out and put into place a new strategy.

South Viet Nam's strategy for survival had two parts: the awesome air and naval power of the United States would shield it from any really egregious aggression from the North, while the ARVN and the auxiliary forces, with American supplies, would fight an indefinite holding action on the ground. But the Congress of the United States made short work of the arrangement: in June 1973, it cut off all funds for U.S. military action in and over Indochina effective August 15, thus inviting the North to attack the South. Then came the controversial War Powers Resolution of November 7, 1973, introducing novel restrictions on the president's constitutional powers as commander in chief of the armed forces. Observing these developments, the Central Committee of the Communist Party in Hanoi decided in the fall of 1973 that the time was once again ripe for a major offensive.[42]

Meanwhile, not content with having fixed things so that the United States could not honor President Nixon's pledges, the lawmakers in Washington now set out to cripple South Viet Nam's ability to protect itself. In 1972–73, South Viet Nam received $2.2 billion in U.S. assistance. In 1973–74, that figure was slashed to $964 million, more than a 50 percent reduction. The following year the South received only $700 million (while the U.S. ambassador in Saigon was saying that the real need was for twice that amount).

In terms of economic aid, military assistance, and warfare, the United States had already spent close to $150 billion in Viet Nam ($400 billion in 2001 dollars);[43] now, for significantly less than 1 percent of that amount, the Washington politicos were going to let all that, and much, much more, go down the drain. (On the other hand, in 1973 Congress managed to scrape together over two billion dollars for Israel. From 1976 to 1980, Israel would receive over $11 billion in grants and credits from the United States, and Egypt would get another $3.6 billion.)[44]

Congress's reduction of assistance to South Viet Nam to below operating levels represented "a decision that seriously undermined South Vietnamese combat power and will to continue the struggle."[45] The last southern offensive operation took place in May 1974; after that, lack of fuel, spare parts, and ammunition continuously reduced the ARVN's mobility. As early as February 1974 aid reduction was seriously affecting ARVN artillery; eventually artillery batteries in the Central Highlands that had previously been firing 100 rounds daily were reduced to firing 4. By that summer, each ARVN soldier received only 85 bullets per month.[46] In the Delta, the most populous part of the country and the area where the Communists had always been weakest, cutbacks to the navy forced it to deactivate half of its units, thus uncovering that whole strategic area. The shortage of new batteries cut army radio communications by 50 percent. Aircraft flew fewer missions, and many planes ceased to fly at all because they lacked replacement parts. About half of the ARVN's truck force was put in mothballs for lack of fuel and parts. Even the bandages of the wounded had to be washed and used again.[47]

The cut-off of U.S. aid to the South, however, had no effect on Communist supplies flowing to the North. The Soviets were supplying 85 percent of the oil and 100 percent of the heavy weapons of the NVA; 50,000 Chinese engineering troops kept the northern transport system operating.[48] The North was receiving roughly twice what the Americans were giving to the South.[49] In the last days of the unequal struggle, one observer wrote that "the most likely single reason for the sudden change of fortune [between the two sides] is the build-up of North Vietnamese forces during the two years since the ceasefire. There has been a corresponding run-down of United States support to the South."[50]

The Communist leaders in Hanoi were deeply impressed with the reduction in aid to the South, which was rendering the ARVN clearly inferior to them.[51] In their eyes, the growing American desertion of Viet Nam represented "a fundamental turning point in the balance of forces."[52] Communist propaganda addressed to the Ruff-Puffs harped on the theme of American abandonment.[53]

Coincidentally with the drastic reduction of U.S. aid came the turmoil of Watergate, which puzzled Hanoi; President Nixon's totally unexpected resignation in August 1974 presented a whole new situation to them, because both North and South had believed that if Hanoi had mounted a major offensive, Nixon would have struck back hard. In view of the fact that Soviet-equipped NVA heavy divisions were much more vulnerable to U.S. airpower than the guerrillas of the Viet Cong had ever been, Nixon's departure was a major development.

In October 1974 the full Politburo and Central Committee met in Hanoi to map strategy; the question to be decided was where to launch the coming major assault. In Military Region I, south of the Demilitarized Zone, the ARVN was too strong; the same was true of MR III (Saigon). MR IV (the Delta) was too far from Communist supply lines. Thus the Central Highlands became the agreed-upon main battlefield for 1975.

In December 1974 the NVA struck its first major blow: an overwhelming assault on Phuoc Long province, on the border of MR III and MR IV. Efforts by the ARVN to counterattack failed. Southern troops who had families in the provincial capital or among the refugees simply disappeared from the ranks, a harbinger of disaster.[54]

The conquest of Phuoc Long was one of the most decisive events of the entire war. It was the first time that an entire province had fallen to the Communists. But the South Vietnamese received a much more severe shock when the president of the United States failed to make any response to this open escalation of aggression; indeed, President Ford, in his first State of the Union message, did not even mention South Viet Nam. A few days later, he announced that he could foresee no circumstances in which the United States would return to the struggle. This declaration that the United States would not lift a finger to preserve South Viet Nam, in which it had invested so much blood and treasure, shook the South Vietnamese like nothing since the Tet Offensive; now their American mentors had not only cut them off materially but disowned them publicly.[55] Above all, Ford's statement convinced Hanoi that the hour had indeed arrived to attempt the final conquest of the South.[56]

13

The Last Days of South Viet Nam

War is mainly a catalog of blunders.

—Clausewitz

THE FALL OF BAN ME THUOT

With their forces having to a great extent recovered from the expensive failure of the 1972 Easter Offensive, and greatly excited by the increasingly obvious American determination to abandon South Viet Nam, the Hanoi leadership planned to make big gains during 1975. The essence of the northern strategy was to mount another effort to cut South Viet Nam in two across the Central Highlands, then make some thrusts in the direction of Saigon. Close to 180,000 North Vietnamese combat troops entered South Viet Nam from the beginning of September 1974 to the end of April 1975.[1] Saigon was unable to counter this massive influx effectively, having neither a mobile reserve nor a second strategic line of defense. Even if there had been a reserve, the lack of fuel and spare parts resulting from the severe reductions in U.S. assistance would have prevented its efficient deployment.

The key to the northern offensive was the city of Ban Me Thuot, about 40 miles east of the Cambodian border in the lower end of the highlands. Defending the city was the 23d Division, a punishment unit for disciplinary cases and other troublesome soldiers. The Communists planned to take Ban Me Thuot by employing all their old and successful tactics: ruse, surprise, and overwhelming force. Attacks were launched against Pleiku and Kontum, important posts to the north of Ban Me Thuot. ARVN intelligence informed General Phu, commanding at Ban Me Thuot, that the attacks to the north of him were distractions. Refusing to believe this, Phu stripped Ban Me Thuot of troops in order to defend Pleiku and Kontum.[2] Because they could choose the times and places of their attacks, while Saigon tried to defend everything, the Hanoi forces were almost always able to assemble overwhelming numbers at any point, and that is what happened to Ban Me Thuot. The North had a superiority of 2.2 to 1 in heavy artillery, and 20 to 1 in overall personnel. Besieged Ban Me Thuot would at one time have been supplied by air, but the rise in oil prices and the cutback in U.S. aid now made this impossible, while the Communist ring around the city made reinforcement by truck exceptionally difficult. On March 11, 1975, Ban Me Thuot fell. This disaster was to change the whole war and indeed seal the destiny of South Viet Nam.

During these dark days, South Viet Nam was finding itself increasingly without friends and alone in the world. For 20 years, the Hanoi leadership had told the world that the fighting in South Viet Nam was between an indigenous, broadly based popular uprising and the tyrannical regime—first Diem's and then Thieu's—that had provoked it. Substantial elements of the U.S. media had at least partially accepted this line, and thus it penetrated an ever-increasing segment of the American people and their elected representatives. In February 1975, the month before the fall of Ban Me Thuot, a high-ranking delegation of South Vietnamese leaders went to Washington, only to be refused an audience by Senate Majority Leader Mansfield and by Minority Leader Scott. When the U.S. Congress appropriated only $700 million of an original $1 billion authorization for defense assistance to South Viet Nam, it had "an errosive effect on the morale of the Republic of Viet Nam Armed Forces."[3] Massive aid cutbacks, and the clearly expressed hostility to South Viet Nam that lay behind them, induced "a growing psychology of accommodation and retreat that sometimes approached despair"[4] and thus "made defeat inevitable."[5]

Aware that the tactics used against Ban Me Thuot could and would be employed elsewhere, high-ranking ARVN officers approached Thieu with demands for a major shift in strategy.[6] On March 14, three days after the fall of Ban Me Thuot and two days after the House Democratic Caucus rejected President Ford's plea for emergency supplemental aid to South Viet Nam, President Thieu announced to ARVN leaders his new strategy. Ban Me Thuot, declared Thieu, must be retaken at all costs; it must become the northern anchor for a consolidated defense of Military Regions III and IV (the Saigon area and the Mekong Delta); in order to accomplish this task, Military Regions I and II (the five northernmost provinces and the Central Highlands), with the exception of the strongholds of Hue and Da Nang, would have to be stripped of troops and abandoned to the enemy.

The decision to retreat from the north and center in order to concentrate in the south was not a bad one in itself: 7 of the ARVN's 13 divisions were deployed in MRs I and II, defending only one-fifth of the population. A consolidated South Viet Nam based on MRs III and IV would constitute a state of well over 12 million people. Clearly, the new concentration strategy depended on the successful extrication and redeployment of ARVN forces from the northern provinces, in the teeth of NVA attacks—the key assumption being that

ARVN divisions in the northern areas could carry out a massive fighting retreat, the most difficult operation known in warfare. "If some revolutions are essentially a collapse of the old order, and others are the product of individual human actions, the Vietnamese revolution is quintessentially an example of the latter."[7] The truth of this statement finds its confirmation in the series of really disastrous decisions and movements in March 1975 that in an amazingly short time completely unravelled the fabric of the South Vietnamese army.

The Airborne Division, along with the marines, had long been the most elite unit in the South Vietnamese armed forces. Rushed to the defense of Quang Tri province during the Easter Offensive, the Airborne Division had done good work but had suffered thousands of killed and wounded. By the spring of 1975, therefore, it was really a new division, filled with relatively unseasoned replacements and lacking the old spirit of self-confidence.[8] Morale was depressed further because while the base of the Airborne was in the south, where the families of its members live, after the 1973 Paris agreements it had been committed to a static defense of Military Region I. The Airborne was nevertheless the symbol of determined resistance to any northern invasion of Military Region I. On March 14, as the overture to Thieu's new strategy, General Truong was ordered to send the Airborne Division from Da Nang to Saigon, preparatory to an offensive to retake Ban Me Thuot. This was indeed a "most disastrous" decision,[9] because to replace the redeployed Airborne troops, the crack Marine Division was moved out of Quang Tri down to Da Nang. This shift left the ancient and symbolic capital city of Hue with inadequate protection. The removal of the Airborne from MR I also set the stage for the torrents of refugees that would soon make the defense of Hue and Da Nang impossible.

DEBACLE IN THE CENTRAL HIGHLANDS

On March 16 began the first major phase of the withdrawal from the Central Highlands. Units from Pleiku and Kontum were to move south and east. The troops in Pleiku were set on their way without anyone having informed the civilian authorities in that town. When people realized what was happening, panic enveloped the population. Physicians abandoned their hospitals, policemen shed their uniforms, arson and looting were rampant.[10] Everyone wanted to join the ARVN troops in leaving the highlands. Inexplicably, no one in authority in Saigon had imagined that a massive exodus of civilians would seek to join the retreating columns of soldiers, becoming entangled with them and bringing the retreat to an effective halt. The retreat from Kontum and Pleiku, through extremely rough country over secondary roads and inadequate or even broken bridges, would in the best of circumstances have been tremendously difficult; with the enemy not only pursuing but somehow all around, with crowds of panic-stricken civilians clogging the roads and blocking army vehicles, it was impossible. The retreat soon disintegrated into anarchy. Tanks and ox-carts became hopelessly entangled, young soldiers jostled venerable farmers, frantic parents searched for lost children, the roar of engines competed with the cries of terrified animals, officers lost control of their units—all while great numbers of helpless civilians and soldiers were being slaughtered by indiscriminate fire from NVA artillery as well as from wayward bombs dropped by South Vietnamese aircraft. The confusion, panic, and tragedy of the retreat from the Central Highlands surpass Hemingway's vivid portrayal of the retreat of the Italian army before the conquering Austro-Germans at the battle of Caporetto.

The retreat from the highlands was unfolding with essentially no plans, with poor intelligence—nobody was even sure which bridges were up and which down—and a total lack of preparation for handling civilian refugees. Scores of good aircraft were left behind for the enemy at Pleiku (as also later at Da Nang).[11] Even the most basic military tactics for a retreat, such as "leapfrogging"—in which some units stand and face the enemy while others retreat behind them, those retreating then taking a stand while the former defending units fall back behind them, and so on—were forgotten. The retreat from Pleiku and Kontum "must rank as one of the worst planned and worst executed withdrawal operations in the annals of military history."[12] In the end, nearly all the military units that began the withdrawal disintegrated. In the face of this and similar catastrophes in MRs I and II, many high-ranking ARVN officers took their own lives.[13]

The unannounced ARVN pullout from Kontum and Pleiku meant that RF-PF units in these areas were to be left behind and exposed to the advancing NVA. News of this abandonment spread rapidly over South Viet Nam and had the predictable effect on the morale of territorial units everywhere.[14]

During the attack on Ban Me Thuot, the retreat from the Central Highlands, and the consequent northern invasion of MR I, the Thieu government made no effective effort to communicate its plans or expectations to the people of South Viet Nam. Nobody knew what was going on, and so the rumor mills inevitably began rolling.[15] The most widespread of these rumors was that Thieu had made a deal with Hanoi: in return for the northern provinces, Hanoi would guarantee the neutrality of the remainder of South Viet Nam.[16] Such rumors were sped along, where they were not actually created, by Communists who had infiltrated both the ARVN and the civilian administration. Their agents included at least one general, Nguyen Huu Hanh; not until after the final surrender of Saigon did everyone realize how numerous and destructive the Communists who had penetrated the Saigon government had been.[17]

The rumors of a deal between Thieu and Hanoi paralyzed top military commanders, who hesitated to waste blood in a resistance to the inevitable.[18] For 20 years the Communists had tried in vain to implant the idea that the ARVN was on the verge of collapse and defection. Now in the spring of 1975 it was all coming true, like some incredible nightmare.

The lack of planning, communication, and leadership would all almost certainly have caused Thieu's redeployment to come unravelled in the end. But the disintegration of the ARVN was hastened by the anxiety of soldiers in MRs I

and II to take care of their families. In an effort to overcome the most fundamental cause of desertion in the military, the Thieu government had made it a
policy to permit and even encourage families of soldiers to live near military
bases. Thus when the withdrawals were ordered, these civilians were exposed
to capture and reprisals at the hands of the advancing NVA. Memories of what
had happened at Hue during Tet 1968 were too fresh in everyone's mind for
any soldier to be able to contemplate the capture of his family by the Communists with anything but despair. Besides, if one believed the rumors that Thieu
had agreed to a new partition, it was imperative that one's family be moved far
enough south to wind up on the non-Communist side of any new dividing line.
Thus many soldiers left their units and the line of retreat to try to find their
families and take them to safety.[19]

While soldiers sought to remove their families from the Communist path, the
same rumors of a new partition produced an inundation of refugees. The numbers of the refugees and their panic overwhelmed any chance of directing them
south in an organized way. Almost the entire population of Quang Tri province,
for example, jammed the roads toward Hue.[20] When it became clear that Hue
could not be held, over a quarter of a million civilians struggled to escape farther
south to what they supposed was the safety of Da Nang.[21] Their headlong flight
away from advancing enemy units clogged the indaequate highways, while their
desperation communicated itself to those troops who were still in some sort of
orderly arrangement.

During the whole period of the second Vietnamese war, huge flights of refugees took place toward the allied lines and away from the Communists. The
meaning of this direction of refugee flight has been a subject of bitter controversy. Apologists for the Hanoi side have often insisted that refugees fled toward
the allies in order to escape bombing or artillery fire directed toward the Communist areas, and in many instances this was undoubtedly true, especially in
periods when it seemed that the allies were winning. But the flight of refugees
southward in March 1975 suggests quite a different explanation. In March 1975,
the B-52s were gone, and the South Vietnamese air force, with little fuel and
no spare parts, was a shadow of its former self. The massive and disorganized
military withdrawals signaled to all who could see that the Saigon government
was in mortal peril, and that, at the least, the whole northern half of South Viet
Nam was going to pass into the hands of the enemy. Nevertheless, from Quang
Tri to Hue, from Hue to Da Nang, from Da Nang toward Saigon, always the
rolling tide of refugees flowed inexorably south, in front of, alongside, or just
behind a clearly beaten ARVN. There seems no other plausible explanation but
that millions of South Vietnamese simply did not wish, whether from anti-
Communist or anti-northern sentiment, or from whatever mixture of motives
and fears, to live under the Hanoi regime. Hard evidence on this question is
limited, but three careful students of the refugee phenomenon conclude that "fear
of the NLF and North Vietnamese forces and their Communist ideology and
practices was the most important motive for refugee movement and was ex-

pressed by Catholic and non-Catholic alike."[22] The fact that refugees during the last weeks of South Vietnamese independence were disproportionately Catholic, northern, and urban make more plausible the belief that political motives were more important than considerations of safety in these flights. And since 1975, almost 1.5 million people have fled what used to be South Viet Nam, the equivalent of 18 million Americans leaving the United States. There is no way of knowing how many might have wished to leave but for one reason or another were unable.

Whatever our judgment on this question, there is no debate that the disintegration of the South Vietnamese armed forces in MRs I and II was due not to the actions of the enemy but to a collapse of morale, and that this in turn was caused above all by the failure of the Thieu government to anticipate or deal adequately with the enormous effusion of refugees let loose by the ARVN redeployment.

THE FALL OF HUE AND DA NANG

President Thieu had originally thought to hold onto Hue and Da Nang while pulling out of the rest of the northern provinces, but the surge of refugees and the attempts of soldiers to find and remove their families made the defense of Hue impossible. On March 24, Thieu ordered the abandonment of Hue and the regroupment of its forces at Da Nang. It was not possible to remove anything like a majority of the troops, not to speak of the refugees, from Hue by ship. The First ARVN Division, pride of the entire army, attempted to reach Da Nang by road, but was smashed to pieces south of Hue between March 24 and 26. Hue was the historical and cultural capital of Viet Nam. Its fall to the Communists, not through conquest but through abandonment, accompanied by the destruction of the First Division, administered a psychological blow to the ARVN from which it would not be able to recover in time.[23] It was amidst the disaster of Hue that the North Vietnamese Politburo met in Hanoi and made the decision to try to end the war in 1975 with a concerted drive to take Saigon, before the arrival of the rains.

All eyes now shifted to the drama of Da Nang, the next major stronghold south of Hue. Da Nang was supposed to be the most heavily defended city in South Viet Nam, even though the principal force around it, the 3d ARVN Division, had been badly mauled during the Easter Offensive. During the last week of March over one million refugees and soldiers poured into the city.[24] Attempts were made to stage a massive airlift; many were fortunate enough to escape, but too often frantic soldiers ordered women and children off the crowded planes to make room for themselves.[25] Soon all chance of escape by air disappeared when the airfield, with almost 200 planes on it, was overrun by hordes of refugees. Panic gripped the city. Many of the troops just arrived in Da Nang had become separated from their units, many units were without officers, commanding generals had left the scene, and no one came or rose up to impose order and infuse purpose into the demoralized defenders. Elite marine units made no effort to defend the city; indeed some of them engaged in looting and even shot their own officers.[26] Communist shelling of the city increased, if possible, the chaos and terror. Thousands fled into the sea, some in small fishing craft, many swimming in hopes of reaching some vessel; untold numbers drowned or eventually went insane from drinking sea water. In all perhaps 60,000 people died trying to escape from Da Nang.[27] The bursting, bleeding, wailing city, scene of the arrival of the first U.S. Marine combat contingents exactly ten years before, fell on March 30. More than 100,000 soldiers, enough if properly commanded to have defended Da Nang indefinitely, were taken prisoner.

The Communists did not conquer MR I and MR II; they were abandoned. That was according to Thieu's plan. What was not according to plan was that the South Vietnamese forces in those regions would be destroyed as fighting units. Yet out of seven divisions stationed in those areas on March 1, only about 40,000 men were able to regroup in MRs III and IV by April 11, including only 4,000 troops from the once-mighty Marine Division. Many officers had been killed or captured or had disappeared, seriously undermining whatever effectiveness remained to these troops. These numbers represented an unparalleled disaster for South Viet Nam. A question mark had always hung over the existence of a South Vietnamese republic; always before, that question had been expressed as "How many years?" Now the question came down to "How many weeks?" This drastic change in South Viet Nam's survival prospects resulted not from a bitter, protracted battle but a bitter, brief debacle.

On April 2, Secretary of Defense James Schlesinger said that what was going on in South Viet Nam was not a great offensive but a collapse, "with very little major fighting."[28] The next day, as if in confirmation of this pronouncement, Dalat, site of the South Vietnamese West Point, was abandoned without a struggle.

Where would the ARVN make a stand? *Would* the ARVN make a stand? Or was the war already over?

Deserted by their American allies, running out of gasoline and ammunition while the Soviets and Chinese poured vast amounts of both into Hanoi, distracted by floods of rumors and refugees, shattered by the debacle of the withdrawal in the north, the morale of the ARVN and other military formations was close to rock bottom. But even in this grimmest hour, it began to seem that the Hanoi offensive had reached its peak and that the tide was ebbing. In the provinces of Tay Ninh, Long Khanh, Binh Long, and Binh Duong—a belt of territory stretching from the Cambodian frontier to the northeast of Saigon—fierce ARVN resistance, displaying "countless instances of great tenacity in defense and awesome valor in combat, even in the face of overwhelming firepower and numbers," forced NVA pullbacks.[29] The Rangers, once an elite formation, had deteriorated badly in the previous few years. But at Duc My camp Ranger elements fought back tenaciously against hopeless odds. The 22d ARVN Division staged an excellent defense of Binh Dinh. In Ninh Thuan province, at the base of the Central Highlands in MR II, President Thieu's home village of Phan Rang was the site of a heroic defense by Airborne and ARVN infantry elements. The first big NVA assault on Phan Rang began on April 9, and a week later the largest NVA attacking force in the history of the war overwhelmed the defenders. During these battles of the spring offensive, defeated ARVN forces were not allowed to surrender; instead they were forced to "adhere to the people"—that is, they had to proclaim that they were defecting to the Communists. When surrendering ARVN units engaged in this semantic exercise, Hanoi publicized to the world that they had "changed sides."[30]

It was at Xuan Loc, the last stop on the main highway to Saigon, only 30 miles away, that ARVN units engaged in probably the best fighting of their 20-year struggle for independence, winning the grudging admiration even of the Communists.[31] The town was defended by the 18th ARVN Division, which no one had ever considered to be any good. Yet the 18th held on through an incredible artillery pounding. Determined to take Xuan Loc and viewing it as a meatgrinder in which to destroy irreplaceable enemy troops, the NVA poured in everything it could scrape together; eventually four NVA divisions encircled the town, while the 18th ARVN Division had been reduced in effect to the size of one regiment.[32] Nevertheless, surviving elements, including Regional and Popular Forces, were able to cut their way out of Xuan Loc on April 21st and reassemble for the final defense of Saigon.[33] If only the evacuation of the north had been half as orderly as the withdrawal from besieged Xuan Loc!

On April 21, 1975, the same day that Xuan Loc fell, President Thieu announced his resignation.

By the end of the first week of April, the ARVN had been largely broken up, and other RVNAF forces were demoralized; yet most of the population of South Viet Nam, in the Saigon area and the Mekong Delta, was still in the hands of the republic. In Saigon, the situation was perilous. A classic battlefront encircled the capital, no more than 30 miles and in some places less than 20 miles from center city. Only 30,000 troops, including Ruff-Puffs, were available to man the defenses of the city, while the NVA and Viet Cong had up to 16 divisions available for the seige, equipped with the latest weapons, including surface-to-air missiles.[34] The voice of the Viet Cong, Liberation Radio, began calling once again on the people of Saigon to rise up against their oppressors. Once again, as in 1968 and 1972, the inhabitants of the city remained strangely impervious to their opportunities to show enthusiasm for a Communist victory. By April 20, a quiet settled down over the battlefields, as the Communist forces tightened their noose and the defenders contemplated their situation and awaited a miracle—or rather, help from their American allies. Most South Vietnamese generals were convinced that, just as the U.S. B-52s had made all the difference in the 1972 offensive, they could stop the 1975 offensive dead in its tracks.[35] Late in March, ARVN leaders pleaded with Washington for some B-52 raids on the huge concentrations of northern troops inside South Viet Nam, raids that could have broken North Viet Nam's military power for years. But the U.S. Congress had slammed the door on any military help to its one-time ally and was firmly tightening the faucet on continued financial assistance as well. Nevertheless, so deep was the belief within the ARVN, from top to bottom, that the Americans would not abandon them in their hour of trial, that the B-52s would suddenly come back and break up the NVA in confusion, that the ARVN's plans and efforts in its own defense undoubtedly suffered as a result.[36] President Thieu himself believed up until almost the last day that the Americans would not, after so many years and so many billions of dollars and so much young blood, condemn him and his countrymen to a Communist conquest that the Americans could prevent merely with the strength of their air force.[37]

THE EVACUATION OF SAIGON

During the month of April, the United States evacuated 130,000 Vietnamese from Saigon, not only government and military figures and their families but many persons of more humble estate as well. Most of these were employees of the U.S. government and their dependents, or persons who had openly sided with the Saigon government or identified themselves as opposed to a Communist takeover of their country. They and their families faced certain persecution, and worse, if they fell into the hands of the Communist forces. Twelve thousand were lifted out of the besieged capital in the last two days of the evacuation alone, April 28 and 29. This was no mean accomplishment, and other scores of thousands got out of the city and the country on their own. But the episode has left behind it much bitter controversy. The U.S. ambassador, Graham Martin, is charged with lack of planning and foresight, and much else.[38] As the days of Saigon were visibly dwindling to a few, the evacuation became more and more a scene of disorganization, betrayal, and tragedy. At Tan Son Nhut air base, guards had to be bribed to let civilians get near evacuation aircraft.[39] Some Americans gave up their seats on busses going to the evacuation site at the U.S. embassy to terrified Vietnamese, confident that they themselves would not be left behind.[40] But the scene at the embassy itself was truly awful. Thousands of Vietnamese, many of them women with young children in their arms, believing themselves to have been promised escape, or simply filled with fear at what would be visited upon them by the Communists, clamored, begged, and wept in front of the gates to be let inside the grounds and carried to safety. As they slowly retreated, floor by floor, up to the roof of the embassy and its helicopter landing pad, Marine guards had to use tear gas and rifle butts to restrain these crowds of desperate Vietnamese civilians. The feelings of many during these bitterest hours were expressed by Sirik Matak, not a Vietnamese but an official in the collapsing Lon Nol government in neighboring Cambodia. As the murderous Khmer Rouge Communist forces closed in on the capital city of Phnom Penh, Matak addressed the following letter to John Gunther Dean, the U.S. ambassador:

Dear Excellency and Friend,

I thank you sincerely for your letter and your offer to transport me toward freedom. I cannot, alas, leave in such a cowardly fashion.

As for you and particularly for your great country, I never believed for a moment that you would have this sentiment of abandoning a people which has chosen liberty. You have refused us your protection and we can do nothing about it. You leave and my wish is that you and your country will find happiness under the sky. But mark it well that, if I shall die here on the spot and in my country that I love, it is too bad because we are all born and must one day die. I have only committed this mistake of believing in you, the Americans.

Please accept, Excellency, my dear friend, my faithful and friendly sentiments.

Sirik Matak[41]

The Americans left behind not merely broken pledges to suffering allies in Saigon. They left behind Vietnamese employees of the U.S. Information Agency, mainly women, as well as South Korean general Rhee Dai Yong and other Korean officers, all of whom had been promised certain airlift out of Saigon.

They left behind computers and tapes with the names and addresses of Vietnamese who had helped the Americans in one way or another, including Vietnamese agents of the United States who had infiltrated the Viet Cong.[42]

They left behind the files of 200,000 ex-Communists who had rallied over the years to the support of the Saigon government.[43]

The Americans were not alone in this bacchanal of betrayal. Taiwan abandoned hundreds of its citizens who were intelligence agents.[44] Airlifts of adopted Vietnamese orphans to Australia were halted by the government of that country after Hanoi protested.[45] British ambassador John Bushnell refused to take any of his Vietnamese staff with him (reports say he referred to them as "coolies").[46] The Canadian embassy informed all its Vietnamese employees that they and their dependents would be taken out of Saigon the following day, but the next morning, when the Vietnamese and their families arrived, the embassy was empty.[47]

THE SURRENDER

In accordance with the South Vietnamese constitution, President Thieu's resignation was followed by the swearing in of aged Vice President Tran Van Huong. But enormous pressure was building for Huong to hand power over to General Duong Van Minh ("Big Minh"). Some believed that Minh would be able to negotiate with the Communists and save what could be saved. Others believed that Minh was to be the man to organize a final stand at Saigon—an Asian Stalingrad—that would win the admiration, and the assistance, of the Americans.[48] On April 28, one week after Thieu's resignation, Huong gave up his office, and the National Assembly chose Minh as the new president of South Viet Nam. By then serious efforts were being made under General Nguyen Van

Toan to organize the defenses of Saigon and the surrounding area.[49] In the whole Mekong Delta region, containing almost half of the total population of South Viet Nam, the authority of the Saigon government and the ARVN was intact: not one of the region's 16 provincial capitals, not even a single district capital, was in Communist hands.[50] In the other direction, at Lai Khe, 30 miles north of Saigon, the 5th ARVN Division was fighting hard and getting ready to attempt a breakthrough to the capital city.[51] And the rains were coming! Any day, any hour now, the rainy season would break over Saigon and the whole south, the rainy season that made infantry movements so difficult and tank advances impossible.

But at 10:20 A.M. April 30, Saigon time, President Minh—assassin of Diem—broadcast a call to all the armed forces to cease resistance. At the conclusion of his message, the heavens opened, and the rains began. Then the first North Vietnamese tanks crashed through the gates of Independence Palace. The Republic of South Viet Nam had ceased to exist.

Minh's surrender order triggered the suicide of many high-ranking military and police officials.[52] And those pilots of the South Vietnamese air force who were unable to reach the Seventh Fleet or Thailand crashed their American-built planes into the South China Sea.[53]

14

Conclusion: Viet Nam and the Future

> A true but complicated idea always has less chance of succeeding than one which is false but simple.
>
> —Tocqueville

Many Americans are eager to derive useful lessons from the Viet Nam War. But in the opening years of this new century, they do not begin to approach a consensus even about what happened during that conflict, not to speak of why it happened, and perhaps they never will.[1]

The lack of agreement on the meaning of Viet Nam is perhaps not as bad a thing as it might seem, because it is easy to get the lessons of great events wrong. Clearly, if the Germans had not broken up the tsarist army, the Bolsheviks could not have seized power when they did; yet both Lenin and Stalin underplayed the relationship between war and revolution in their instructions to foreign Communist parties. When Che Guevara analysed Castro's victory in Cuba, he forgot that Castro had won broad support by presenting himself not as a Communist but as a democrat; consequently Guevara met his bloody death in the mountains of Bolivia. Both Lin Piao and the Hanoi Politburo, in explaining Mao's triumph in China, took little note of the fact that Japan had been defeated not by guerrillas but by the United States. Therein lay the tap-root of the failure of the Viet Cong.[2]

The chances for getting the Viet Nam case wrong are high, not only because of its emotional impact but also because it is a particularly complex one to figure out. Consider, for example, the nearly ideal conditions enjoyed by the Viet Cong guerrrillas. Most of the terrain of South Viet Nam was perfect for guerrilla operations. The guerrillas had accumulated years of experience fighting against the French, during which time they trained their cadres and perfected their tactics. The Viet Cong inherited the prestige of the former Viet Minh. They received plenty of outside aid. They enjoyed extensive sanctuaries. The government of South Viet Nam was new and shaky. The strategy of the American and Vietnamese allies—attrition, in a country completely open to invasion—was deeply flawed. The Americans labored under the further grave handicaps of being racially and linguistically alien; finally—not least—the United States was very far away. In spite of this impressive array of advantages, the Viet Cong failed to conquer the South or even to win a single important engagement against U.S. forces. The most salient military aspect of the American experience in Viet Nam is that U.S. conventional forces defeated, however expensively, the Communist guerrillas. That is why the conquest of South Viet Nam required the departure of the Americans and an invasion by conventional northern armies.[3]

Strategists, political scientists, historians, and others will debate for years the causes of the fall of South Viet Nam. As for now, any preliminary explanation of those events will have to include a comparative inventory of northern strengths and southern weaknesses that is something like the following.

THE STRENGTHS OF HANOI

Basking in the prestige of the Viet Minh victory over the French, determined to extend its rule to the South, the Hanoi leadership had powerful political cards to play, of which two, at least, were outstanding.

The first was the presentation of an attractive program: expel the foreigner, give the land to the peasants, and unite the nation. The Communists had the enormous advantage of being able to promise that all the country's ills (many of them aggravated or caused by the insurgency/invasion itself) would completely disappear after their victory. Whatever else it brought, a northern triumph would mean unification, while a northern failure would mean continued partition, probably for generations. (Unification, however, was more popular in the North than in the South, and "land-to-the-tiller" was of course a fraud.)

The North's second political card was the totalitarian control the Politburo exercised over its society. Ho Chi Minh and his successors made it utterly clear that in order to unite all of Viet Nam on their terms and on their timetable, they were willing to spend any number of lives and extract any amount of suffering from their own people. The familiar machinery of the totalitarian state translated such priorities into policy. Therein lay the essential flaw in the U.S. "attrition strategy." Then, prepared as they were to sacrifice untold hecatombs to confront even the awesome power of the Americans, the northern leaders were both surprised and gratified when it became clear to them (very early in fact) that the administration of Lyndon Johnson had no intention of unleashing that power against them. Instead, American might would be doled out carefully and sparingly, just as if time favored the Americans rather than the North Vietnamese. Hanoi's ruthless determination to conquer the South had the further effect of undermining the southern government both at home and in the United States from the first hour, because "peace" could come only if Saigon surrendered.

In addition to these political strengths, Hanoi and the Viet Cong had two key military advantages.

First, the Communists possessed military doctrine and fielded armed forces well suited to both the aims and the territory for which they were fighting. The effectiveness of their approach was magnified because the Americans applied inappropriate military doctrine, and therefore inappropriate forces, in Viet Nam. The Americans also strove, unfortunately with much success, to create a South Vietnamese army in their own image (see chapters 6 and 8).[4]

Second, Communist forces fighting in the South enjoyed the inestimable advantage of having sanctuaries in neighboring Cambodia and Laos, and in North Viet Nam itself. These areas served not only the traditional function of sanctuaries, to provide safe places for resting guerrillas and stockpiling supplies. Much more importantly, they made possible, especially during the last seven years of the war, the pursuit by Hanoi of a sort of latter-day, slow-motion Schlieffen Plan: the destruction of South Viet Nam through a gigantic, continuous envelopment via the Ho Chi Minh Trail.

THE WEAKNESSES OF SAIGON

Complementing Hanoi's peculiar strengths in the conflict were Saigon's peculiar weaknesses.

Most visibly, the South Vietnamese suffered the effects of inadequate leadership. Confronted with mortal challenges in the forms of systematic assassination, guerrilla revolt, and conventional invasion, the state of South Viet Nam at the same time lacked the stability that the possession of ancient political institutions would have provided. In circumstances like these, leadership assumes supreme importance. Leaders of national stature, who led their people by the example of their own dedication, rectitude, and austerity, could have made up for many of the country's disadvantages. The successors of President Diem did not begin to measure up to such requirements.

Rooted in the French colonial experience, the weaknesses of the post-Diem southern leaders flourished in the hothouse atmosphere of the U.S. alliance. The North Vietnamese fought a total war. The Americans (like the French before them) fought a limited war; the South Vietnamese fought a limited war as well, their frightful casualty lists notwithstanding. The ARVN's lack of consistent aggressiveness, of a sense of urgency, its preoccupation with politics, derived in large part from its belief in the invincibility of its American allies and the confidence that those allies would never desert it. The dulling of ARVN's fighting edge by the overwhelming American presence was perhaps beyond the control of any post-Diem southern leadership. But South Vietnamese leaders grew only in their dependence on the Americans, not in their understanding of them. Above all, President Thieu and his closest advisers never really grasped the profound political shifts taking place in America as a result of both Tet and Watergate. Thus they could neither predict nor deflect the gathering hostility toward the South Vietnamese within the U.S. Congress.

But without question, the decisive disadvantage of South Viet Nam was its geography. Had Viet Nam been an island like Taiwan, a peninsula like Malaya or South Korea, or an archipelago like the Philippines, the fighting there would have proceeded and ended quite differently. But, as an open society sharing a border with a totalitarian enemy and outflanked by its enemy's sanctuaries, South Viet Nam was in a very grave position. The North's systematic and massive violation of the neutrality of Laos and Cambodia meant not only that the war would be fought on southern soil but also that Communist forces could always have a numerical advantage over South Vietnamese forces at any point they chose to attack.

The South's geography worked against it in another way: there was too much of it. Most of the territory between the 17th parallel and Saigon was sparsely populated; within that area, the defense of places such as the prestigious city of Hue imposed great burdens on the South Vietnamese armed forces, with no military returns whatsoever. Trying to hold all this area both overstrained the South's resources and exposed it to constant flanking movements from Hanoi's sanctuaries. There was no reason in logic or history why the South Vietnamese had to attempt to hold so much territory in the Central Highlands. After all, it was not they but the French who had drawn the partition line. Being both on the strategic defensive and over-extended as well, the armed forces of South Viet Nam were in an ultimately untenable position. Their situation would have been incomparably stronger if the northern boundary had been along the 15th or even the 13th parallel. As early as 1963 Senator Mansfield advised President Johnson that South Viet Nam should contract its boundaries. Indeed it was in a late but logical effort to retrench, to create a more defensible super-enclave in the deep south, that President Thieu led his people to their final calamity.[5]

As South Viet Nam's territory was too large, so was its army. In the ARVN, pay for enlisted men and care for dependents were low, political education was poor, and training was sketchy. All of these ills stemmed mainly from the ARVN's great size. Besides, a big ARVN required a big draft, which lowered the proportion of volunteers inside the army, inflated the desertion rates, and often produced recruits for the Viet Cong (see chapter 5). But perhaps the most practical consideration of all is that a trimmed-down ARVN would clearly have been unable to defend Viet Nam from the Ca Mau Peninsula all the way up to the Demilitarized Zone. It is therefore very likely that a strategic retreat to more defensible boundaries would have occurred much earlier, while (or even before) large numbers of U.S. combat troops were still in the country.

In spite of so many daunting burdens and menacing conditions, South Viet Nam was in good shape at the beginning of 1973, better actually than ever before. The government's extensive land reform program had largely eliminated a major weapon from the Viet Cong arsenal. The prospect of compulsory unification under the Hanoi Politburo repelled large segments of the southern population, especially Catholics, the sects, northern refugees, the urban middle class, and ethnic minorities.[6] A separate state of South Viet Nam not only had historical precedent and regional and religious bases; more than one million Vietnamese in uniform would be killed or wounded in its defense. All-out northern efforts to shatter the southern government and armed forces during Tet and again in the Easter Offensive had—in a word—failed. In 1974, a noted British military expert ranked the ARVN second among free-world armies only to Israel's in land fighting capability.[7] There was a lot of good human material around in South Viet Nam, both civilian and military; given sufficient time, suitable leadership might well have emerged. Even after they had been saddled with the terribly one-sided Paris settlement, there was good reason to expect that with continued supplies from the United States and especially the help of the B-52s, the ARVN and the territorial forces would continue to stand up to the best units of the North Vietnamese regular army.

The scenario did not unfold that way. Rejected morally and abandoned materially by the Americans, South Viet Nam could not resist northern military advantages and efficiency. It was the force of these circumstances that drove President Thieu to his catastrophic retreat from the Central Highlands. Yet even in the last desperate days of southern resistance, U.S. air strikes against Communist forces beseiging Xuan Loc (the kind of strikes President Nixon had promised) would have crippled northern military power for years.

Here, then, we arrive at the final weakness of the South Vietnamese side: the American alliance.

WASHINGTON VERSUS SAIGON

"A democracy," wrote Tocqueville, "finds it difficult to coordinate the details of a great undertaking and to fix on some plan and carry it through with determination in spite of obstacles." (Or in the words of George Marshall, "No democracy can fight a Seven Years' War.")

These observations did not need to wait very long for the Americans to give them fresh confirmation. The massive investments of U.S. troops and treasure in South Viet Nam did not seem to be producing results quickly enough. Growing American restlessness with the war manifested itself in an increasing tendency to challenge its moral validity.

Such a challenge was of course not without basis. The damage inflicted on civilian life and property in the South (especially as presented by the news media) disturbed and eventually alienated ever-increasing segments of American society. For instance, the use of burning oil (in Vietnam, napalm) in combat is older than the Greeks, but employing it in or close to populated areas was one of the less inspired, indeed less comprehensible, aspects of the U.S. effort.[8] If there are any universally and perpetually valid lessons to be taken from the bitter American experience in Viet Nam, one of them is surely that the United

States must adopt or invent methods of fighting guerrillas that are far less devastating to civilians.

Increasingly, however, Americans challenged the moral validity of the war through criticism of perceived flaws in the government or people of South Viet Nam.

Many, for example, held the government of President Thieu to be unworthy of assistance, because it was not democratic enough—this in South Viet Nam, to whose culture Western-style democracy was utterly alien, whose territory was torn by civil war and invasion, in a region of the world where functioning democracies were notably scarce. In fact, of course, the Thieu government held office as a result of elections that were far more competitive and honest than those in most member states of the United Nations, and immeasurably more so than in North Viet Nam.

Another proof of the unworthiness of South Viet Nam to receive U.S. help was corruption. The impression grew in the United States that the South Vietnamese were hardly more than a gaggle of hustlers and prostitutes, perfectly happy to have the Americans do their fighting for them while they themselves, from President Thieu on down, indulged in a bacchanal of graft.[9] Clearly, there was considerable corruption within the government and the ARVN. Equally clearly, much of it was produced by the presence both of enemy forces and of the Americans: "The South Vietnamese may have their fair share of corruption, but they have also been corrupted."[10] Having to fight the war on its own soil aggravated South Viet Nam's grave internal weaknesses and even created some of these weaknesses: not only through the unravelling of southern society by Viet Cong terrorism and the operations of the NVA but by the omnipresence of rich, young, unattached Americans as well.

It is not pleasant to imagine what the world would look like today if the Americans and their leaders had insisted on high standards of financial ethics and "real" democracy from their allies in World War II. Surely, one must at some point respond to the criticisms of southern Vietnamese shortcomings with the question: undemocratic and corrupt compared with what? Whatever anyone may think or wish the Viet Cong represented at one time or another, after 1968 the struggle was between two governments, North and South. One was an admittedly corrupt government, with at least some of the institutions and mechanisms of democracy and capable of further democratic evolution; the other was a totalitarian state explicitly contemptuous of all the political values of the American people. As it turns out, by the admission of their own leaders, totalitarian Viet Nam too is riddled with corruption. This was a big surprise to many Americans, though it is not clear why; indeed, one could define totalitarianism—the denial of any valid or binding distinction between the private and the political, of any limitations on those who possess power—as the quintessence of corruption.

Some members of the Congress who were too embarrassed to assume the fashionable posture of moral superiority toward the South Vietnamese embraced another tactic. Especially in the spring of 1975, when President Ford made his emergency pleas to Congress to rush aid to a stricken Saigon, one heard the argument that since the United States had already poured so many billions into South Viet Nam, and that country still was not safe and self-sufficient, what good would another billion dollars accomplish? And yet, more than five decades after they first landed in Korea, American forces still stand watch on the 38th parallel, while U.S. military assistance and grants and credits to South Korea since 1953 exceed $20 billion.[11]

But Congress was determined to wash its hands of the Vietnamese.

THE MEANING OF THE SOUTH'S DEFEAT

That South Viet Nam, an open society cut off from vital supplies by its U.S. allies, so that in the last weeks of the fighting many of its units had neither gasoline nor bullets nor even clean bandages—that this South Viet Nam was defeated by the Soviet- and Chinese-equipped armies of totalitarian North Viet Nam constitutes no great mystery. But what does indeed constitute a mystery is why, to so many American minds, the South's military defeat somehow proves its lack of political viability. The victory of the northern military machine does not demonstrate underlying southern popular support for such a denouement but rather the opposite. Saigon did not fall to rioting revolutionary mobs, much less to the pajama-clad guerrillas of American mythology, but to well-trained and well-equipped conventional armies from the North. The major point to be held in mind above all others about the fall of South Viet Nam is this: *North Viet Nam had to take over the South by military means because it could not do so by political means.* Clearly, North Viet Nam was militarily more efficient than the South, especially after U.S. aid cutbacks. If the efficiency of a country's military is the moral measure of its policies, then "Hitler would have had the most desirable political system in the mid-twentieth century."[12] Despite their increasing isolation, the South Vietnamese fought on. The length of time between the withdrawal of the last U.S. ground combat troops and the fall of Saigon is comparable to that between Pearl Harbor and Normandy, or between the election of Lincoln and the battle of Gettysburg.

To insist on the political and military viability of South Viet Nam is of course to deny neither the charismatic appeal of Ho Chi Minh (who died in 1969), nor the organizational virtuosity of Vietnamese Communism, nor the strategic dilemmas, uninspired leadership, and social contradictions of the South. No one can be sure what would eventually have happened if the Americans had continued the kind of material support to the South Vietnamese guaranteed to them by President Nixon. But the reason why South Viet Nam fell in 1975 was Thieu's bungled pullback, which had been precipitated and was to be followed by denial of U.S. aid.

In 1966, a seasoned observer of Viet Nam penned a grim prophecy: "My heart goes out to the Vietnamese people—who have been sold out again and again, whose long history could be written in terms of betrayal and who, based on this long and bitter experience, can only expect that eventually America too will sell them out."[13] Another wrote, "I also came to understand that [American abandonment] represented a broken promise to millions of Vietnamese—not just a few corrupt generals—who depended on American protection against a ruthless and determined enemy. Abandoning our Viet Nam effort was a necessary act, in terms of our own needs, but it was also an act of betrayal."[14]

The United States could have pursued a less extravagant and destructive course in Viet Nam—a demographic strategy, rural security, closing the Ho Chi Minh Trail—but chose not to. The United States could have sustained the southern armed forces indefinitely, but chose not to. The United States could have stopped the final offensive against Saigon dead in its tracks with airpower alone, but chose not to. And so in a real sense the Americans defeated the South Vietnamese, and themselves.

At least one distinguished European, having watched the unfolding of these miserable events, has concluded that "perhaps the major lesson of the Viet Nam war is: do not rely on the United States as an ally."[15]

The story of the Vietnamese people since 1975 has been infinitely sad. The victorious North Vietnamese executed at least 65,000 persons. Of the 400,000 South Vietnamese sent to prison camps, perhaps 200,000 died in them. Many thousands more perished from being forced to clear minefields without detectors. Of the one million "boat people" who sought safety on the sea, unknown numbers died, while others wound up in pirate slavery. The South Vietnamese diaspora eventually exceeded two million.[16]

Those who could not flee and were not killed suffered economic deprivation, political repression, and yet more fighting—against the Cambodians, against the Chinese, against the Thais. All this has deeply disillusioned some of the more thoughtful of those Americans who once were so vociferously critical of the South Vietnamese.[17] It is now painfully clear that "however repressive the Saigon regime may have appeared, there was more freedom in the South than in the North."[18] At the time, however, many Americans did not wish to make the effort to distinguish between what is bad and what is worse. And now it is too late.

Epilogue 2001:
South Viet Nam's Defeat Revisited

The Johnson administration made a disproportionate and destructive commitment to the Viet Nam conflict. To reverse this policy would therefore have been intelligent. But the Americans changed their minds about the war largely because they misunderstood the Tet Offensive. They then decided that reversing a wrong decision justified abandoning the millions of South Vietnamese who had assumed a public anti-Communist stance. The bill for this cruel desertion remains to be paid.

Since 1975, many have said that the Viet Nam War was not fought in vain, because it gave the states of Southeast Asia a clear view of what Communism really was and time to take internal measures against it. By delaying the fall of the dominoes, the war permanently prevented it. Whatever the merits of this view, it is probably of little comfort to the South Vietnamese people, whose sacrifices were followed by abandonment, repression, poverty, emigration, and execution.

But in fact that sad conflict did have the most profound effects on the course of world politics, in a way that perhaps no one could have predicted. The Soviet Union of Leonid Brezhnev saw the self-inflicted American defeat in Viet Nam as signaling a true shift in the "correlation of forces";[1] that is, the tides of world politics were definitely flowing toward Communism. The Soviets became much more self-confident and aggressive, from Angola and Libya to Ethiopia and Nicaragua. In the eyes of Washington observers, Soviet military and intelligence advisers were seemingly everywhere, and the Soviet military buildup was ominous.[2] In December 1979, with the invasion of Afghanistan, Soviet ground forces for the first time crossed a border outside the recognized Soviet bloc.

This unprecedented Soviet forward policy produced at least two fateful consequences. First, the Soviet Union's intercontinental activism required it to com-mit not only prestige but also resources. The CIA estimated that between 1981 and 1986 Soviet support to its clients in Afghanistan, Angola, and Nicaragua alone cost $13 billion, with another $6 billion dollars a year just for Cuba.[3] This turned out to be far beyond what the USSR could afford. Second, all this highly visible Soviet global activity, coming on the heels of the debacle in South Viet Nam and then U.S. national humiliation in Iran, helped turn political opinion in the United States in favor of more spending on defense and intelligence.[4] The buildup began in the last year of the Jimmy Carter administration. It culminated under President Ronald Reagan in the strategy of breaking the power of the USSR through overwhelming technological challenges, a strategy that was unexpectedly effective.

Thus, in one of modern history's most stupendous ironies, one can quite plainly trace real world–historical linkages between the fall of the Vietnamese republic and the collapse of the Soviet empire.

Notes

PREFACE TO SECOND EDITION

1. Douglas Pike, *PAVN* (Novato, CA: Presidio, 1986), p. 5.

PREFACE TO FIRST EDITION

1. Dennis J. Duncanson, *Government and Revolution in Viet Nam* (New York: Oxford University, 1968), p. 1.

CHAPTER 1

1. Ellen J. Hammer, *The Struggle for Indochina, 1940–1955* (Stanford, CA: Stanford University, 1966), p. 62.
2. Douglas Pike, *Viet Cong: The Organization and Techniques of the National Liberation Front of South Viet Nam* (Cambridge, MA: MIT, 1966), p. 6.
3. Truong Nhu Tang, *A Viet Cong Memoir* (New York: Harcourt Brace, 1985), p. 283.
4. Pike, *Viet Cong*, p. 5; Tran Van Don, *Our Endless War* (San Rafael, CA: Presidio, 1978), p. 6.
5. Hoang Van Chi, *From Colonialism to Communism: A Case History of North Viet Nam* (New York: Praeger, 1964), p. 5.
6. Hoang Van Chi, *From Colonialism to Communism*, p. 6; John T. McAlister, *Viet Nam: The Origins of Revolution* (Garden City, NY: Doubleday Anchor, 1971), p. 271.
7. Joseph Buttinger, *Viet Nam: A Political History* (New York: Praeger, 1968), chapter 3.
8. Duncanson, *Government and Revolution*, p. 39; Robert F. Turner, *Vietnamese Communism: Its Origins and Development* (Stanford, CA: Hoover Institution, 1975), p. 4 n.

9. Duncanson, *Government and Revolution*, p. 19.

10. Ibid., p. 75.

11. Ibid., p. 103.

12. Ibid., p. 81.

13. See, for example, Eric Wolf, *Peasant Wars of the Twentieth Century* (New York: Harper and Row, 1969).

14. See Samuel L. Popkin, *The Rational Peasant* (Berkeley: University of California, 1979).

15. Duncanson, *Government and Revolution*, p. 110; Hammer, *Struggle*, p. 64.

16. K. M. Panikkar, *Asia and Western Dominance* (New York: John Day, 1950).

17. Hammer, *Struggle*, p. 69.

18. Duncanson, *Government and Revolution*, p. 132.

19. Bernard Fall, *The Two Viet Nams: A Political and Military Analysis*, 2d rev. ed. (New York: Praeger, 1967), p. 28.

20. John F. Cady, *The Roots of French Imperialism in Eastern Asia* (Ithaca, NY: Cornell University, 1954).

21. Duncanson, *Government and Revolution*, p. 133.

22. See Vilfredo Pareto, *Les systèmes socialistes*, and *The Mind and Society*, vol. 2.

CHAPTER 2

1. See Anthony James Joes, *From the Barrel of a Gun: Armies and Revolutions* (McLean, VA: Pergamon-Brassey's, 1986). Many would argue that the third condition—including confusion and division within the established ruling class—is by far the most important.

2. Fall, *Two Viet Nams*, p. 35.

3. Duncanson, *Government and Revolution*, p. 103.

4. Fall, *Two Viet Nams*, p. 35.

5. Duncanson, *Government and Revolution*, p. 103.

6. Hammer, *Struggle*, p. 73.

7. McAlister, *Viet Nam*, pp. 300–301.

8. Ibid., p. 74.

9. Duncanson, *Government and Revolution*, p. 128.

10. Hammer, *Struggle*, p. 79.

11. Besides Ho Chi Minh, alumni of the school include Ngo Dinh Diem (son of the school's founder), Vo Nguyen Giap, and Pham Van Dong.

12. Fall, *Two Viet Nams*, p. 92.

13. Truong Nhu Tang, *Viet Cong Memoir*, p. 190.

14. Turner, *Vietnamese Communism*, p. 5; William J. Duiker, *The Communist Road to Power in Viet Nam* (Boulder, CO: Westview, 1981), p. 16; Ho Chi Minh, "The Path Which Led Me to Leninism," in Ho Chi Minh, *On Revolution*, ed. Bernard Fall (New York: Praeger, 1967).

15. Hammer, *Struggle*, p. 75.

16. Robert M. Blum, *Drawing the Line: The Origin of the American Containment Policy in East Asia* (New York: Norton, 1982), p. 218.

17. Hoang Van Chi, *From Colonialism to Communism*, p. 44; Douglas Pike, *A History*

of Vietnamese Communism, 1925–1976 (Stanford, CA: Hoover Institution, 1978), p. 29; Turner, *Vietnamese Communism*, pp. 8, 9, 11.

18. Fall, *Two Viet Nams*, p. 83.

19. Duncanson, *Government and Revolution*, p. 144; Democratic Republic of Viet Nam, *Thirty Years of Struggle of the Party* (Hanoi, 1960).

20. Pike, *History*, p. 20.

21. Duncanson, *Government and Revolution*, p. 140.

22. Duiker, *Communist Road*, p. 45.

23. Joseph Buttinger, *A Dragon Defiant: A Short History of Viet Nam* (New York: Praeger, 1972), p. 72.

24. Duiker, *Communist Road*, p. 26.

25. Ibid., pp. 58–59.

26. Chalmers Johnson, *Autopsy on People's War* (Berkeley: University of California, 1973), p. 10. See also Hoang Van Chi, *From Colonialism to Communism*, p. 30.

27. Popkin, *Rational Peasant*, p. 218.

28. On the essential nature of the "revolutionary alliance" between intelligentsia and peasantry, and the role nationalism plays in this alliance, see Samuel Huntington, *Political Order in Changing Societies* (New Haven, CT: Yale University, 1968), chapter 5.

29. Johnson, *Autopsy*, p. 12.

30. This is very much like the program the Fascist revolutionary Mussolini advocated after the First World War, except that his conversion to nationalism was not merely tactical. See Anthony James Joes, *Mussolini* (New York: Franklin Watts, 1982).

31. Paul Ely, *Lessons of the War in Indochina*, vol. 2 (Santa Monica, CA: Rand Corporation, 1967), p. 32.

32. Duiker, *Communist Road*, pp. 70–71.

33. Alexander Woodside, *Community and Revolution in Modern Viet Nam* (Boston: Houghton Mifflin, 1976).

34. Robert J. O'Neill, *General Giap* (New York: Praeger, 1969), p. 29.

35. McAlister, *Viet Nam*, p. 318.

36. Duiker, *Communist Road*, p. 103.

37. McAlister, *Viet Nam*, p. 318.

38. See Joes, *From the Barrel of a Gun*.

39. Duiker, *Communist Road*, p. 107; McAlister, *Viet Nam*, p. 149; Hammer, *Struggle*, p. 101.

40. Duiker, *Communist Road*, p. 107; Joseph Buttinger, *Viet Nam: A Dragon Embattled*, vol. 1 (New York: Praeger, 1967), pp. 292–300.

41. Philippe Devillers, *Histoire du Viet-Nam de 1940 à 1952*, 3d ed. (Paris: Éditions du Seuil, 1952), p. 186.

42. Fall, *Two Viet Nams*, p. 65. See also Joyce Lebra, *Japanese-Trained Armies in Southeast Asia* (New York: Columbia University, 1977).

43. Buttinger, *Dragon Defiant*, p. 85.

44. Hoang Van Chi, *From Colonialism to Communism*, p. 44; Buttinger, *Dragon Defiant*, p. 86.

45. Buttinger, *Dragon Embattled*, p. 399.

46. Ibid., p. 408.

47. Ibid., p. 409. For more on this issue see Truong Chinh, *Primer for Revolt*, p. 24; Fall, *Two Viet Nams*, p. 101; McAlister, *Viet Nam: Origins*, pp. 190–192; Lucien Bodard,

The Quicksand War: Prelude to Viet Nam (Boston: Little, Brown, 1967), pp. 208–209; Hammer, *Struggle*, pp. 158, 176.

48. Buttinger, *Dragon Embattled*, p. 412.

49. Fall, *Two Viet Nams*, p. 101.

50. Devillers, *Histoire*, p. 201; Turner, *Vietnamese Communism*, p. 48; McAlister, *Viet Nam*, p. 221.

CHAPTER 3

1. Fall, *Two Viet Nams*, pp. 72–73; Devillers, *Histoire du Viet-Nam*, pp. 248–271.

2. O'Neill, *General Giap*, p. 31.

3. McAlister, *Viet Nam*, p. 233.

4. Fall, *Two Viet Nams*, p. 76.

5. Ibid., p. 77.

6. George K. Tanham, *Communist Revolutionary Warfare: From the Viet Minh to the Viet Cong*, rev. ed. (New York: Praeger, 1967), p. 84.

7. Tanham, *Communist Revolutionary Warfare*, p. 64.

8. Hammer, *Struggle*, p. 248.

9. O'Neill, *General Giap*, p. 45.

10. Pike, *Viet Cong*, p. 48.

11. Fall, *Two Viet Nams*, p. 101.

12. Ibid., p. 203.

13. Ibid., p. 212; *The Pentagon Papers: The Defense Department History of United States Decisionmaking on Viet Nam*, vol. 1, Senator Gravel Edition (Boston: Beacon, 1971), pp. 57–67. This agreement was reconfirmed by the Elysée Treaty of March 1949.

14. Fall, *Two Viet Nams*, p. 213.

15. Ronald B. Spector, *Advice and Support: The Early Years, 1941–1960* (Washington, DC: U.S. Army Center of Military History, 1983), p. 203.

16. Heuri Navarre, *Agonie de l'Indochine* (Paris: Plon, 1956), p. 46.

17. Paul Ely, *Lessons of the War in Indochina*, p. 59.

18. Fall, *Two Viet Nams*, p. 220.

19. Michael Carver, *War since 1945* (New York: Putnam, 1981), p. 112.

20. Duncanson, *Government and Revolution*, p. 189.

21. O'Neill, *General Giap*, p. 69. It is difficult to see, however, how Giap's logistical system could have coped with a larger number of men.

22. Fall, *Two Viet Nams*.

23. Tanham, *Communist Revolutionary Warfare*, pp. 107–110; Bernard Fall, *Street without Joy* (Harrisburg, PA: Stackpole, 1964), p. 242.

24. Denis Warner, *Certain Victory: How Hanoi Won the War* (Kansas City, KS: Sneed, Andrews and McMeel, 1978), p. 89.

25. Phillip B. Davidson, *Viet Nam at War: The History, 1946–1975* (Novato, CA: Presidio, 1988), p. 49; Tanham, *Communist Revolutionary Warfare*, p. 9; Bodard, *Quicksand War*, p. 13.

26. Ely, *Lessons of the War*, p. 193.

27. Ibid., p. 217.

28. Ibid., p. 158.

29. Ibid., pp. 93, 216.

30. Ibid., p. 200.

31. Ibid., p. 76.

32. Fall, *Street without Joy*, p. 354.

33. Bodard, *Quicksand War*, p. 239.

34. Tanham,*Communist Revolutionary Warfare*, p. 90.

35. Donald Lancaster, *The Emancipation of French Indochina* (London: Oxford University, 1961), p. 218.

36. Fall, *Street without Joy*, p. 30.

37. O'Neill, *General Giap*, pp. 90–99.

38. Davidson, *Viet Nam at War*, p. 275. Emphasis in original.

39. Bernard Fall, *Hell in a Very Small Place* (Philadelphia: Lippincott, 1967), p. 225.

40. Ibid., p. 8.

41. Ibid., p. 255.

42. Ibid., p. 337.

43. Ibid., p. 266. The Chinese provided 100 artillery pieces, 60,000 shells, and 2.4 million rounds of ammunition for the battle at Dien Bien Phu; Chen Jian, "China and the First Indo-China War, 1950–1954," *China Quarterly*, no. 133 (March 1993), pp. 85–110. From 1956 to 1963, Chinese aid to North Viet Nam included 10,000 artillery pieces and 28 naval vessels. Chinese antiaircraft troops defended important sites in the North. A total of 320,000 Chinese engineer and other troops served in North Viet Nam. "Without that support, the history, even the outcome, of the Viet Nam War might have been different"; Chen Jian, "China's Involvement in the Viet Nam War, 1964–1969," *China Quarterly*, no. 142 (June 1995), pp. 356–388, quotation on p. 380.

44. From a story in *Le Monde*, quoted in Fall, *Hell in a Very Small Place*, pp. 20–21.

45. Richard Nixon, *No More Viet Nams* (New York: Arbor House, 1985), p. 31. On the U.S. decision not to intervene at Dien Bien Phu, see Dwight D. Eisenhower, *Mandate for Change: 1953–1956* (Garden City, NY: Doubleday, 1963), pp. 332–356; Richard Nixon, *RN: The Memoirs of Richard Nixon* (New York: Grosset and Dunlap, 1978), pp. 150–155; *The Pentagon Papers*, vol. 1, pp. 97–106; Stephen E. Ambrose, *Eisenhower*, vol. 2, *The President* (New York: Simon and Schuster, 1984), pp. 173–186; Melanie Billings-Yun, *Decision against War: Eisenhower and Dien Bien Phu 1954* (New York: Columbia University, 1980); Robert A. Divine, *Eisenhower and the Cold War* (New York: Oxford University, 1981), pp. 39–51.

46. Duiker, *Communist Road*, p. 152.

47. Fall, *Two Viet Nams*, p. 229.

48. Ibid., p. 223.

49. Numbers, of course, vary. I have derived these figures mainly from Fall, *Street without Joy*, and Edgar O'Ballance, *The Indochina War, 1945–1954* (London: Faber and Faber, 1964); Thomas C. Thayer, *War without Fronts: The American Experience in Viet Nam* (Boulder, CO: Westview, 1986), p. 9; Pike, *Viet Cong*, p. 49 n.

50. Fall, *Street without Joy*, p. 45.

51. Ibid., p. 136.

52. Ibid., p. 242.

53. Tanham, *Communist Revolutionary Warfare*, p. 7.

CHAPTER 4

1. Roy Jumper and Marjorie Normand, "Viet Nam", in *Government and Politics in Southeast Asia*, ed. George McT. Kahin (Ithaca, NY: Cornell University, 1964), p. 437.

2. Hammer, *Struggle*, p. 345; Duncanson, *Government and Revolution*, p. 401; P. J. Honey, ed., *North Viet Nam Today: Profile of a Communist Satellite* (New York: Praeger, 1962), p. 6.

3. Peter L. Berger, "Underdevelopment Revisited," *Commentary* 78, no. 1 (July 1984), p. 43.

4. Honey, *North Viet Nam*, p. 8.

5. Hoang Van Chi, *From Colonialism to Communism*, p. 167.

6. Fall, *Two Viet Nams*, pp. 155–156; Honey, *North Viet Nam*, p. 8; Hoang Van Chi, *From Colonialism to Communism*, p. 72.

7. Fall, *Two Viet Nams*, pp. 155–156.

8. Hoang Van Chi, *From Colonialism to Communism*, p. 189.

9. Ibid., p. 190.

10. Turner, *Vietnamese Communism*, pp. 141–142.

11. Fall, *Two Viet Nams*, pp. 156–157.

12. Turner, *Vietnamese Communism*, p. 162.

13. Bernard Fall in Wesley Fishel, ed., *Viet Nam: Anatomy of a Conflict* (Itasca, IL: Peacock, 1968), p. 148.

14. Fall, *Two Viet Nams*, p. 244.

15. Ibid., p. 239.

16. Robert Scigliano, *South Viet Nam: Nation under Stress* (Boston: Houghton Mifflin, 1964), p. 16.

17. Ibid., p. 17.

18. Devillers, *Histoire du Viet-Nam*, p. 63.

19. Ibid., p. 126.

20. Fall, *Two Viet Nams*, p. 240.

21. Robert Shaplen, *The Lost Revolution: The U.S. in Viet Nam, 1946–1966* (New York: Harper and Row, 1966), p. 110.

22. Jean Lacouture and Philippe Devillers, *La fin d'une guerre: Indochine 1954* (Paris: Seuil, 1960), quoted in Scigliano, *South Viet Nam*, p. 64.

23. Scigliano, *South Viet Nam*, p. 17.

24. Jumper and Normand, "Viet Nam," p. 399.

25. Spector, *Advice and Support*, p. 238.

26. Scigliano, *South Viet Nam*, p. 183; William Henderson in Fishel, *Viet Nam*, p. 187.

27. Scigliano, *South Viet Nam*, p. 18.

28. Jumper and Normand, "Viet Nam," p. 431.

29. Jumper and Normand, "Viet Nam." But Scigliano thinks the Catholic population was only 7 percent (*South Viet Nam*, p. 53).

30. Scigliano, *South Viet Nam*, p. 53.

31. Spector, *Advice and Support*, pp. 321–322.

32. Pike, *Viet Cong*, p. 59.

33. Popkin, *Rational Peasant*, p. 240.

34. Ibid., p. 242.

35. Ibid., p. 211.

36. Edward G. Lansdale, *In the Midst of Wars: An American's Mission to Southeast Asia* (New York: Harper and Row, 1972), p. 178; Cecil B. Currey, *Edward Lansdale. The Unquiet American* (Boston: Houghton Mifflin, 1988).

37. "Memorandum for the President," March 16, 1964, *Pentagon Papers*, vol. 3, pp. 499–500.

38. Ibid. The Communists certainly believed in the domino theory; see Timothy Lomperis, *The War Everyone Lost—and Won: America's Intervention in Viet Nam's Twin Struggles*, 2d ed. (Baton Rouge: Louisiana University, 1984), pp. 3, 138–139.

39. Hammer, *Struggle*, p. 356; Jumper and Normand, "Viet Nam," p. 400.

40. Sen. Mike Mansfield in *Harper's*, January 1956, p. 48.

41. *Pentagon Papers*, vol. 1, p. 297.

42. *Vital Speeches*, vol. 22 (August 1, 1956), p. 618.

43. William Henderson, "South Viet Nam Finds Itself," *Foreign Affairs*, January 1957; quoted in Fishel, *Viet Nam*, p. 183.

44. Warner, *Certain Victory*, p. 88.

45. *Pentagon Papers*, vol. 1, p. 293.

46. Lansdale, *In the Midst of Wars*, p. 258.

47. Ibid., p. 177.

48. Scigliano, *South Viet Nam*, p. 22.

49. See the article in *Harper's* by Senator Mansfield.

50. Jumper and Normand, "Viet Nam," p. 401.

51. Denis Warner, *The Last Confucian* (New York: Macmillan, 1963), p. 73.

52. Scigliano, *South Viet Nam*, p. 57.

53. Tran Van Don, *Our Endless War* (San Rafael: Presidio, 1978), p. 62.

54. Fall, *Two Viet Nams*, p. 314.

55. Scigliano, *South Viet Nam*, p. 101.

56. Ibid., pp. 105–106.

57. Fall, *Two Viet Nams*, p. 315.

58. The authors of *The Pentagon Papers* maintain that the erection of two jurisdictions in Viet Nam made reunification elections exceedingly improbable; *Pentagon Papers*, vol. 1, pp. 161–166. Victor Bator concurs in this judgment: see his *Viet Nam, A Diplomatic Tragedy: The Origins of U.S. Involvement* (London: Faber and Faber, 1965); so does R. B. Smith, *An International History of the Viet Nam War*, vol. 1, *Revolution and Containment 1955–1961* (New York: St. Martin's, 1983), pp. 20, 30. In his magisterial study of the Geneva agreements, Robert F. Randle writes that in light of "the very profound ambiguities in the relevant Geneva documents" and the "ambiguities and incompleteness of the final declaration, it does no justice to the complexities of the Vietnamese situation, either in fact or in legal theory, to speak glibly of 'violations' of the 'Geneva Accords' "; *Geneva 1954: The Settlement of the Indochinese War* (Princeton, NJ: Princeton University, 1969), pp. 444–445. Note that only the French military and the Viet Minh signed the agreement of cessation of hostilities in Viet Nam, and nobody at all signed the so-called Final Declarations. See the relevant Geneva documents in Randle, *Geneva 1954*, pp. 569–607, and in Turner, *Vietnamese Communism*, pp. 365–381.

59. Fishel, *Viet Nam*, p. 147; *Pentagon Papers*, vol. 1, p. 245.

60. Truong Nhu Tang, *Viet Cong Memoir*, p. 203.

61. *Pentagon Papers*, vol. 1, p. 284; Duiker, *The Communist Road to Power*, pp. 172–173; Smith, *An International History of the Viet Nam War*, vol. 1, pp. 28–31.

62. Pike, *Viet Cong*, p. 53.

CHAPTER 5

1. Johnson, *Autopsy*, p. 5.

2. Ibid., p. 7. See also Geoffrey Fairbairn, *Revolutionary Guerrilla Warfare: The Countryside Version* (Harmondsworth, England: Penguin, 1974).

3. Fall, *Two Viet Nams*, p. 316.

4. Lomperis, *The War Everyone Lost—and Won*, p. 57.

5. Duiker, *The Communist Road to Power*, p. 199; see also Douglas Pike in Peter Braestrup, ed., *Viet Nam as History* (Washington, DC: University Press of America, 1984), p. 73; Guenter Lewy, *America in Viet Nam* (New York: Oxford University, 1978), p. 40 and passim; Turner, *Vietnamese Communism*, pp. 229–232; Jeffrey Race, *War Comes to Long An: Revolutionary Conflict in a Vietnamese Province* (Berkeley: University of California, 1972), pp. 104–107; "Viet Nam: We Lied to You," *Economist*, February 26, 1983; Smith, *International History*, vol. 1, pp. 16–17. After its conquest of the South, Hanoi did not try to hide its instigation and direction of the war. See, *inter alia*, General Van Tien Dung, *Our Great Spring Victory* (New York: Monthly Review 177), p. 206 and passim, and Bui Tin, *Following Ho Chi Minh: Memoirs of a North Vietnamese Colonel* (Honolulu: University of Hawaii, 1995), p. 41.

6. Wolf Ladejinsky in Michigan State University Social Science Research Bureau, *Problems of Freedom* (Glencoe, IL: Free Press, 1961), p. 175; Ellen Hammer, "South Viet Nam: The Limits of Political Action," *Pacific Affairs* 35, no. 1 (Spring 1962); Lansdale, *In the Midst of Wars*, also believes that Hanoi made the decision for forcible unification on the basis of its unwillingness to be compared with the South.

7. Duiker, *The Communist Road to Power*, p. 180; Douglas Pike, *PAVN: People's Army of Viet Nam* (Novato, CA: Presidio, 1986), p. 215.

8. Stuart A. Herrington, *Silence Was a Weapon: The Viet Nam War in the Villages* (Novato, CA: Presidio, 1982), p. 137.

9. On the centrality of good local administration, see Duncanson, *Government and Revolution*, passim. On the assassination campaigns see Fall, *Two Viet Nams*, p. 281, and Race, *War Comes to Long An*, p. 83.

10. Race, *War Comes to Long An*, p. 83; Duiker, *The Communist Road to Power*, p. 180.

11. Robert Shaplen, quoted in *Pentagon Papers*, vol. 1, p. 334; see also Eric M. Bergerud, *The Dynamics of Defeat: The Viet Nam War in Hau Nghia Province* (Boulder, CO: Westview, 1991), p. 67–68.

12. Scigliano, *South Viet Nam*, p. 140.

13. Robert Thompson, *Defeating Communist Insurgency: The Lessons of Malaya and Viet Nam* (New York: Praeger, 1966), p. 27; See also Stephen T. Hosmer, *Viet Cong Repression and its Implications for the Future* (Santa Monica, CA: Rand Corporation, 1970).

14. Duncanson, *Government and Revolution*, p. 261.

15. Scigliano, *South Viet Nam*, p. 117.

16. Thompson, *Defeating Communist Insurgency*, p. 39.

17. Herrington, *Silence*, passim.

18. *Pentagon Papers*, vol. 2, pp. 697–698.

19. Duncanson, *Government and Revolution*, p. 14.

20. William R. Andrews, *The Village War: Vietnamese Communist Revolutionary Ac-*

tivities in Dinh Tuong Province, 1960–1964 (Columbia: University of Missouri, 1973), pp. 56–60.

21. Thomas Dooley, *Deliver Us from Evil*. See also Duncanson, *Government and Revolution*.

22. *Pentagon Papers*, vol. 1, p. 333.

23. Duiker, *Communist Road to Power*, pp. 183–184; Spector, *Advice and Support*, pp. 315–316 and 326.

24. Duiker, *Communist Road to Power*, pp. 186–188; Dong Van Khuyen, *The RVNAF* (Washington, DC: U.S. Army Center of Military History, 1980), p. 312.

25. Spector, *Advice and Support*, p. 330; Truong Nhu Tang, *Viet Cong Memoir*, p. 240.

26. John C. Donnell, *Viet Cong Recruitment: Why and How Men Join* (Santa Monica, CA: Rand Corporation, 1975), passim; Truong Nhu Tang, *Viet Cong Memoir*.

27. Gerald C. Hickey, *Village in Vietnam* (New Haven, CT: Yale University, 1964, pp. 233–247.

28. Nathan Leites, *The Viet Cong Style of Politics* (Santa Monica, CA: Rand Corporation, 1969).

29. See, for example, ibid.

30. Donnell, *Recruitment*, passim.

31. See, for example, Herrington, *Silence*, p. 31.

32. Leites, *Viet Cong Style*, p. xxv.

33. Donnell, *Recruitment*, passim.

34. Leites, *Viet Cong Style*, passim.

35. Ibid., pp. 49–51.

36. Ibid., p. xxiii.

37. Warner, *Last Confucian*, p. 18.

38. Truong Nhu Tang, *Viet Cong Memoir*, p. 166.

39. See, for example, Stuart A. Herrington, *Peace with Honor?* (Novato, CA: Presidio, 1983), p. 60.

40. Bergerud, *Dynamics of Defeat*, pp. 23 and 326. "No matter how hard a government village chief worked, he could never hope to be more than a village chief, whereas a poor peasant [in the Viet Cong] could hope to become a village secretary, the district secretary, or even higher—his lack of education and his inability to speak flawless French would not weigh against him. In fact, they would be in his favor." Race, *War Comes to Long An*, p. 170. Douglas Blaufarb emphasizes that joining the party often meant breaking ties with one's family, village, and clan; thus one's dedication to the party and its aims became total. *The Counterinsurgency Era: U.S. Doctrine and Performance* (New York: Free Press, 1977), p. 8.

41. Leites, *Viet Cong Style*, p. 3.

42. Ibid., p. 129 and passim.

43. Donnell, *Recruitment*, passim.

44. Leites, *Viet Cong Style*, p. 43.

45. Ibid., pp. 111, 173.

46. Pike, *Viet Cong*, pp. 283–284, 376–377.

47. Truong Nhu Tang, *Viet Cong Memoir*, p. 167.

48. Donnell, *Recruitment*, p. 14.

49. Ibid., p. x.

50. Duiker, *Communist Road to Power*, p. 262.

51. Duncanson, *Government and Revolution*, p. 297.
52. Duiker, *Communist Road to Power*, p. 250.
53. Herrington, *Silence*, p. 168.
54. Duiker, *Communist Road to Power*, p. 276.

CHAPTER 6

1. There are many good studies of guerrilla tactics; see especially Napoleon Valeriano and C. T. R. Bohannan, *Counter-Guerrilla Operations: The Philippine Experience* (New York: Praeger, 1962); Peter Paret and John Shy, *Guerrillas in the 1960s*, rev. ed. (New York: Praeger, 1962); Samuel B. Griffith, *Mao Tse-tung on Guerrilla Warfare* (New York: Praeger, 1961); Fairbairn, *Revolutionary Guerrilla Warfare*; Anthony James Joes, *Modern Guerrilla Insurgency* (Westport, CT: Praeger, 1992), and *Guerrilla Warfare: A Historical, Biographical and Bibliographical Sourcebook* (Westport, CT: Greenwood, 1996).

2. Johnson, *Autopsy.*

3. Duncanson, *Government and Revolution*, p. 367; Richard L. Clutterbuck, *The Long, Long War: Counterinsurgency in Malaya and Viet Nam* (New York: Praeger, 1966), pp. 65–66.

4. Gerald Chaliand, ed., *Guerrilla Strategies* (Berkeley: University of California, 1982), p. 10. See also Cao Van Vien and Dong Van Khuyen, *Reflections on the Viet Nam War* (Washington, DC: U.S. Army Center of Military History, 1980), p. 149—"It was the VC [infrastructure], not the guerrillas or local forces, which was the foundation of the insurgency"; and Robert Thompson, *No Exit from Viet Nam* (New York: David McKay, 1969), p. 32.

5. Thompson, *Defeating Communist Insurgency*, pp. 55–56.

6. Thompson, *No Exit*, p. 150.

7. Thompson, *Defeating Communist Insurgency*, p. 27.

8. Race, *War Comes to Long An*, p. 83.

9. Thompson, *Defeating Communist Insurgency*, p. 39.

10. Duncanson, *Government and Revolution*, p. 367.

11. Warner, *Certain Victory*, p. 136.

12. Duncanson, *Government and Revolution*, p. 187.

13. Valeriano and Bohannan, *Counter-Guerrilla Operations*, p. 115.

14. Duncanson, *Government and Revolution*, p. 364.

15. Leites, *Viet Cong Style*, p. 17.

16. Thompson, *Defeating Communist Insurgency*, p. 54; Fall, *Two Viet Nams*, p. 273.

17. Valeriano and Bohannan, *Counter-Guerrilla Operations*, p. 206.

18. Clutterbuck, *The Long, Long War*, pp. 51–52.

19. Cao Van Vien and Dong Van Khuyen, *Reflections*, pp. 31–32.

20. Allan E. Goodman, *An Institutional Profile of the South Vietnamese Officer Corps* (Santa Monica, CA: Rand Corporation, 1970), p. 3; Cao Van Vien and Dong Van Khuyen, *Reflections*, p. 147.

21. Thompson, *Defeating Communist Insurgency*, pp. 146–147.

22. Ely, *Lessons of the War*, p. 275; David Galula, *Counter-Insurgency Warfare: Theory and Practice* (New York: Praeger, 1964), p. 32.

23. Ely, *Lessons*, p. 110.

24. Edward Mead Earle, *Makers of Modern Strategy* (Princeton, NJ: Princeton University, 1948).

25. Thompson, *Defeating Communist Insurgency*, pp. 57–59; Paret and Shy, *Guerrillas*, p. 41.

26. Clutterbuck, *The Long, Long War*, p. 50.

27. Paret and Shy, *Guerrillas*, pp. 41–42; Joes, *From the Barrel of a Gun*, chapter 7.

28. See W. Scott Thompson and D. D. Frizzell, eds., *The Lessons of Viet Nam* (New York: Crane, Russak, 1977), p. 229 and passim; Andrew F. Krepinevich, Jr., *The Army and Viet Nam* (Baltimore: Johns Hopkins University, 1986), pp. 172–193.

29. *Pentagon Papers*, vol. 2, p. 142.

30. Duncanson, *Government and Revolution*, pp. 315–316.

31. Warner, *Last Confucian*, p. 17.

32. Clutterbuck, *The Long, Long War*, p. 67; Thompson, *Defeating Communist Insurgency*, chapter 12.

33. Cao Van Vien and Dong Van Khuyen, *Reflections*, p. 27 n.

34. The helicopter gunship changed the face of anti-guerrilla warfare in Viet Nam and continued to do so later in places like Afghanistan and Cambodia; some of Mao's ideas about secure guerrilla bases may need revision.

35. James W. Dunn, "Province Advisers in Viet Nam, 1962–1965," in Richard A. Hunt and Richard H. Shultz, Jr., eds., *Lessons from an Unconventional War* (New York: Pergamon, 1982), pp. 1–23.

36. *Pentagon Papers*, vol. 2, p. 686.

37. Duncanson, *Government and Revolution*, p. 319.

38. *Pentagon Papers*, vol. 2, p. 129.

39. Scigliano, *South Viet Nam*, p. 183.

40. *Pentagon Papers*, vol. 2, p. 756.

41. Thompson, *Defeating Communist Insurgency*, p. 154.

42. Clutterbuck, *The Long, Long War*, pp. 52–53; Ely, *Lessons*, p. 162.

43. Valeriano and Bohannan, *Counter-Guerrilla Operations*, pp. 97–98.

44. Clutterbuck, *The Long, Long War*, p. 109.

45. Thompson, *Defeating Communist Insurgency*, chapter 8.

46. Duncanson, *Government and Revolution*, pp. 320–321.

47. Herrington, *Silence*, p. 19.

48. Clutterbuck, *The Long, Long War*, p. 110 n. See the important study by Jeanette A. Koch, *The Chieu Hoi Program in South Viet Nam 1963–1971* (Santa Monica, CA: Rand Corporation, January 1973), as well as Thayer, *War without Fronts*, and Hunt, *Pacification*.

49. Duncanson, *Government and Revolution*, p. 300.

50. See, as just one example, Paret and Shy, *Guerrillas*, p. 71.

51. Thompson, *Defeating Communist Insurgency*, pp. 48–49.

52. Ibid., p. 176.

53. Ibid., chapter 9.

54. *Pentagon Papers*, vol. 1, p. 256.

55. Duncanson, *Government and Revolution*, p. 258.

56. Herrington, *Silence*, p. 201.

57. Lewy, *America in Viet Nam*, p. 186.

58. Herrington, *Silence*, p. 123.

59. Can Van Vien and Dong Van Khuyen, *Reflections*, p. 37; Duncanson, *Government*

and Revolution, p. 288; James L. Collins, *The Development and Training of the South Vietnamese Army, 1950–1972* (Washington, DC: Department of the Army, 1975), p. 10.

60. Ngo Quang Truong, *Territorial Forces* (Washington, DC: U.S. Army Center of Military History, 1981), p. 335.

61. Dong Van Khuyen, *The RVNAF*, p. 335.

62. Can Van Vien and Dong Van Khuyen, *Reflections*, p. 42.

63. Paradoxically, poorly trained troops seem to do better on the offensive rather than on the defensive: Ely, *Lessons*, p. 151; Ngo Quang Truong, *Territorial Forces*, p. 83.

64. Tanham, *Communist Revolutionary Warfare*, pp. 159–160.

65. Herrington, *Silence*, pp. 50–51.

66. Thompson and Frizzell, *Lessons*, p. 257.

67. Ngo Quang Truong, *Territorial Forces*, pp. 66–68.

68. Ibid., p. 133.

69. Thompson and Frizzell, *Lessons*, pp. 256–161; Ngo Quang Truong, *Territorial Forces*, p. 77.

70. Ngo Quang Truong, *Territorial Forces*, p. 128.

71. Thomas C. Thayer, in Thompson and Frizzell, *Lessons*, p. 258.

72. Thayer in Thompson and Frizzell, *Lessons*, pp. 258–260.

CHAPTER 7

1. Duncanson, *Government and Revolution*, p. 225.

2. Scigliano, *South Viet Nam*, p. 186.

3. Spector, *Advice and Support*, p. 288 and passim.

4. Duncanson, *Government and Revolution*, p. 238; Tran Van Don, *Our Endless War*, p. 67.

5. Duncanson, *Government and Revolution*, p. 377.

6. Fishel, *Viet Nam*, p. 515; Galula, *Counter-Insurgency Warfare*, p. 30.

7. Duncanson, *Government and Revolution*, p. 256.

8. Scigliano, *South Viet Nam*, p. 185.

9. Warner, *Last Confucian*, p. 95. See the portrait of Diem in *The Pentagon Papers*, vol. 1, pp. 253–260.

10. Duncanson, *Government and Revolution*, p. 259.

11. Ibid., p. 371.

12. Hammer, *Struggle*, p. 350.

13. Thompson, *No Exit from Viet Nam*, p. 118.

14. Pike, *Viet Cong*, p. 57.

15. Scigliano, *South Viet Nam*, p. 189.

16. *New York Times*, April 10, 1961.

17. Collins, *Development and Training*, pp. 23–24.

18. Thompson, *No Exit from Viet Nam*, p. 107; *Pentagon Papers*, vol. 2, p. 225.

19. "I believe now, however, that the crisis was a Viet Cong conspiracy." Frederick Nolting, *From Trust to Tragedy: The Political Memoirs of Frederick Nolting, Kennedy's Ambassador to Diem's Viet Nam* (New York: Praeger, 1988), p. 115. See also Duncanson, *Government and Revolution*, p. 330 n, and Francis X. Winters, *The Year of the Hare* (Athens: University of Georgia, 1997), p. 73.

20. Roger Lalouette, the French ambassador to Saigon, told Henry Cabot Lodge that

"in the days of the French administration [of Viet Nam] suicides of Buddhists were very common and had no effect whatever on the population. They create much more excitement abroad than in Viet Nam" See message of Lodge to Kennedy, August 30, 1963, U.S. Department of State, *Foreign Relations of the United States* [hereafter *FRUS*] *1961–1963: Viet Nam*, vol. 4, (Washington, DC: U.S. Government Printing Office), p. 58.

21. Duncanson, *Government and Revolution*, p. 335; *Pentagon Papers*, vol. 2, p. 226; Winters, *Year of the Hare*, p. 25. There was great confusion within the State Department on this point; even decades later, Dean Rusk could still write that "Diem had to reconcile with the [*sic*] Buddhists, who amounted to 95% of the population." Dean Rusk, *As I Saw It: A Secretary of State's Memoirs* (London: Tauris, 1990), p. 379.

22. Ellen J. Hammer, *A Death in November: America in Viet Nam 1963* (New York: Dutton, 1987), p. 45; Maxwell Taylor, *Swords and Plowshares* (New York: Norton, 1972), p. 300; Nolting, *From Trust to Tragedy*, pp. 86 and 116. In July 1963 Assistant Secretary of State Manning complained to President Kennedy of the "correspondents' hostility to the [Diem] government", *FRUS 1961–1963: Viet Nam*, vol. 3, p. 531. On the politicization of American correspondents in Saigon see William Prochnau, *Once upon a Distant War: Young War Correspondents and the Early Viet Nam Battles* (New York: Times Books, 1995). See also Anne Blair, *Lodge in Viet Nam* (New Haven, CT: Yale University, 1995). David Halberstam of the *New York Times*, a vociferous critic of Diem, was 29 years old during the crisis.

23. *Pentagon Papers*, vol. 2, p. 232; Nolting, *From Trust to Tragedy*, p. 121.

24. Scigliano, *South Viet Nam*, p. 220.

25. See Hammer, *Death in November*, pp. 220–232; Mieczyslaw Maneli, *War of the Vanquished* (New York: Harper and Row, 1971). For French activities in the contacts between Nhu and Hanoi, see Georges Chaffard, *Les deux guerres du Viet Nam* (Paris: Table Rond, 1969).

26. See Hammer, *Death in November*, as well as Winters, *Year of the Hare*, and Blair, *Lodge in Viet Nam*.

27. See Hammer, *Death in November*, pp. 179–180; Winters, *Year of the Hare*, pp. 56–57; *Pentagon Papers*, vol. 2, p. 235.

28. Scigliano, *South Viet Nam*, p. 222; Jumper and Normand, "Viet Nam," p. 434; Hammer, *Death in November*, passim.

29. Actually, at the time of the Buddhist crisis, only 4 of the 17 cabinet ministers were Christians; Nolting, *From Trust to Tragedy*, p. 107.

30. *Pentagon Papers*, vol. 2, p. 265.

31. Duncanson, *Government and Revolution*, p. 339.

32. On October 10, 1963, Director of Central Intelligence McCone told the Senate Foreign Relations Committee that "We have not seen a successor government in the wings that we could say positively would be an improvement over Diem"; Harold P. Ford, *CIA and the Viet Nam Policymakers: Three Episodes 1962–1968* (Washington, DC: Central Intelligence Agency, Center for the Study of Intelligence, 1998), p. 36. For more on McCone's doubts about the coup, see Senate Select Committee to Study Governmental Operations, *Alleged Assassination Plots Involving Foreign Leaders* (Washington, DC: U.S. Government Printing Office, 1975), p. 221, and *FRUS 1961–1963: Viet Nam*, vol. 4, pp. 406–407.

33. Conference with President Kennedy, August 28, 1963, *in FRUS 1961–1963: Viet Nam*, vol. 4, p. 3.

34. Hammer, *Death in November*, p. 276; William Colby, *Lost Victory: A Firsthand*

Account of America's Sixteen-Year Involvement in Vietnam (Chicago: Contemporary Books, 1989), pp. 151–152.

35. *FRUS 1961–1963: Viet Nam*, vol. 4, p. 465 n.

36. Ibid., p. 470. Previously, ambassador to India John Kenneth Galbraith had informed Kennedy that he need not worry about who or what would come after Diem, because "nothing succeeds like successors": *Pentagon Papers*, vol. 2, p. 124. The lack of concern in Washington about who or what would come after Diem is incredible; see Colby, *Lost Victory*, pp. 133, 141, and 147.

37. Tran Van Don, *Our Endless War*, p. 107; *Pentagon Papers*, vol. 2, p. 269; Hammer, *Death in November*, p. 293.

38. Tran Van Don, *Our Endless War*, p. 112; Warner, *Certain Victory*, p. 129; Hammer, *Death in November*, pp. 298–299.

39. Tran Van Don, *Our Endless War*, p. 112.

40. Duncanson, *Government and Revolution*, p. 341; Hammer, *Death in November*, p. 306.

41. Winters, *Year of the Hare*, p. 157.

42. Ibid., p. 60.

43. Ibid., p. 86.

44. Duncanson, *Government and Revolution*, p. 339.

45. Ibid., p. xi.

46. *FRUS 1961–1963: Viet Nam*, vol. 4, p. 578.

47. Nolting, *From Trust to Tragedy*, p. 3.

48. Colby, *Lost Victory*, p. 158.

49. Henry Kissinger, *White House Years* (Boston: Little, Brown, 1979), pp. 231 and 1034; Pike, *Viet Cong*, pp. 163–164.

50. *FRUS 1961–1963: Viet Nam*, vol. 4, p. 736.

51. Patrick Lloyd Hatcher, *The Suicide of an Elite: American Internationalism and Viet Nam* (Stanford, CA: Stanford University, 1990), p. 317. William Colby agrees with this judgment, see his *Lost Victory*, p. 366. So did Edward Lansdale; see Cecil B. Currey, *Edward Lansdale: The Unquiet American* (Boston: Houghton Mifflin, 1988).

52. *Pentagon Papers*, vol. 2, p. 372.

53. Duncanson, *Government and Revolution*, p. 342.

54. Allan E. Goodman, *Politics in War: The Bases of Political Community in South Viet Nam* (Cambridge, MA: Harvard University, 1973), p. 43.

55. Duncanson, *Government and Revolution*, p. 342.

56. Ibid.

57. Hoang Ngoc Lung, *The General Offensives of 1968–1969* (Washington, DC: U.S. Army Center of Military History, 1981), p. 1.

58. Duncanson, *Government and Revolution*, p. 356.

59. Cao Van Vien and Dong Van Khuyen, *Reflections on the War in Viet Nam* (Washington, DC: U.S. Army Center of Military History, 1980), p. 77.

60. Duiker, *Communist Road to Power*, pp. 221–223.

61. Dong Van Khuyen, *The RVNAF*, pp. 12–13.

62. Lewy, *America in Viet Nam*, p. 56.

63. Alan Dawson, *55 Days: The Fall of South Viet Nam* (Englewood Cliffs, NJ: Prentice-Hall, 1977), p. 222; Hammer, *Death in November*, p. 287.

64. Arnold Isaacs, *Without Honor: Defeat in Viet Nam and Cambodia* (New York: Vintage, 1984), p. 114.

65. Taylor, *Swords and Plowshares*, p. 345.

66. Allan E. Goodman, *Politics in War: The Bases of Political Community in South Viet Nam* (Cambridge, MA: Harvard University, 1973) p. 41.

67. Ibid., p. 44.

68. Ibid., p. 55.

69. Howard R. Penniman, *Elections in South Viet Nam* (Washington, DC: American Enterprise Institute, 1972), p. 89.

70. Goodman, *Politics in War*, p. 62.

71. Robert Shaplen, *The Road from War* (New York: Harper and Row, 1971), p. 83.

72. Penniman, *Elections in South Viet Nam*.

CHAPTER 8

1. Spector, *Advice and Support*, p. 131; Hammer, *Struggle*, p. 287; Navarre, *Agonie de l'Indochine*, p. 46; Douglas Pike, *PAVN: People's Army of Vietnam* (Novato, CA: Presidio, 1986), p. 5.

2. See Bui Diem, *In the Jaws of History* (Boston: Houghton Mifflin, 1987). For recognitions, see Hammer, *Struggle*, p. 321.

3. Spector, *Advice and Support*, p. 255.

4. Collins, *Development and Training*, p. 97.

5. Spector, *Advice and Support*, p. 282.

6. Allan E. Goodman, *An Institutional Profile of the South Vietnamese Officer Corps* (Santa Monica, CA: Rand Corporation, 1970), p. 9.

7. Ibid., p. 9.

8. Ibid., p. v.

9. Collins, *Development and Training*, pp. 78–79.

10. Lewy, *America in Viet Nam*, p. 170.

11. Goodman, *Institutional Profile*, p. vi.

12. Ibid., p. 9.

13. Duncanson, *Government and Revolution*, p. 290.

14. Spector, *Advice and Support*, p. 278.

15. See Gordon W. Prange, *At Dawn We Slept* (New York: Penguin Books, 1982), pp. 108–109.

16. Lewy, *America in Viet Nam*, p. 170.

17. G. H. Turley, *The Easter Offensive: Viet Nam 1972* (Novato, CA: Presidio), p. 146.

18. Thomas C. Thayer, *War without Fronts* (Boulder, CO: Westview, 1985), p. 68.

19. Ibid., pp. 60–63.

20. Warner, *Last Confucian*, p. 108.

21. Bruce Palmer, Jr., *The 25-Year War: America's Military Role in Viet Nam* (Lexington: University Press of Kentucky, 1984). See also Harry Summers, *On Strategy: A Critical Assessment of the Viet Nam War* (Novato, CA: Presidio, 1982).

22. Lewy, *America in Viet Nam*, p. 182.

23. Duncanson, *Government and Revolution*, p. 323.

24. Maj. Gen. Richard Lee, quoted in Collins, *Development and Training*, p. 75.

25. Thompson, *Defeating Communist Insurgency*, pp. 58–62.

26. Douglas S. Blaufarb, "The Sources of U.S. Frustration in Viet Nam," in *Lessons*

from an Unconventional War, ed. Richard A. Hunt and Richard H. Shultz, Jr. (New York: Pergamon, 1982), p. 150.

27. Spector, *Advice and Support*, p. 354.

28. Thomas Thayer, "How to Analyze a War without Fronts," *Journal of Defense Research* (Fall 1975), p. viii; Thayer, *War without Fronts*, p. 71.

29. Collins, *Development and Training*, p. 122; Tran Van Dong, *The RVNAF*, p. 72; Thayer, *War without Fronts*, p. 72.

30. Collins, *Development and Training*, p. 75.

31. Lewy, *America in Viet Nam*, pp. 177–178.

32. Herrington, *Silence was a Weapon*, p. 211.

33. Collins, *Development and Training*, p. 151.

34. Machiavelli, *The Art of War*, Book VI.

35. Ely, *Lessons of the War*, p. 219.

36. Lewy, *America in Viet Nam*, p. 164; Collins, *Development and Training*, p. 47.

37. Collins, *Development and Training*, p. 101.

38. Lewy, *America in Viet Nam*, p. 166–167.

39. Spector, *Advice and Support*, p. 353.

40. Steven Hosmer, Konrad Kellen, and Brian M. Jenkins, *The Fall of South Viet Nam: Statements by Vietnamese Military and Civilian Leaders* (New York: Crane Russak, 1980), p. 84.

41. Collins, *Development and Training*, p. 120–130.

42. Spector, *Advice and Support*, pp. 291–293; Cao Van Vien et al., *The U.S. Adviser* (Washington, DC: U.S. Army Center of Military History, 1980).

43. Collins, *Development and Training*, p. 92.

44. Soldiers in the Chinese People's Liberation Army during the Korean War (and probably at other times) had no definite enlistment period and no clear way to get out of the PLA besides death. See Alexander George, *The Chinese Communist Army in Action* (New York: Columbia University, 1966).

45. Lewy, *America in Viet Nam*, p. 173.

46. Collins, *Development and Training*, p. 60.

47. Dong Van Khuyen, *The RVNAF*, p. 152.

48. Pike, *PAVN*, p. 244.

49. Lewy, *America in Viet Nam*, p. 173.

50. Thayer, *War without Fronts*, p. 75.

51. Pike, *PAVN*, p. 244; Lewy, *America in Viet Nam*, p. 172; William E. Le Gro, *Viet Nam from Ceasefire to Capitulation* (Washington, DC: U.S. Army Center of Military History 1981), p. 34; Tanham, *Communist Revolutionary Warfare*, maintains that even among ARVN members taken prisoner by the enemy, few changed sides.

52. Thayer, *War without Fronts*, p. 202.

53. Bruce Catton, *The Army of the Potomac: Glory Road* (Garden City, NY: Doubleday, 1952), pp. 102 and 255.

54. Allan Nevins, *The War for the Union: The Organized War 1863–1864* (New York: Scribner's, 1971), p. 131.

55. Spector, *Advice and Support*, p. 344–348.

56. Lewy, *America in Viet Nam*, p. 184. For weaknesses at the top of ARVN, see Lewis Sorley, *A Better War: The Unexamined Victories and Final Tragedy of America's Last Years in Viet Nam* (New York: Harcourt, Brace, 1999).

CHAPTER 9

1. Don Oberdorfer, *Tet!* (Garden City, NY: Doubleday, 1971), p. 81; Hoang Ngoc Lung, *The General Offensives of 1968–1969* (Washington, DC: U.S. Army Center of Military History, 1981), p. 22.

2. William D. Henderson, *Why the Viet Cong Fought: A Study of Motivation and Control in a Modern Army in Combat* (Westport, CT: Greenwood, 1979), p. xv.

3. Hoang, *General Offensive*, p. 21.

4. *Washington Post*, April 6, 1969.

5. Henderson, *Why the Viet Cong Fought*, p. 23.

6. Fall, *Viet Nam Witness*.

7. Oberdorfer, *Tet!* p. 45.

8. James J. Wirtz, *The Tet Offensive: Intelligence Failure in War* (Ithaca, NY: Cornell University, 1991), pp. 23 and 60.

9. Whether or not the siege of Khe Sanh was intended as a distraction or was an integral part of Giap's offensive plans is still disputed. See Wirtz, *Tet Offensive*, pp. 63, 81, and 98, and Gabriel Kolko, *Anatomy of a War* (New York: Pantheon, 1985), p. 305. Davidson rejects the view of Khe Sanh as merely a diversion; *Viet Nam at War*, pp. 444–445. Consult also John Prados and R. W. Stubbe, *Valley of Decision: The Siege of Khe Sanh* (Boston: Houghton Mifflin, 1991).

10. Wirtz, *Tet Offensive*, p. 265.

11. Dave Richard Palmer, *Summons of the Trumpet: U.S.–Viet Nam in Perspective* (San Rafael, CA: Presidio, 1978), p. 180.

12. "The South Vietnamese, like the Americans, could not believe that the enemy would adopt a strategy guaranteeing his own disaster." Davidson, *Viet Nam at War*, p. 545.

13. Wirtz, *Tet Offensive*, pp. 82, 245.

14. Ibid., p. 84. But see also Ronnie Ford, *Tet 1968: Understanding the Surprise* (London: Frank Cass, 1995).

15. Oberdorfer, *Tet!* p. 121.

16. Davidson, *Viet Nam at War*, p. 483.

17. Lyndon B. Johnson, *The Vantage Point* (New York: Holt, Rinehart, Winston, 1971), p. 380.

18. Wirtz, *Tet Offensive*, p. 1. Johnson's lack of leadership was a decisive influence on the outcome of the conflict; as late as June 1967 a Gallup Poll reported that fully half of the American people had no idea why the United States was engaged in Viet Nam.

19. Peter Braestrup, *Big Story*, vol. 1 (Boulder, CO: Westview, 1977), p. 444.

20. Hoang, *General Offensives*, p. 138; Sorley, *A Better War*, p. 164.

21. Wirtz, *Tet Offensive*, p. 224.

22. Palmer, *Summons of the Trumpet*, p. 210. "The professionalism and steadfastness of ARVN during the Tet offensive surprised not only the enemy, but the Americans and themselves as well." Davidson, *Viet Nam at War*, p. 546. "The South Vietnamese had fully vindicated my trust." Westmoreland, *A Soldier Reports*, p. 332.

23. Hoang, *General Offensives*, p. 150.

24. Thompson, *No Exit from Viet Nam*, p. 124.

25. Hoang, *General Offensives*, pp. 22–23.

26. Wirtz, *Tet Offensive*, p. 224.

27. Palmer, *Summons of the Trumpet*, p. 246.

28. Davidson, *Viet Nam at War*, p. 447. See also Kolko, *Anatomy of a War*, pp. 327–334.

29. Taylor, *Swords and Plowshares*, p. 383; Robert S. Shaplen, *The Road from War: Viet Nam 1965–1971* (New York: Harper and Row, 1971), p. 219. Communist losses from Tet were "cripplingly high"; Turley, *Second Indochina War*, p. 108. For a Communist estimate of the disaster (quickly supressed), see Tran Van Tra, *Concluding the 30-Years War* (Rosslyn, VA: Foreign Broadcast Information Service, 1983).

30. Kolko, *Anatomy of a War*, p. 327.

31. Davidson, *Viet Nam at War*, p. 475. Ambassador Bunker cabled President Johnson: "The enemy has suffered a major military defeat"; *Bunker Papers*, vol. 2, p. 328.

32. See, among others, Truong Nhu Tang, *A Viet Cong Memoir* (New York: Harcourt, 1987), and F. Charles Parker, *Viet Nam: Strategy for a Stalemate* (New York: Paragon, 1989). General Giap himself had never been very optimistic about the Offensive's prospects.

33. Kolko, *Anatomy of a War*, pp. 371, 334; Thayer, *War without Fronts*, p. 92.

34. See Tran Van Tra, *Concluding the 30-Year's War*, p. 35. See also Richard A. Hunt, *Pacification: The American Struggle for Viet Nam's Hearts and Minds* (Boulder, CO: Westview, 1995), chapter 10ff.

35. Hoang, *General Offensives*, p. 136.

36. Oberdorfer, *Tet!* p. 201; see also Alan Dawson, *55 Days: The Fall of South Viet Nam* (Englewood Cliffs, NJ: Prentice-Hall, 1977), p. 92.

37. Oberdorfer, *Tet!* p. 232.

38. Ibid., pp. 200ff.

39. Samuel Popkin, "The Village War," in *Viet Nam as History*, ed. Peter Braestrup (Washington, DC: University Press of America, 1984), p. 102. Ater Tet, "the population had substantially abandoned the VC cause" (while not necessarily embracing that of Saigon); Douglas Blaufarb, *The Counterinsurgency Era*, p. 271. To make up their heavy losses, the VC drastically increased their forcible recruitment of peasants; at the same time, increased mobilization by Saigon decreased the numbers available for this forcible Communist recruitment.

40. Palmer, *Summons of the Trumpet*, p. 201. On the Viet Cong military debacle, see Duiker, *the Communist Road to Power*, p. 269; Lewy, *America in Viet Nam*, p. 76. See also Thayer, *War without Fronts*, p. 92; Shaplen, *Bitter Victory*, pp. 188–189; Blaufarb, *Counterinsurgency Era*, pp. 261–262.

41. Pike, *PAVN*, p. 227.

42. Timothy Lomperis, *From People's War to People's Rule: Insurgency, Intervention, and the Lessons of Vietnam* (Chapel Hill: University of North Carolina, 1996), p. 321.

43. "People's War, as a banner that had led the Party through a generation of trials, was finished"; Lomperis, *From People's War to People's Rule*, pp. 341 and 340. "Never again was the Tet 1968 strategy repeated," Kolko, *Anatomy of a War*, p. 334. See also Chalmers Johnson's little classic, *Autopsy on People's War*.

44. Controversy has surrounded the question of whether Hanoi was consciously aiming Tet at American opinion; both Sir Robert Thompson (in Thompson and Frizzell, *Lessons of Viet Nam*, p. 120) and Phillip Davidson (in *Secrets of the Viet Nam War*, p. 101) believe that it was not.

45. Braestrup, *Big Story*, vol. 1, p. 695.

46. Ibid., p. 449.

47. Ibid., p. 450; Alan Goodman in Braestrup, ed., *Viet Nam as History*, p. 90.

48. Braestrup, *Big Story*, vol. 1, p. 461.

49. Ibid., p. 475.

50. On CBS TV, February 14, 1968; see Braestrup, *Big Story*, vol. 1, pp. 175 and 468.

51. See Associated Press and UPI accounts of the Communist having seized "the first five floors of the U.S. Embassy" in Oberdorfer, *Tet!* pp. 30–31.

52. Oberdorfer, *Tet!* p. 332.

53. Ibid., p. 242.

54. Lewy, *America in Viet Nam*, p. 434. See also Parker, *Viet Nam: Strategy for a Stalemate*, pp. 204–205.

55. Braestrup, *Big Story*, vol. 1, pp. 162, 184, 531.

56. Ibid., p. 705. Things did not improve over time. In 1973 the secretary of state declared that "in the U.S. all the press, the media and the intellectuals have a vested interest in our defeat." Kissinger, *White House Years*, p. 1390. And see Sorley, *A Better War*, p. 225 and passim.

57. Braestrup, *Big Story*, vol. 1, p. 708.

58. Ibid., passim, especially p. 495.

59. Pike, PAVN, p. 242.

60. See Olivier Todd, *Cruel April: The Fall of Saigon* (New York: Norton, 1990), pp. 95, 253, and 398; and "The Reporter Was a Spy," *New York Times*, April 28, 1997, p. A8.

61. Lewy, *American in Viet Nam*, pp. 400, 401.

62. Braestrup, *Big Story*, pp. 531, 492, 716.

63. Warner, *Certain Victory*, p. 205.

64. Marc Leepson, "Viet Nam War Reconsidered," *Editorial Research Reports* (March 1983). p. 195. The French journalist Olivier Todd makes an almost identical criticism in *Cruel April*, p. 139.

65. *Economist*, May 13, 1972, p. 34.

66. Douglas Pike, quoted in Warner, *Certain Victory*, p. 183.

67. See Sorley, *A Better War*, especially pp. 219ff.

68. In 1994, Senate majority leader Mitchell (D.-Maine) said that the American news industry was "more destructive than constructive *than ever*." Representative Barney Frank (D.-Mass.) opined that "you people [the media] celebrate failure and ignore success. *Nothing about government is done as incompetently as the reporting of it.*" *New York Times*, October 1, 1994, my italics. Now, if persons in responsible positions are taken seriously when they publicly declare that American media personnel are unable to present a generally accurate picture of what happens in Washington, where they speak the language and know the culture, it is neither seemly nor permissible to dismiss or attack questions about the quality of the reporting out of Saigon.

CHAPTER 10

1. Nixon, *Memoirs*, p. 450.

2. Nixon, *No More Viet Nams*, p. 122.

3. Duiker, *Communist Road to Power*, p. 286; Dave Richard Palmer, *Summons of*

the Trumpet: U.S.–Viet Nam in Perspective (San Rafael, CA: Presidio, 1978), p. 236; J. D. Coleman, *Incursion* (New York: St. Martin's, 1991); Tran Dinh Tho, *The Cambodian Incursion* (Washington, DC: U.S. Army Center of Military History, 1979).

4. Palmer, *25-Year War*, pp. 103–104.

5. Message from Ambassador Bunker to the president, March 30, 1971, *Bunker Papers*, vol. 3, pp. 820–821. Lam Son saw the first major tank battles of the war.

6. Palmer, *The 25-Year War*, p. 13; Nixon, *Memoirs*, p. 499. Estimates of enemy deaths range from 13,000 to 18,000; Sorley, *A Better War*, pp. 243–261.

7. Hammond Rolph, "Vietnamese Communism and the Protracted War," *Asian Survey* 12 (September 1972), pp. 785 and 789.

8. Blaufarb, "Sources of Frustration," p. 147.

9. Lewy, *America in Viet Nam*, p. 196.

10. *Economist*, June 17, 1972, p. 16.

11. Ibid., April 15, 1972, p. 15.

12. Turley, *The Easter Offensive*, p. 27. The North's Soviet-made tanks were far superior to the ARVN's U.S.-made light tanks; Jeffrey J. Clarke, *Advice and Support: The Final Years, 1965–1973.* (Washington, DC: U.S. Army Center of Military History, 1988), p. 482.

13. *Economist*, April 22, 1972, p. 16.

14. Turley, *Easter Offensive*, p. 104.

15. Lewy, *America in Viet Nam*, p. 197.

16. *Economist*, May 6, 1972, p. 39.

17. Ibid., May 13, 1972, p. 31.

18. Ibid., June 24, 1972, p. 28.

19. Ibid., May 6, 1972, p. 39.

20. Herrington, *Silence Was a Weapon*, p. 210.

21. Lewy, *America in Viet Nam*, p. 198; Herrington, *Silence Was a Weapon*, p. 210.

22. Lewy, *America in Viet Nam*, pp. 199–200; Sorley, *A Better War*, chapter 20.

23. Pike, *PAVN*, p. 229.

24. Palmer, *The 25-Year War*, p. 122. Pike, in *PAVN*, says the ARVN fought "heroically"; Sorley, in *A Better War*, gives the Territorials very high grades.

25. Le Gro, *Viet Nam from Ceasefire to Capitulation*, p. 174; Collins, *Development and Training*, p. 122; Palmer, *Summons of the Trumpet*, p. 255.

26. Summers, *On Strategy*, p. 138.

CHAPTER 11

1. On this entire topic of Viet Nam's place in U.S. foreign policy planning, see Leslie Gelb and Richard K. Betts, *The Irony of Viet Nam: The System Worked* (Washington, DC: Brookings Institute, 1979). See also Fredrik Logevall, *Choosing War: The Lost Chance for Peace and the Escalation of the War in Viet Nam* (Berkeley: University of California, 1999).

2. *Pentagon Papers*, vol. 1, p. 615.

3. John F. Kennedy, "America's Stake in Viet Nam," reprinted in Wesley Fishel, *Viet Nam*, pp. 144–145.

4. Lin Piao, *Long Live the Victory of People's War* (Peking: n.p., 1965).

5. Hubert Humphrey, *The Education of a Public Man* (Garden City, NY: Doubleday, 1976), p. 333.

6. Donald Vought, "American Culture and American Arms: The Case of Viet Nam," in *Lessons from an Unconventional War*, ed. Hunt and Shultz, pp. 171–172.

7. Herrington, *Silence Was a Weapon*, p. 214.

8. Ibid., p. 213.

9. *New York Times*, December 7, 1967.

10. Thompson, *No Exit from Viet Nam*, p. 53; Krepinevich, *The Army and Viet Nam*, p. 197.

11. Clausewitz wrote: "Casualty reports on either side are never accurate. . . . [T]hat is why guns and prisoners have always counted as the real trophies of victory." *On War*, book 4, chapter 4.

12. Thompson, *No Exit*, p. 143.

13. Pike, *PAVN*, p. 227.

14. Henderson, *Why the Viet Cong Fought*, p. xviii.

15. Thayer, *War without Fronts*, p. 114. General Westmoreland came to regret the one-year tour; see his *A Soldier Reports* (Garden City, NY: Doubleday, 1976), p. 417.

16. The Marine experiment with village security, called CAPS (combined action platoons) was the basis for a much more effective response to the guerrillas, but the hostility of General Westmoreland and others to the program withered it. See F. J. West, *Small Unit Action in Viet Nam* (Quantico, VA: U.S. Marine Corps, 1967), and *The Village* (New York: Harper and Row, 1972); Al Hemingway, *Our War Was Different: Marine Combined Action Platoons in Viet Nam* (Annapolis, MD: Naval Institute Press, 1994); Michael A. Hennessy, *Strategy in Viet Nam* (Westport, CT: Praeger, 1997); Michael E. Peterson, *The Combined Action Platoons* (New York: Praeger, 1989); Herrington, *Silence Was a Weapon*. See also the incisive and prophetic critique of American strategy entitled *The Program for the Pacification and Long-term Development of South Viet Nam* [PROVN], a study commissioned by the Army Chief of Staff that appeared in March 1966; excerpts and critiques of PROVN are found, *inter alia*, in *The Pentagon Papers*, vol. 2, pp. 576ff; this study suggested many of the reforms carried out later by General Creighton Abrams, Westmoreland's successor in Viet Nam.

17. Taylor, *Swords and Plowshares*, p. 247; *Pentagon Papers*, vol. 2, p. 636; Arthur Schlesinger, *A Thousand Days: John F. Kennedy in the White House* (Boston: Houghton Mifflin, 1965), p. 163; Nixon, *No More Viet Nams*, p. 60. Eisenhower stated further that if necessary the United States should act alone to close the Laotian route; Lyndon Johnson, *The Vantage Point* (New York: Holt, Rinehart, Winston, 1971), p. 51. In Henry Kissinger's view, "Eisenhower turned out to have been right. . . . Even though Laos was a remote and landlocked country, the North Vietnamese, as feared and hated foreigners, could not have waged a guerrilla war on its soil. America could have fought there the sort of conventional war for which its army had been trained." *Diplomacy* (New York: Simon and Schuster, 1994), p. 647.

18. Norman B. Hannah, *The Key to Failure: Laos and the Viet Nam War* (Lanham, MD; Madison Books, 1987), p. xv.

19. Palmer, *The 25-year War*, p. 105; Oberdorfer, *Tet!* p. 268. See Westmoreland, *A Soldier Reports*, p. 148.

20. Palmer, *The 25-Year War*, pp. 182–186. Summers endorses General Palmer's conclusion that three divisions in Laos, with five along the DMZ, would have been sufficient to isolate South Viet Nam from invasion; Summers, *On Strategy*, pp. 122–123. "There

is little doubt that the U.S. Army had the capabilities, especially if reinforced, to have cut the Ho Chi Minh Trail, neutralized the sanctuaries, and isolated Front [VC] forces from outside aid"; Eric Bergerud, *The Dynamics of Defeat: The Viet Nam War in Hau Nghia Province* (Boulder, Co: Westview, 1991), p. 330.

21. Shaplen, *Bitter Victory*, p. 158.

22. Johnson, *Vantage Point*, p. 369.

23. Hammer, *Death in November*, p. 31. The reader may recall the primary role Harriman played in the assassination of President Diem.

24. Johnson, *Vantage Point*, p. 370 (my italics). "One further point which was a key element in the Viet Nam war and one which people do not realize was probably its turning point was the Laos Agreement of 1962. Because it kept the United States out of Laos and gave North Vietnamese a free run it made the war almost unwinnable." Robert Thompson, "Regular Armies and Insurgency", in *Regular Armies and Insurgency*, ed. Ronald Haycock (London: Croom Helm, 1979), p. 17.

25. Shaplen, *Bitter Victory*, pp. 148, 157; Douglas Pike, "Road to Victory," in *War in Peace*, vol. 5 (London: Orbis, 1984); Richard H. Shultz, Jr., *The Secret War against Hanoi* (New York: HarperCollins, 1999), pp. 205–206.

26. Thompson, "Regular Armies and Insurgency," p. 18.

27. Bunker in Hannah, *Key to Failure*, p. 217. Bunker urged President Johnson to invade Laos; ibid., pp. 236–237.

28. Ibid., p. 183.

29. Smith, *International History*, vol. 2, p. 102. See the discussion of an American barrier across Laos in Wirtz, *Tet Offensive*, pp. 120ff.

30. In fact, this turned out to be not entirely true; the Nixon bombing of December 1972 shocked the leadership of Hanoi.

31. See U. S. Grant Sharp, *Strategy for Defeat: Viet Nam in Retrospect* (San Rafael, CA: Presidio, 1978).

32. *Pentagon Papers*, vol. 2, p. 384. For a Defense Department view of the bombing, see vol. 4, pp. 1–259. "The idea that destroying, or threatening to destroy, North Viet Nam's industry would pressure Hanoi into calling it quits seems, in retrospect, a colossal misjudgment" (vol. 4, p. 57).

33. Douglas Pike, *Masters of Deceit* (unpublished ms), p. 44.

34. Ibid., p. 31.

35. Allan E. Goodman, *The Lost Peace: America's Search for a Negotiated Settlement of the Viet Nam War* (Stanford, CA: Hoover Institution, 1978) p. 161.

36. Duncanson, *Government and Revolution*, p. 21; Norman Podhoretz, *Why We Were in Viet Nam* (New York: Simon and Schuster, 1982).

37. Lewy, *America in Viet Nam*, p. 432.

38. See, for example, Theodore H. White, *The Making of the President 1972* (New York: Athenaeum, 1973).

39. Kissinger, *White House Years*, pp. 255–256.

40. Richard M. Nixon, *United States Foreign Policy for the 1970s* (Washington, DC: U.S. Government Printing Office, 1971).

41. Douglas Pike in Braestrup, *Viet Nam as History*, p. 88; Palmer, *The 25-Year War*, pp. 140–141; George C. Herring, "The Nixon Strategy in Viet Nam," in Braestrup, *Viet Nam as History*, p. 57.

42. Lewy, *America in Viet Nam*, pp. 203–204.

43. Isaacs, *Without Honor*, p. xii.

CHAPTER 12

1. Dawson, *55 Days*, p. 123.

2. Hosmer et al., *The Fall of South Viet Nam*, p. 30. "The Paris Agreement was served on South Viet Nam like a death warrant"; Cao Van Vien, *The Final Collapse*, p. 6; "The Paris peace agreements of 1973 were in effect a surrender"; Dean Rusk, *As I Saw It*, p. 431.

3. Nixon, *No More Viet Nams*, p. 170.

4. Nixon, *RN: The Memoirs*, pp. 202–203; Lewy, *America in Viet Nam*, pp. 202–203; Nguyen Tien Hung and Jerrold L. N. Schecter, *The Palace File: Viet Nam Secret Documents* (New York: Harper and Row, 1986), especially pp. 149ff.

5. Kissinger, *White House Years*, pp. 1459–1460, 1469.

6. Vo Nguyen Giap, *How We Won the War* (Philadelphia: Recon, 1976), p. 26.

7. Le Gro, *Viet Nam*, p. 32.

8. Ibid., p. 78.

9. Ibid., p. 30.

10. Hosmer et al., *The Fall of South Viet Nam*, p. 132.

11. Cao Van Vien, *Final Collapse*, p. 39.

12. Communist writers are very critical of Thieu for his hold-all strategy. See for example Tran Van Tra, *Concluding the 30-Years War*, pp. 63, 72.

13. Dong Van Thuyen, *The RVNAF*, p. 330; Le Gro, *Viet Nam* pp. 69–70.

14. Dong Van Khuyen, *The RVNAF*, p. 236.

15. Goodman, *Institutional Profile*, p. 21.

16. Kolko, *Anatomy*, p. 256.

17. Le Gro, *Viet Nam*, p. 72.

18. Hosmer et al., *Fall of South Viet Nam*, p. 119.

19. Cao Van Vien, *Final Collapse*, p. 45.

20. Stuart A. Herrington, *Peace with Honor?* (Novato, CA: Presidio, 1983), p. 36.

21. Braestrup, *Big Story*, vol. 1, p. 498.

22. Truong Nhu Tang, *Viet Cong Memoir*, passim.

23. William S. Turley, *The Second Indochina War: A Short Political and Military History, 1954–1975* (Boulder, CO: Westview, 1986).

24. Lomperis, *The War Everyone Lost*, p. 167.

25. See, among others, Fairbairn, *Revolutionary Guerrilla Warfare: The Countryside Version*; Edgar O'Ballance, *The Algerian Insurrection 1954–1962* (Hamden, CT: Archon, 1967); George T. Kelly, *Lost Soldiers: The French Army and Empire in Crisis* (Cambridge, MA: MIT, 1965); Bergerud, *Dynamics of Defeat*.

26. Charles Stuart Callison, *Land-to-the-Tiller in the Mekong Delta* (Lanham, MD: University Press of America, 1983), p. iii. The Thieu land reform was called "the most imaginative and progressive non-Communist land reform in the twentieth century"; Thompson and Frizzell, *Lessons*, p. 218.

27. Lewy, *America in Viet Nam*, p. 189; Duiker, *Communist Road*, p. 290.

28. Callison, *Land to the Tiller*, p. 337.

29. Kolko, *Anatomy*, p. 482.

30. Le Gro, *Viet Nam*, p. 91.

31. Robert A. Scalapino in the *New York Times Magazine*, December 11, 1966, quoted in Fishel, *Viet Nam*, p. 780.

32. Quoted in Fishel, *Viet Nam*, pp. 653 and 659.

33. Kolko, *Anatomy*, p. 250; Thompson, *No Exit*, p. 65. Race agrees that the Viet Cong were a minority; *War Comes to Long An*, p. 188.

34. Penniman, *Elections*, p. 199; Malcolm Salmon, "After Revolution, Evolution," *Far Eastern Economic Review*, December 12, 1975, pp. 32–34. Duncanson, *Government and Revolution*, estimates the Communists had the support of one in four Vietnamese. Robert Thompson and John Paul Vann concurred in the collapse of support for the Communists in the rural areas. See Sorley, *A Better War*, pp. 348 and 356.

35. Thayer, *War without Fronts*, p. 35.

36. Penniman, *Elections*, p. 195.

37. Lewy, *America in Viet Nam*, p. 173.

38. Le Gro, *Viet Nam*, p. 60.

39. Ibid., p. 15.

40. Allan E. Goodman, "The Dynamics of the United States–South Vietnamese Alliance: What Went Wrong?" in Braestrup, *Viet Nam as History*, p. 90. South Vietnamese and US military deaths compare as follows:

Year	U.S.	RVNAF
1965	1369	11,242
1966	5008	11,953
1967	9377	12,716
1968	14,589	27,915
1969	9414	21,833
1970	4221	23,346
1971	1381	22,738
1972	300	39,587
1973	237	27,901
1974	207	31,219

Adapted from Jeffery J. Clarke, *Advice and Support: The Final Years* (Washington, DC: U.S. Army Center of Military, 1988,) p. 275.

41. Hoang Ngoc Lung, *General Offensives*, pp. 142–143. But see Sorley's sympathetic portrait in *A Better War*.

42. Lewy, *America in Viet Nam*, p. 205.

43. Thayer, *War without Fronts*, p. 23.

44. *Statistical Abstract of the United States, 1986* (Washington, DC: U.S. Department of Commerce, 1985).

45. Le Gro, *Viet Nam*, p. 88.

46. Lewy, *America in Viet Nam*, p. 208. These figures are accepted as valid by North Vietnamese sources; see Van Tien Dung, *Our Great Spring Victory*, pp. 17–18.

47. Lewy, *America in Viet Nam*, p. 208; Dong Van Khuyen, *The RVNAF*, pp. 287–288; Le Gro, *Viet Nam*, pp. 84–87.

48. Lomperis, *The War Everyone Lost*, p. 75.

49. Goodman, *The Lost Peace*, p. 175.

50. Richard West, "Saigon Keeps Its Vigil," *New Statesman*, April 4, 1975.

51. Le Gro, *Viet Nam*, p. 132.

52. Vo Nguyen Giap, *How We Won*, p. 24.

53. Dong Van Khuyen, *The RVNAF*, p. 287.

54. Can Van Vien, *Final Collapse*, p. 51.

55. Ibid., pp. 67–68.

56. Le Gro, *Viet Nam*, pp. 138–139; Dawson, *55 Days*, p. 27; Lewy, *America in Viet Nam*, p. 211; Duiker, *Communist Road to Power*, p. 309. The Communists were deeply impressed with the events after Phuoc Long; see Tran Van Tra, *Concluding the 30-Years War*, p. 134.

CHAPTER 13

1. Lewy, *America in Viet Nam*, p. 213.

2. Le Gro, *Viet Nam*, p. 149; Vo Nguyen Giap, *How We Won*, p. 49; Dawson, *55 Days*, p. 47.

3. Defense Attaché Office, *RVNAF Final Assessment*, June 15, 1975, p. 16-B-1.

4. Lewy, *America in Viet Nam*, p. 208.

5. Cao Van Vien, *The Final Collapse*, p. 7.

6. Duiker, *Communist Road to Power*, pp. 310–311.

7. Ibid., p. 325.

8. Le Gro, *Viet Nam*, p. 61.

9. W. Scott Thompson, "The Indochinese Debacle and the United States," *Orbis* 19 (Fall 1975), p. 996.

10. Warner, *Certain Victory*, pp. 60–61.

11. Herrington, *Peace with Honor?* p. 123.

12. Hosmer et al., *Fall of South Viet Nam*, p. 194.

13. Cao Van Vien, *Final Collapse*, p. 118.

14. Cao Van Vien and Dong Van Khuyen, *Reflections*, p. 128.

15. Cao Van Vien, *Final Collapse*, pp. 109–110.

16. Herrington, *Peace with Honor?* p. 128.

17. Dawson, *55 Days*, p. 13; Cao Van Vien, *Final Collapse*, p. 146.

18. Warner, *Certain Victory*, p. 70.

19. Defense Attaché Office, *RVNAF Final Assessment*, p. 16-B-5.

20. Le Gro, *Viet Nam*, p. 155.

21. Dawson, *55 Days*, p. 108.

22. Le Thi Que, A. Terry Rambo, and Gary D. Murfin, "Why They Fled: Refugee Movement during the Spring 1975 Communist Offensive in South Viet Nam," *Asian Survey* 16 (September 1976), p. 863.

23. Dawson, *55 Days*, p. 147.

24. Lewy, *America in Viet Nam*, p. 213.

25. Warner, *Certain Victory*, p. 74.

26. Ibid.

27. Ibid., p. 75.

28. Le Gro, *Viet Nam*, p. 171.

29. Ibid., pp. 170, 172.

30. Dawson, *55 Days*, p. 134.

31. Van Tien Dung, *Our Great Spring Victory*, pp. 165ff.

32. Le Gro, *Viet Nam*, pp. 173–175; Dawson, *55 Days*, pp. 234ff.

33. Cao Van Vien, *Final Collapse*, pp. 132–133.

34. Dawson, *55 Days*, has 10 NVA divisions besieging Saigon, p. 298; Le Gro, *Viet Nam*, places 16 NVA divisions in Military Region III (which included Saigon), p. 177; Cao Van Vien, *Final Collapse*, says 15 combat divisions attacked Saigon, supplemented by others, p. 129.

35. Hosmer et al., *Fall of South Viet Nam*, p. 133.

36. Ibid., pp. 237–238; Cao Van Vien, *Final Collapse*, p. 5.

37. Truong Nhu Tang, *Viet Cong Memoir*, pp. 137–138; Dong Van Khuyen, *The RVNAF*, p. 387.

38. See, for example, Dawson, *55 Days*.

39. Ibid., p. 307.

40. Ibid.

41. Warner, *Certain Victory*, p. 208.

42. Dawson, *55 Days*, p. 352; Warner, *Certain Victory*, p. 246.

43. Warner, *Certain Victory*, p. 203.

44. Dawson, *55 Days*, p. 339.

45. Ibid., p. 306.

46. Ibid., p. 305.

47. Warner, *Certain Victory*, p. 237.

48. Dawson, *55 Days*, p. 305.

49. Hosmer et al., *Fall of South Viet Nam*, p. 247.

50. Cao Van Vien, *Final Collapse*, p. 140.

51. In the event, this effort was defeated by the well-armed and numerous NVA; the Fifth Division's commander, Brig. Gen. Le Nguyen Vy, committed suicide after his failure.

52. Dawson, *55 Days*, pp. 1–17.

53. Herrington, *Peace with Honor?* p. 146.

CHAPTER 14

1. See, for example, David Franklin and James Chace, "The Lessons of Viet Nam?" *Foreign Affairs* 63 (Spring 1985).

2. Johnson, *Autopsy*.

3. Some observers identify the absence of a consolidated American-ARVN command as a key to the failure in Viet Nam. They point to the U.S. success in defending South Korea, where the Americans exercised overall military command, and especially to the defeat of Communist guerrillas in Malaya, where the British directed both the civilian government and the military campaigning. The validity of this principle is not totally clear. U.S. forces in South Korea were only to a small degree concerned with counter-guerrilla operations; most of the time they were fighting a conventional war, at which they excel (recall the Persian Gulf conflict of 1991). The French directed both civilian and military affairs in Indochina, but this availed them little in the absence of both a sound strategy and sufficient military means. Infinitely more important than the problem of divided command was the failure to adapt strategy to geography: the Americans fundamentally erred in waging a war of attrition while at the same time leaving South Viet Nam open to continuous, systematic invasion via the Ho Chi Minh Trail (see chapter

11). A useful principle for any future U.S. counter-guerrilla operation might be: If you can't seal the place off, write it off.

4. See Krepinevich, *The Army and Viet Nam.*

5. Sharp, *Strategy for Defeat*, p. 30.

6. It was much more unpopular than victory by the early Viet Cong had ever been.

7. Robert Thompson, *Peace Is Not at Hand* (New York: David McKay, 1974), p. 169.

8. Thompson, *No Exit*, p. 164.

9. Dawson, *55 Days*, p. 593.

10. Thompson, *No Exit*, p. 146.

11. *Statistical Abstract 1986*, p. 337. In the spring of 1952 the United States had 770,000 troops in South Korea, far more than were ever in South Viet Nam at one time.

12. *Economist*, May 6, 1972, p. 12.

13. Pike, *Viet Cong*, p. xii.

14. Arnold Isaacs, *Without Honor: Defeat in Viet Nam and Cambodia* (New York: Vintage, 1984), p. xii.

15. Thompson, *Peace Is Not at Hand*, p. 200 n. 66.

16. See Jacqueline Desbarats and Karl Jackson, "Viet Nam 1975–1982: The Cruel Peace," *Washington Quarterly* 8, no. 5 (1985). See also Sorley, *A Better War*, 457–458.

17. "It seemed to me then and still seems to me today that those of us who were opposed to the American effort in Indochina should be humbled by the scale of suffering inflicted by the Communist victors—especially in Cambodia but in Viet Nam and Laos as well." William Shawcross, author of *Sideshow, New York Review of Books*, August 12, 1993, p. 381.

18. Lomperis, *The War Everyone Lost*, p. 162.

EPILOGUE 2001

1. Martin Malia, *The Soviet Tragedy* (New York: Free Press, 1994), pp. 374ff. "The degree to which this perception predominated was so great that it is difficult to communicate to a generation that never experienced it"; Timothy Lomperis, *From People's War to People's Rule: Insurgency, Intervention, and the Lessons of Viet Nam* (Chapel Hill; University of North Carolina, 1996), p. 315. In particular, the Vietnamese Communists had apparently perfected a strategy "for which *there is no known proven counterstrategy*"; Douglas Pike, *PAVN*, p. 213, italics in original.

2. Robert M. Gates, *From the Shadows: The Ultimate Insider's Story of Five Presidents and How They Won the Cold War* (New York: Simon and Schuster, 1996), p. 174.

3. Ibid., p. 427.

4. Ibid., p. 175ff.

Select Bibliography

Ambrose, Stephen E. *Eisenhower*. Vol. 2, *The President*. New York: Simon and Schuster, 1984.

Andradé, Dale. *Ashes to Ashes: The Phoenix Program and the Vietnam War*. Lexington, MA: Lexington, 1990.

Andrews, William R. *The Village War: Vietnamese Communist Revolutionary Activities in Dinh Tuong Province 1960–1964*. Columbia: University of Missouri, 1973.

Bao Dai. *Dragon d'Annam*. Paris: Plon, 1980.

Bator, Victor. *Viet Nam, A Diplomatic Tragedy: The Origins of U.S. Involvement*. London: Faber and Faber 1965.

Bergerud, Eric M. *The Dynamics of Defeat: The Viet Nam War in Hau Nghia Province*. Boulder, CO: Westview, 1991.

Berman, Larry. *Planning a Tragedy: The Americanization of the War in Viet Nam*. New York: Norton, 1982.

Billings-Yun, Melanie. *Decision against War: Eisenhower and Dien Bien Phu 1954*. New York: Columbia University, 1988.

Blair, Anne. *Lodge in Viet Nam*. New Haven, CT: Yale University, 1995.

Blaufarb, Douglas. *The Counterinsurgency Era: U.S. Doctrine and Performance*. New York: Free Press, 1977.

——. "The Sources of Frustration in Viet Nam." In Richard A. Hunt and Richard H. Shultz, eds., *Lessons from an Unconventional War*. New York: Pergamon, 1982.

Blum, Robert M. *Drawing the Line: The Origin of the American Containment Policy in East Asia*. New York: Norton, 1982.

Bodard, Lucien. *The Quicksand War: Prelude to Viet Nam*. Boston: Little, Brown, 1967.

Boyer de LaTour, Pierre. *La martyre de l'armée française: De l'Indochine à l'Algérie*. Paris: Presses du Mail, 1962.

Braestrup, Peter. *Big Story*. Boulder, CO: Westview, 1977.

Braestrup, Peter, ed. *Viet Nam as History*. Washington, DC: University Press of America, 1984.

Browne, Malcolm. *The New Face of War*. New York: Bobbs-Merrill, 1965.

Bui Diem. *In the Jaws of History*. Boston: Houghton Mifflin, 1987.

Bui Tin. *Following Ho Chi Minh: Memoirs of a North Vietnamese Colonel*. Honolulu: University of Hawaii, 1995.

Bunker, Ellsworth. *The Bunker Papers: Reports to the President from Viet Nam, 1967– 1973*. Ed. Douglas Pike, 3 vols. Berkeley: University of California, 1990.

Buttinger, Joseph. *A Dragon Defiant: A Short History of Viet Nam*. New York: Praeger, 1972.

———. *The Smaller Dragon: A Political History of Viet Nam*. New York: Praeger, 1958.

———. *Viet Nam: A Dragon Embattled*. New York: Praeger, 1967. 2 vols.

———. *Viet Nam: A Political History*. New York: Praeger, 1968.

Cable, Larry. *Conflict of Myths: The Development of American Counterinsurgency Doctrine and the Viet Nam War*. New York: Free Press, 1986.

Cady, John F. *The Roots of French Imperialism in Eastern Asia*. Ithaca, NY: Cornell University, 1954.

Callison, Charles Stuart. *Land-to-the-Tiller in the Mekong Delta*. Lanham, MD: University Press of America, 1983.

Cantwell, Thomas. *The Army of South Viet Nam: A Military and Political History, 1955– 1975*. Doctoral dissertation, University of New South Wales, 1989.

Cao Van Vien. *The Final Collapse*. Washington, DC: U.S. Army Center of Military History, 1983.

Cao Van Vien and Dong Van Khuyen. *Reflections on the Viet Nam War*. Washington, DC: U.S. Army Center of Military History, 1980.

Cao Van Vien et al. *The U.S. Adviser*. Washington, DC: U.S. Army Center of Military History, 1980.

Carver, Michael. *War since 1945*. New York: Putnam, 1981.

"Causes, Origins, and Lessons of the Viet Nam War." Hearings before the Committee on Foreign Relations of the United States Senate, Washington, DC: U.S. Government Printing Office, 1973.

Chaliand, Gerard, ed. *Guerrilla Strategies*. Berkeley: University of California, 1982.

Chen Jian. "China and the First Indo-China War, 1950–1954." *China Quarterly*, no. 133 (March 1983).

———. "China's Involvement in the Viet Nam War, 1964–1969." *China Quarterly*, no. 142 (June 1995).

Clarke, Jeffrey J. *Advice and Support: The Final Years, 1965–1973*. Washington, DC: U.S. Army Center of Military History, 1988.

Clausewitz, Carl von. *On War*. Edited and Translated by Michael Howard and Peter Paret. Princeton, NJ: Princeton University, 1976.

Clodfelter, Mark. *The Limits of Air Power: The American Bombing of North Viet Nam*. New York: Free Press, 1989.

Clutterbuck, Richard L. *The Long, Long War: Counterinsurgency in Malaya and Viet Nam*. New York: Praeger, 1966.

Colby, William. *Lost Victory: A Firsthand Account of America's Sixteen-Year Involvement in Vietnam*. Chicago: Contemporary Books, 1989.

Collins, James L. *The Development and Training of the South Vietnamese Army, 1950– 1972*. Washington, DC: Department of the Army, 1975.

Cooper, Chester L. *The Lost Crusade: America in Viet Nam*. New York: Dodd, Mead, 1970.

Cross, J. E. *Conflict in the Shadows*. New York: Doubleday, 1963.

Crozier, Brian. *The Rebel: A Study of Postwar Insurrections.* Boston: Beacon, 1960.

Currey, Cecil B. *Edward Lansdale: The Unquiet American.* Boston: Houghton Mifflin, 1988.

——. *Victory at Any Cost: The Genius of Viet Nam's General Vo Nguyen Giap.* Washington, DC: Brassey's, 1997.

Davidson, Phillip B. *Viet Nam at War: The History, 1946–1975.* Novato, CA: Presidio, 1988.

Davidson, W. Phillips. *Some Observations on Viet Cong Operations in the Villages.* Santa Monica, CA: Rand Corporation, 1968.

Dawson, Alan. *55 Days: The Fall of South Viet Nam.* Englewood Cliffs, N.J.: Prentice-Hall, 1977.

Defense Attaché Office. *RVNAF: Final Assessment.* Washington, DC: U.S. Government Printing Office, 1975.

Democratic Republic of Viet Nam. *Thirty Years of Struggle of the Party.* Hanoi: 1960.

Department of the Army. *A Program for the Long-Term Pacification and Development of Viet Nam.* Washington, DC: Department of the Army, 1966.

Desbarats, Jacqueline, and Karl Jackson. "Viet Nam 1975–1982: The Cruel Peace." *Washington Quarterly* 8, no. 5 (1985).

Devillers, Philippe. *Histoire du Viet-Nam de 1940 à 1952.* 3d edition. Paris: Éditions du Seuil, 1952.

Divine, Robert A. *Eisenhower and the Cold War.* New York: Oxford University, 1981.

Doan Van Toai and David Chanoff. *The Vietnamese Gulag.* New York: Simon and Schuster, 1985.

Dong Van Khuyen. *The RVNAF.* Washington, DC: U.S. Army Center of Military History, 1980.

Donnell, John C. *Viet Cong Recruitment: Why and How Men Join.* Santa Monica, CA: Rand Corporation, 1975.

Dooley, Thomas. *Dr. Tom Dooley's Three Great Books.* New York: Farrar, Strauss and Cudahy, 1960.

Duiker, William J. *The Communist Road to Power in Viet Nam.* Boulder, CO: Westview, 1981.

——. *The Rise of Nationalism in Viet Nam, 1920–1941.* Ithaca, NY: Cornell University, 1976.

——. *Sacred War: Nationalism and Revolution in Divided Viet Nam.* New York: McGraw-Hill, 1995.

Duncanson, Dennis J. *Government and Revolution in Viet Nam.* New York: Oxford University, 1968.

Eisenhower, Dwight D. *Mandate for Change, 1953–1956.* Garden City, NY: Doubleday, 1963.

Ely, Paul. *Lessons of the War in Indochina.* Vol. 2. Santa Monica, CA: Rand Corporation (translation), 1967.

——. *L'Indochine dans la tourmente.* Paris: Plon, 1964.

Engelmann, Larry. *Tears before the Rain: An Oral History of the Fall of South Viet Nam.* New York: Oxford University, 1990.

Fairbairn, Geoffrey. *Revolutionary Guerrilla Warfare: The Countryside Version.* Harmondsworth, England: Penguin, 1974.

Fall, Bernard. *Hell in a Very Small Place.* Philadelphia: Lippincott, 1967.

——. *Street without Joy.* Harrisburg, PA: Stackpole, 1964.

————. *The Two Viet Nams: A Political and Military Analysis*. 2d revised edition. New York: Praeger, 1967.

————. *Viet Nam Witness, 1953–1966*. New York: Praeger, 1966.

Fishel, Wesley, ed. *Viet Nam: Anatomy of a Conflict*. Itasca, IL: Peacock, 1968.

Ford, Ronnie E. *Tet 1968: Understanding the Surprise*. London: Frank Cass, 1995.

Foreign Relations of the United States, 1961–1963: Viet Nam. Washington, DC: U.S. Government Printing Office, 1988–1991.

Fromkin, David, and James Chace. "The Lessons of Viet Nam?" *Foreign Affairs* 63 (Spring 1985).

Gallucci, Robert. *Neither Peace nor Honor: The Politics of American Military Policy in Viet Nam*. Baltimore: Johns Hopkins University, 1975.

Galula, David. *Counter-Insurgency Warfare: Theory and Practice*. New York: Praeger, 1964.

Gates, Robert M. *From the Shadows: The Ultimate Insider's Story of Five Presidents and How They Won the Cold War*. New York: Simon and Schuster, 1966.

Gelb, Leslie, and Richard K. Betts. *The Irony of Viet Nam: The System Worked*. Washington, DC: Brookings Institution, 1979.

Goodman, Allan E. *An Institutional Profile of the South Vietnamese Officer Corps*. Santa Monica, CA: Rand Corporation, 1970.

————. *The Lost Peace: America's Search for a Negotiated Settlement of the Viet Nam War*. Stanford, CA: Hoover Institution, 1978.

————. *Politics in War: The Bases of Political Community in South Viet Nam*. Cambridge, MA: Harvard University, 1973.

Grant, J. A. C. "The Vietnamese Constitution of 1956." *American Political Science Review* 52 (June 1958).

Greene, T. N., ed. *The Guerrilla—and How to Fight Him*. New York: Praeger, 1962.

Griffith, Samuel B. *Mao Tse-tung on Guerrilla Warfare*. New York: Praeger, 1961.

Grinter, Lawrence E. "How They Lost: Doctrines, Strategies and Outcomes of the Viet Nam War." *Asian Survey* 15 (December 1975).

Guevara, Che. *Guerrilla Warfare*. New York: Vintage, 1961.

Gurtov, Melvin, and Konrad Kellen. *Viet Nam: Lessons and Mislessons*. Santa Monica, CA: Rand Corporation, 1969.

Haley, P. Edward. *Congress and the Fall of South Viet Nam and Cambodia*. Rutherford, NJ: Fairleigh Dickinson University, 1982.

Hammer, Ellen J. *A Death in November: America in Viet Nam 1963*. New York: Dutton, 1987.

————. "South Viet Nam: The Limits of Political Action." *Pacific Affairs* 35, no. 1 (Spring 1962).

————. *The Struggle for Indochina, 1940–1955*. Stanford, CA: Stanford University, 1966.

Hannah, Norman B. *The Key to Failure: Laos and the Viet Nam War*. Lanham, MD: Madison, 1987.

Hemingway, Al. *Our War Was Different: Marine Combined Action Platoons in Viet Nam*. Annapolis, MD: Naval Institute Press, 1994.

Henderson, William D. *Why the Viet Cong Fought: A Study of Motivation and Control in a Modern Army in Combat*. Westport, CT: Greenwood, 1979.

Hennessy, Michael A. *Strategy in Viet Nam: The Marines and Revolutionary Warfare in I Corps, 1965–1972*, Westport, CT: Praeger, 1997.

Herring, George C. *America's Longest War*. 2d edition. New York: Knopf, 1986.

Herrington, Stuart A. *Silence Was a Weapon: The Viet Nam War in the Villages*. Novato, CA: Presidio, 1982.

————. *Peace with Honor?* Novato, CA: Presidio, 1983.

Hickey, Gerald C. *Village in Viet Nam*. New Haven, CT: Yale University, 1964.

Ho Chi Minh. "The Path Which Led Me to Leninism." In Bernard Fall, ed., *Ho Chi Minh on Revolution: Selected Writings*. New York: Praeger, 1967.

————. *Selected Writings*. Hanoi: Foreign Languages Publishing House, 1977.

The Ho Chi Minh Trail. Hanoi: Foreign Languages Publishing House, 1985.

Hoang Ngoc Lung. *The General Offensives of 1968–1969*. Washington, DC: U.S. Army Center of Military History, 1981.

Hoang Van Chi. *From Colonialism to Communism: A Case Study of North Viet Nam*. New York: Praeger, 1964.

Honey, P. J., ed. *North Viet Nam Today: Profile of a Communist Satellite*. New York: Praeger, 1962.

Horn, Keith. *Battle for Hue: Tet 1968*. Novato, CA: Presidio, 1983.

Hosmer, Stephen T. *Viet Cong Repression and Its Implications for the Future*. Santa Monica, CA: Rand Corporation, 1970.

Hosmer, Stephen; Konrad Kellen, and Brian M. Jenkins. *The Fall of South Viet Nam: Statements by Vietnamese Military and Civilian Leaders*. New York: Crane, Russak, 1980.

Humphrey, Hubert. *The Education of a Public Man*. Garden City, NY: Doubleday, 1976.

Hung P. Nguyen. "Communist Offensive Strategy and the Defense of South Viet Nam," in Lloyd J. Matthews and Dave E. Brown, eds., *Assessing the Viet Nam War*. McLean, VA: Pergamon-Brassey's, 1987.

Hunt, Richard A. *Pacification: The American Struggle for Viet Nam's Hearts and Minds*. Boulder, CO: Westview, 1995.

Hunt, Richard A., and Richard H. Shultz, Jr., eds. *Lessons from an Unconventional War*. New York: Pergamon, 1982.

Huynh Kim Khanh. *Vietnamese Communism 1925–1945*. Ithaca, NY: Cornell University, 1982.

Isaacs, Arnold. *Without Honor: Defeat in Viet Nam and Cambodia*. New York: Vintage, 1984.

Joes, Anthony James. *From the Barrel of a Gun: Armies and Revolutions*. McLean, VA: Pergamon-Brassey's, 1986.

Johnson, Chalmers. *Autopsy on People's War*. Berkeley: University of California, 1973.

Johnson, Lyndon B. *The Vantage Point*. New York: Holt, Rinehart, Winston, 1971.

Joint Low-Intensity Conflict Project. *Analytical Review of Low-Intensity Conflict*. Fort Monroe, VA: U.S. Army, 1986.

Jumper, Roy, and Marjorie Weiner Normand. "Viet Nam." In George McT. Kahin, ed., *Government and Politics of Southeast Asia*. Ithaca, NY: Cornell University, 1964.

Kahin, George McT. *Intervention: How America Became Involved in Viet Nam*. New York: Knopf, 1986.

Kellen, Konrad. *A View of the VC*. Santa Monica, CA: Rand Corporation, 1969.

Kelly, George T. *Lost Soldiers: The French Army and Empire in Crisis*. Cambridge, MA: MIT, 1965.

Kinnard, Douglas. *The War Managers*. Hanover, NH: University Press of New England, 1977.

Kissinger, Henry. *White House Years*. Boston: Little, Brown, 1979.

Kolko, Gabriel. *Anatomy of a War*. New York: Pantheon, 1985.

Komer, Robert W. *Bureaucracy at War: U.S. Performance in the Viet Nam Conflict*. Boulder, CO: Westview, 1986.

Krepinevich, Andrew F., Jr. *The Army and Viet Nam*. Baltimore: John Hopkins University, 1986.

Lacouture, Jean. *Ho Chi Minh: A Political Biography*. Trans. Peter Wiles. London: Penguin, 1968.

Lam Quang Thi. *Autopsy: The Death of South Viet Nam*. Phoenix, AZ: Sphinx, 1986.

Lancaster, Donald. *The Emancipation of French Indo-China*. London: Oxford University, 1961.

Lanning, Michael Lee, and Dan Cragg. *Inside the VC and the NVA*. New York: Fawcett Columbine, 1992.

Lansdale, Edward G. *In the Midst of Wars: An American's Mission to Southeast Asia*. New York: Harper and Row, 1972.

Le Gro, William E. *Viet Nam from Cease-Fire to Capitulation*. Washington, DC: U.S. Army Center of Military History, 1981.

Leites, Nathan. *The Viet Cong Style of Politics*. Santa Monica, CA: Rand Corporation, 1969.

Lessons from the Viet Nam War. London: Royal United Service Institution, 1969.

Le Thi Que, A. Terry Rambo, and Gary D. Murfin. "Why They Fled: Refugee Movement during the Spring 1975 Communist Offensive in South Viet Nam." *Asian Survey* 16 (September 1976).

Lewy, Guenter. *America in Viet Nam*. New York: Oxford University, 1978.

———. "Some Political-Military Lessons of the Viet Nam War." In Lloyd J. Matthews and Dave E. Brown, eds., *Assessing the Viet Nam War*. McLean, VA: Pergamon-Brassey's, 1987.

Lind, Michael. *Viet Nam: The Necessary War*. New York: Free Press, 1999.

Lindholm, Richard W., ed. *Viet Nam: The First Five Years*. East Lansing: Michigan State University, 1959.

Lin Piao. *Long Live the Victory of People's War*. Peking: n.p., 1965.

Lockhart, Greg. *Nation in Arms: The Origins of the People's Army of Viet Nam*. Boston: Allen and Unwyn, 1989.

Logevall, Fredrik. *Choosing War: The Lost Chance for Peace and the Escalation of War in Viet Nam*. Berkeley: University of California, 1999.

Lomperis, Timothy. *From People's War to People's Rule: Insurgency, Intervention, and the Lessons of Viet Nam*. Chapel Hill: University of North Carolina, 1996.

———. *The War Everyone Lost—and Won: American Intervention in Viet Nam's Twin Struggles*. Baton Rouge: Louisiana State University, 1984.

McAlister, John T. *Viet Nam: The Origins of Revolution*. Garden City, NY: Doubleday Anchor, 1971.

McGarvey, Patrick J. *Visions of Victory: Selected Vietnamese Communist Military Writings 1965–1968*. Stanford, CA: Hoover Institute, 1969.

McMaster, H. R. *Dereliction of Duty*. New York: HarperCollins 1997.

Machiavelli, Niccolò. *The Art of War*. New York: Da Capo, 1965.

Malia, Martin. *The Soviet Tragedy*. New York: Free Press, 1994.

Maneli, Mieczyslaw. *War of the Vanquished*. New York: Harper and Row, 1971.

Mangold, Tom. *The Tunnels of Cu Chi*. New York: Random House, 1985.

Mao Tse-tung. *Report on an Investigation of the Peasant Movement in Hunan* [1927]. Peking: Foreign Languages Press, 1967.

Marchand, Jean. *L'Indochine en guerre.* Paris: Pouzet, 1955.

Marr, David G. *Vietnamese Anticolonialism, 1885–1925.* Los Angeles: University of California, 1971.

Matthews, Lloyd J., and Dave E. Brown. *Assessing the Viet Nam War.* McLean, VA: Pergamon-Brassey's, 1987.

Michigan State University Social Science Research Bureau. *Problems of Freedom: South Viet Nam since Independence.* Glencoe, IL: Free Press, 1961.

Moore, Harold G., and Joseph L. Galloway. *We Were Soldiers Once . . . and Young: Ia Drang, the Battle That Changed the War in Vietnam.* New York: Random House, 1992.

Moyar, Mark. *Phoenix and the Birds of Prey: The CIA's Secret Campaign to Destroy the Viet Cong.* Annapolis, MD: Naval Institute Press, 1997.

Navarre, Henri. *Agonie de l'Indochine.* Paris: Plon, 1956.

Ngo Quang Truong. *The Easter Offensive of 1972.* Washington, DC: U.S. Army Center of Military History, 1980.

————. *Territorial Forces.* Washington, DC: U.S. Army Center of Military History, 1981.

Nguyen Duy Hinh. *Lam Son 719.* Washington, DC: U.S. Army Center of Military History, 1979.

————. *Vietnamization and the Cease-Fire.* Washington, DC: U.S. Army Center of Military History, 1980.

Nguyen Tien Hung and Jerrold L. Schecter. *The Palace File: Viet Nam Secret Documents.* New York: Harper and Row, 1986.

Nighswonger, William A. *Rural Pacification in Viet Nam.* New York: Praeger, 1966.

Nixon, Richard M. *No More Viet Nams.* New York: Arbor House, 1985.

————. *RN: The Memoirs of Richard Nixon.* New York: Grosset and Dunlap, 1978.

————. *United States Foreign Policy for the 1970s.* Washington, DC: U.S. Government Printing Office, 1971.

Nolan, Keith William. *Battle for Hue: Tet 1968.* Novato, CA: Presidio, 1983.

Nolting, Frederick. *From Trust to Tragedy: The Political Memoirs of Frederick Nolting, Kennedy's Ambassador to Dien's Viet Nam.* New York: Praeger, 1988.

O'Ballance, Edgar. *The Indo-China War 1945–1954.* London: Faber and Faber, 1964.

Oberdorfer, Don. *Tet!* Garden City, NJ: Doubleday, 1971. Reissued 1984 by Da Capo.

Olson, James S., and Randy Roberts. *Where the Domino Fell: America and Viet Nam 1945–1990.* New York: St. Martin's, 1991.

O'Neill, Robert J. *General Giap.* New York: Praeger, 1969.

Osanka, Franklin Mark, ed. *Modern Guerrilla Warfare.* New York: Free Press, 1962.

Palmer, Bruce, Jr. *The 25-Year War: America's Military Role in Viet Nam.* Lexington: University of Kentucky, 1984.

Palmer, Dave Richard. *Summons of the Trumpet.* San Rafael, CA: Presidio, 1978.

Panikkar, K. M. *Asia and Western Dominance.* New York: John Day, 1950.

Paret, Peter, and John Shy. *Guerrillas in the 1960s.* Revised edition. New York: Praeger, 1962.

Parker, F. Charles. *Strategy for a Stalemate: Viet Nam.* New York: Paragon, 1989.

Penniman, Howard R. *Elections in South Viet Nam.* Washington, DC: American Enterprise Institute, 1972.

The Pentagon Papers: The Defense Department History of United States Decisionmaking on Viet Nam. Senator Gravel edition. 4 vols. Boston: Beacon, 1971.

People's Army of Viet Nam. *Viet Nam. The Anti-U.S. Resistance War for National Salvation*. Hanoi: PAVN Publishing House, 1980.

Peterson, Michael E. *The Combined Action Platoons: The U.S. Marines' Other War in Viet Nam*. New York: Praeger, 1989.

Pike, Douglas. *History of Vietnamese Communism, 1925–1976*. Stanford, CA: Hoover Institution, 1978.

———. *PAVN: People's Army of Viet Nam*. Novato, CA: Presidio, 1986.

———. *Viet Cong: The Organization and Techniques of the National Liberation Front of South Viet Nam*. Cambridge, MA: MIT, 1966.

———. *Viet Nam and the Soviet Union: Anatomy of an Alliance*. Boulder, CO: Westview, 1987.

———. *War, Peace, and the Viet Cong*. Cambridge, MA: MIT Press, 1969.

Pimlott, John, ed. *Viet Nam: The History and the Tactics*. New York: Crescent, 1982.

Plaster, John L. *SOG: The Secret Wars of America's Commandos in Viet Nam*. New York: Penguin 1997.

Podhoretz, Norman. *Why We Were in Viet Nam*. New York: Simon and Schuster, 1982.

Popkin, Samuel L. *The Rational Peasant*. Berkeley: University of California, 1979.

Porter, Gareth. *Viet Nam: The Definitive Documentation of Human Decisions*. 2 vols. Stanfordville, NY: Coleman Enterprises, 1979.

Prados, John. *The Blood Road: The Ho Chi Minh Trail and the Viet Nam War*. New York: Wiley, 1999.

———. *The Hidden History of the Vietnam War*. Chicago: Ivan R. Dee, 1995.

Prados, John, and R. W. Stubbe. *Valley of Decision: The Siege of Khe Sanh*. Boston: Houghton Mifflin, 1991.

Prochnau, William. *Once Upon a Distant War: Young War Correspondents and the Early Viet Nam Battles*. New York: Times Books, 1995.

Race, Jeffrey. *War Comes to Long An: Revolutionary Conflict in a Vietnamese Province*. Berkeley; University of California, 1972.

Record, Jeffrey. *The Wrong War: Why We Lost in Viet Nam*. Annapolis, MD: Naval Institute Press, 1998.

Rolph, Hammond. "Vietnamese Communism and the Protracted War." *Asian Survey* 12 (September 1972).

Roy, Jules. *The Battle of Dien Bien Phu*. New York: Harper and Row, 1965.

Rusk, Dean. *As I Saw It: A Secretary of State's Memoirs*. London: Tauris, 1991.

Santoli, Al, ed. *To Bear Any Burden*. New York: Dutton, 1985.

Schell, Jonathan. *The Village of Ben Suc*. New York: Random House, 1967.

Scigliano, Robert. *South Viet Nam: Nation under Stress*. Boston: Houghton Mifflin, 1964.

Shaplen, Robert. *Bitter Victory*. New York: Harper and Row, 1986.

———. *The Lost Revolution: The U.S. in Viet Nam, 1946–1966*. New York: Harper and Row, 1966.

———. *The Road from War: Viet Nam 1965–1971*. New York: Harper and Row, 1971.

Sharp, U. S. Grant. *Strategy for Defeat: Viet Nam in Retrospect*. San Rafael, CA: Presidio, 1978.

Sharp, U. S. Grant, and W. Westmoreland. *Report on the War in Viet Nam*. Washington, DC: U.S. Government Printing Office, 1968.

Sheehan, Neil. *A Bright, Shining Lie: John Paul Vann and America in Viet Nam.* New York: Random House, 1988.

Short, Anthony. *The Origins of the Viet Nam War.* London: Longman, 1989.

Shultz, Richard H., Jr. *The Secret War against Hanoi.* New York: HarperCollins, 1999.

Smith, R. B. *An International History of the Viet Nam War.* Vol. 1, *Revolution vs. Containment 1955–1961.* New York: St. Martin's, 1983.

———. *An International History of the Viet Nam War.* Vol. 2, *The Kennedy Strategy.* New York: St. Martin's 1985.

Sorley, Lewis. *A Better War: The Unexamined Victories and Final Tragedy of America's Last Years in Viet Nam.* New York: Harcourt, Brace, 1999.

———. *Thunderbolt: General Creighton Abrams and the Army of His Times.* New York: Simon and Schuster, 1992.

Spector, Ronald. *Advice and Support: The Early Years, 1941–1960.* Washington, DC: U.S. Army Center of Military History, 1983.

Stanton, Shelby L. *The Rise and Fall of an American Army: U.S. Ground Forces in Viet Nam, 1965–1973.* New York: Dell, 1985.

Stevens, Richard. *The Trail.* New York: Garland, 1993.

Summers, Harry G. *On Strategy: A Critical Analysis of the Viet Nam War.* Novato, CA: Presidio, 1982.

Tanham, George K. *Communist Revolutionary Warfare: From the Viet Minh to the Viet Cong.* Revised edition. New York: Praeger, 1967.

Taylor, Maxwell. *Swords and Plowshares.* New York: Norton, 1972.

Thayer, Thomas C. *War without Fronts: The American Experience in Viet Nam.* Boulder, CO: Westview, 1986.

Thompson, Robert. *Defeating Communist Insurgency: The Lessons of Malaya and Viet Nam.* New York: Praeger, 1966.

———. *No Exit from Viet Nam.* New York: David McKay, 1969.

———. *Peace Is Not at Hand.* New York: David McKay, 1974.

———. "Revolutionary War in Southeast Asia." *Orbis* 19 (Fall 1975).

Thompson, W. Scott. "The Indochina Debacle and the United States." *Orbis* 19 (Fall 1975).

Thompson, W. Scott, and Donaldson D. Frizzell. *The Lessons of Viet Nam.* New York: Crane, Russak, 1977.

Thornton, Thomas P. "The Emergence of Communist Revolutionary Doctrine." In C. E. Black and T. P. Thornton, eds., *Communism and Revolution: The Strategic Uses of Political Violence.* Princeton, NJ: Princeton University, 1964.

Tilford, Earl H., Jr. *Setup: What the Air Force Did in Viet Nam and Why.* Maxwell Air Force Base, Ala: Air University, 1991.

Todd, Olivier. *Cruel April: The Fall of Saigon.* New York: Norton, 1990.

Tran Dinh Tho. *The Cambodian Incursion.* Washington, DC: U.S. Army Center of Military History, 1979.

———. *Pacification.* Washington, DC: U.S. Army Center of Military History, 1980.

Tran Van Don. *Our Endless War.* San Rafael, CA: Presidio, 1978.

Tran Van Tra. *Concluding the 30-Years War.* Rosslyn, VA: Foreign Broadcast Information Service, 1983.

Trinquier, Roger. *Modern Warfare: A French View of Counterinsurgency.* New York: Praeger, 1964.

Truong Chinh. *Primer for Revolt: The Communist Takeover in Viet Nam.* New York: Praeger, 1963.

Truong Nhu Tang. *A Viet Cong Memoir.* New York: Harcourt, 1987.

Tucker, Spencer C. *Viet Nam.* London: University Center of London 1999.

Turley, G. H. *The Easter Offensive: Viet Nam 1972.* Novato, CA: Presidio, 1985.

Turley, William S. *The Second Indochina War: A Short Political and Military History 1954–1975.* Boulder, CO: Westview, 1986.

———. *Vietnamese Communism in Comparative Perspective.* Boulder, CO: Westview, 1980.

Turner, Robert F. *Vietnamese Communism: Its Origins and Development.* Stanford, CA: Hoover Institution, 1975.

Valeriano, Napoleon, and C.T.R. Bohannan. *Counter-Guerrilla Operations: The Philippine Experience.* New York: Praeger, 1962.

VanDeMark, Brian. *Into the Quagmire: Lyndon Johnson and the Escalation of the Viet Nam War.* New York: Oxford University, 1991.

Van Tien Dung. *Our Great Spring Victory.* New York: Monthly Review, 1977.

Vo Nguyen Giap. *Dien Bien Phu.* Hanoi. Foreign Languages Publishing House, 1964.

———. *How We Won the War.* Philadelphia: Recon, 1976.

———. *The Military Art of People's War.* New York: Monthly Review, 1970.

———. *People's War, People's Army.* New York: Praeger, 1962.

———. *Unforgettable Days.* Hanoi: Foreign Languages Publishing House, 1975.

Walt, Lewis W. *Strange War, Strange Strategy.* New York: Funk and Wagnalls, 1970.

Warner, Denis. *Certain Victory: How Hanoi Won the War.* Kansas City, KS: Sheed, Andrews and McMeel, 1978.

———. *The Last Confucian.* New York: Macmillan, 1963.

Westmoreland, William. *A Soldier Reports.* Garden City, NY: Doubleday, 1976.

Wheeler, John. "Coming to Grips with Viet Nam." *Foreign Affairs* 68 (Spring 1985).

White, Theodore. *The Making of the President 1972.* New York: Atheneum, 1973.

Winters, Francis X. *The Year of the Hare.* Athens: University of Georgia, 1997.

Wirtz, James J. *The Tet Offensive: Intelligence Failure in War.* Ithaca, NY: Cornell University, 1991.

Wolf, Charles, Jr. *The Logic of Failure: A Viet Nam "Lesson."* Santa Monica, CA: Rand Corporation, 1971.

Wolf, Eric. *Peasant Wars of the Twentieth Century.* New York: Harper and Row, 1969.

Woodside, Alexander. *Community and Revolution in Modern Viet Nam.* Boston: Houghton Mifflin, 1976.

Zasloff, Joseph J. *Origins of the Insurgency in South Viet Nam, 1954–1960.* Santa Monica CA: Rand Corporation, 1967.

Index

About the Author

ANTHONY JAMES JOES is Professor of Political Science and Director of the International Relations Program at Saint Joseph's University in Philadelphia. He is the author or contributing editor of ten books, has published numerous articles in professional journals, and has traveled and lectured on four continents.